Praise for Forbidden *Mysteries of Faery Witch*

"Storm Faerywolf writes so that we can understand, use, practice, and be informed in specific active magical work. The words *grimoire* (medieval), *gramarye* (poetic romantic), and *grammeree* (folkloric term for magic) are all derived from a root word that becomes *grammar*. While the grammar of grimoires was often incomprehensible, the grammar of this book is clear. It describes what can be done, tells you how to do it, and details what you might experience from doing it…even if it is not what you would expect. There is enough grammeree here to last the magical practitioner a long time. Take that step of abandonment into these forbidden mysteries, and you will not regret it."

—R. J. Stewart, author of *The Living World of Faery*

"What strikes me about Storm Faerywolf's work in the Craft is that it is highly innovative yet still stands firmly in the Feri tradition. This book continues his personal work of holding tension between innovation and tradition."

—Anaar, Grandmaster of the Feri tradition and archivist
for the Victor & Cora Anderson Archives

"Storm Faerywolf's *Forbidden Mysteries of Faery Witchcraft* provides a unique, compelling, synergistic, and deliciously 'edgy' view of the Faery Tradition and Witchcraft. He gives considerable attention to primal and chthonic aspects of both traditions and how they marry within his practice, especially working with the underworld. His exercises provide the reader with a means to encounter their reflection in the darkness so they may unearth what is hidden, till what is fertile, encounter what is powerful, and engage with the enchanted. Such treasures are surely forbidden mysteries!"

—Orion Foxwood, author of *The Faery Teachings*

"Storm has gifted the occult community with yet another treasure box of tools. Far from a dry primer, this book is a poetic dance through the most powerful work of Witchcraft, leaving the reader ready to inhale the art of Magick."

—Courtney Weber, author of *Brigid: History, Mystery,*
and Magick of the Celtic Goddess

"*Forbidden Mysteries of Faery Witchcraft* artfully explores and constructively illuminates the often-misunderstood shadow aspects of Witchcraft. Weaving myth, poetry, history, and ritual, Storm guides the reader through the liminal realms of our multifaceted world. In the darkness, we encounter divine beings, elemental spirits, the Mighty Dead, and the keys to understanding ourselves and claiming our own power. With practical exercises, Storm lays out essential tools that a Witch needs to experience magic and these mysteries on their own. Those seeking to deepen their practice will definitely be both challenged and inspired."

—Laura Tempest Zakroff, author of *Sigil Witchery* and *The Witch's Cauldron*

FORBIDDEN MYSTERIES
OF

F·A·E·R·Y

WITCHCRAFT

About the Author

Storm Faerywolf is a professional author, experienced teacher, visionary poet, and practicing warlock. He is an initiate of the Faery Tradition and has been practicing the magical arts since he was just a boy. He holds the Black Wand of a Faery Master and has been teaching both privately and publicly for more than twenty years. He is the founder of BlueRose, a lineage of the Faery Tradition, and is one of the founding teachers of Black Rose, a school and style of practical folkloric Witchcraft.

He is the author of *Betwixt and Between* and *The Stars Within the Earth* and has contributed to various magazines, podcasts, and blogs.

He lives with his two loving partners in the San Francisco Bay Area where together they own and run The Mystic Dream, a spiritual and occult supply shop which offers magical products and spiritual services. For more information about his classes, travel schedule, books, art, or other projects, visit his website at Faerywolf.com.

FORBIDDEN MYSTERIES

OF

F·A·E·R·Y

WITCHCRAFT

STORM FAERYWOLF

Llewellyn Publications
Woodbury, Minnesota

FIRST EDITION
Sixth Printing, 2024

Cover design by Kevin R. Brown
Cover illustration by Chris Nurse/Début Art
Editing by Brian R. Erdrich
Interior illustrations by Llewellyn Art Department and the author
Art on page 35 drawn by W. E. Hill from the Library of Congress (1915)

Llewellyn Publications is a registered trademark of Llewellyn Worldwide Ltd.

Library of Congress Cataloging-in-Publication Data
Names: Faerywolf, Storm, author.
Title: Forbidden mysteries of Faery witchcraft / by Storm Faerywolf.
Description: First edition. | Woodbury, Minnesota : Llewellyn Publications,
   [2018] | Includes bibliographical references and index.
Identifiers: LCCN 2018035836 (print) | LCCN 2018047304 (ebook) | ISBN
   9780738756646 (ebook) | ISBN 9780738756523 (alk. paper)
Subjects: LCSH: Fairies. | Witchcraft.
Classification: LCC BF1552 (ebook) | LCC BF1552 .F345 2018 (print) | DDC
   133.4/3--dc23
LC record available at https://lccn.loc.gov/2018035836

Llewellyn Publications
A Division of Llewellyn Worldwide Ltd.
2143 Wooddale Drive
Woodbury, MN 55125-2989
www.llewellyn.com

Printed in the United States of America

Other Books by Storm Faerywolf

Betwixt and Between

The Stars Within the Earth

Awakening the BlueLotus: A Reiki Level One Handbook

Becoming the BlueLotus: A Reiki Level Two Handbook

Also featured in:

Llewellyn's 2018 Witches' Companion

Llewellyn's 2019 Witches' Spell-a-Day Almanac

Llewellyn's 2019 Magical Almanac

This book is dedicated to the loving memory of Victor and Cora Anderson,
Grandmasters of our tradition, as well as the late Gwydion Pendderwen.
What is remembered lives.

Acknowledgments

In our world, there is no such thing as "doing it on our own." We all are in debt to those who help maintain the systems that support us, as well as to those who have gone before, paving the way so that our world is made even possible. I must first thank my ancestors, whose stories filled my childhood with magic and song and set the stage for me to find myself on the fae-touched path. To all of you, known and unknown, I thank you.

I must next thank my beloved partners, Chas Bogan and Devin Hunter. Were it not for them, I would not have been able to write this book, and for that I am eternally grateful. Grateful for the many long nights spent listening to me go on and on about how a certain subject or symbol was inspiring my work. Grateful for the patience they displayed when I continued to go on and on about some detail of Craft lore or history. Grateful for the many extra shifts they covered at our store so that I could stay home and write. Grateful for the many meals cooked, the errands run, and the housework done so that I could have the time necessary to devote to making this book a reality. Grateful for the love and support that they have both shown me for this, and for my many other half-finished projects that maybe one day I will get back to. I could not have done any of this without you.

I am also grateful to my co-religionists who have inspired and supported me throughout the years: Anaar, Onyx, SoulFire, Karina, Veedub, Thorn, M, Mitchell, Q, Dominic, and Tommie. You have all in your own way helped to make this work possible. To my own community of BlueRose: I feel so honored to have you on this journey with me. Thank you for your support, your love, and your laughter, as we travel together along this winding, beautiful, and sometimes treacherous road.

To Orion Foxwood and RJ Stewart, Faery brothers of another tribe: though our paths differ in style and lineage, we have shared in the deep magic that beats at the heart of Faery and have been changed by it. I am honored to be in this service with you, committed to bringing that magic more fully into this world. Thank you both for your support and inspiration.

To the Witches, both living and dead, of the lineage that brought the Old Craft to me and whose work has served as a foundation for my own: thank you for your teachings and your wisdom. If I stand tall, it is because I am standing on your shoulders.

And to all the other initiates, dedicants, students, and practitioners of the varied lines of our shared tradition, as well as to the many Witches of other traditions, solitaries, and seekers, who have shared their experiences and their magic with me over the years... To everyone who has participated in a ritual I led or attended a workshop I offered... Thank you for your presence and for your feedback. I am a better warlock because of it. You have encouraged me to stay the course and to keep sharing the magic with others, and it is because of you that I continue to do what I do. Without you none of this would be possible. IO EVOHE! Blessed be.

Contents

List of Exercises, Myths, Rituals, Rites, Spells, and Journaling

FOREWORD

Folklore abounds with warnings against engaging with faerys and their bewildering realm, and with good reason, for not only are dangers to be found there, but the agents of Faery are often manipulative and full of false promises. A trustful guide is essential, and is the reason why I am eager to promote the work of Storm Faerywolf, such as this book you are about to read. Throughout the many years that I have known him—as a colleague and my husband—Storm has traversed the misty mounds and violet lit chambers within the lands of Faery, while in the day-to-day world achieving success in his career and gaining an esteemed reputation among his peers. It is his ability to dwell successfully in both worlds that makes him such an excellent teacher. When looking for a useful guidebook, you want one composed from a perspective familiar with your own, so that you might come to understand what queer customs and potential provocations await you at your destination. Storm does a poet's job of translating the magic of Faery for those who wish to quest there on their own. Whether your call to this subject is academic or spiritual, you will be presented with much to contemplate and directly experience. As a keeper of tradition and lover of folklore, Storm presents the modern tradition of Faery Witchcraft as well as the breadth of lore at the heart of fairy tales.

As an initiate and teacher of Faery Tradition I am excited by the wealth of information and practices that Storm has made available herein. Many of the practices he writes about are familiar to me, from my own training and teaching, and it benefits me to read how fully Storm has explored them, to understand his insights, as well as to learn techniques he has expanded on and created anew. Storm and I began taking classes on the Faery Tradition together back in the early nineties. We were two different types of student: he, studious and diligent, myself … well, less so. Were I ever in need of cheating, his would be the paper I would sneak a peek off, which is perhaps the best compliment I can give someone. The dedication he has for retaining the lore of our tradition may only be outshined at times by his love for *Doctor Who* trivia. While there are many different types of students and teachers, I believe anyone interested in the tradition of Faery Witchcraft has something they can learn from Storm, and from this book particularly.

There is much material in this book that is part of traditional lore and practice that until now has not been widely available. Storm's dedication to preserving and promoting the Faery Tradition is a task he has long been involved with, and continues with this book. Academically, Faery Tradition is defined as a *mystery tradition*, meaning that it is understood through direct experience, as opposed to consisting of information alone. If we were giving kudos solely for the achievement of propagating information, Storm could be commended for making as much accessible as he has. For instance, he helped our community take its beginning steps into the digital age with the website FeriTradition.com. Furthermore, his branch of the tradition, known as BlueRose, has made Faery accessible to seekers across the globe. Yet it is in service to the ineffable mysteries of Faery that he has accomplished the most, by providing tools and guidance so that those looking to engage the mysteries of Faery are able to encounter them more fully. With this book, he greatly expands on that work, leading seekers to fully embody what are referred to as *forbidden mysteries*. In this turn of phrase, the word "forbidden" serves a hyperbolic purpose, suggesting taboo. These mysteries are not forbidden in any dogmatic sense (either by traditional codes of secrecy or injunction), but are not meant for the inexperienced and ill-intentioned—who would wisely forbid themselves to dabble with ways that might risk their serenity. But for those who are wise in their preparation, this book provides you the tools and map needed for your adventure into the wild depths of Faery.

What has often been missed in other publications on the subject of Faery magic are those elements known to be pernicious and feral. These fiercer characteristics of the fae are often overlooked in favor of more twee and ephemeral qualities, but any who seek to truly understand this magical race must not overlook the cautionary tales told by those who have encountered these beings. Storm presents these traditional tales, along with narratives born from his own intimate experiences with the Fae, preparing you for the perils that await you down this dark, brambly road.

In this book, the Dark Fae make their presence felt, sometimes merely mischievous, other times more twisted, but always lending insight into our own existence, and connecting us to those tameless parts of ourselves that society would have us keep in the dark. He shares how best to protect yourself and what threats to watch out for, all the while urging the willing deeper down into the underworld. As an emissary between the world of humankind and kingdom of the fae, he knows the powers who operate on the other side, and leads you into individual relationships with them, that they may serve as your allies.

Not only will you meet other entities in different realms, but you will have the opportunity to better understand yourself. Drawing on the transformational work inherent in the Faery Tradition, the work of this book seeks also to strengthen you in your fullness as a human being. Whether your intention is to know yourself better, or to develop the level of insight that leads to pronounced psychic abilities and magical acumen, this book will help unlock potential you may never have known existed in you.

Even so, this book is not simply another self-help program dressed up as Witchcraft. The powers you will encounter are not mere folklore, nor are they just reflections of the human psyche à la Jung, but are instead living beings with their own consciousness and motivations. Some of these exercises teach us how to better understand our own so-called personal demons, but even so, demons and faerys quite separate from us prowl our magic circles, and this book helps to better see them for what they are.

Forbidden Mysteries has so much of what one ought to want from a Witchcraft book: lessons on necromancy, hellfire, demons, demons who want to get sexy, possession, and of course, cursing work. Storm leads you through introspective exercises aimed at helping you understand your ethics, and for those of you who choose to take the offensive in your magic, he provides the basics for understanding how curses are to be thrown and enemies undone.

Forbidden Mysteries of Faery Witchcraft is certain to be considered a seminal book on the subject of Faery magic and something that no true lover of faerys should be without.

Chas Bogan
Author of *The Secret Keys of Conjure*

INTRODUCTION

The Faery[1] tradition is a rich and sensual path of sorcerous soul development. A mystery tradition of Witchcraft originating with the teachings of the blind shaman and poet Victor Anderson, its core is passed mainly orally from a priesthood of initiates who operate in covens and lineages that are wildly diverse in practice. Drawing from many different cultural and literary exemplars, our path weaves together a praxis containing elements of psychicism, ceremonial and folk magic, sexual mysticism, and spirit contact.

While the core of the oral tradition is secret, there has been a wealth of material that has grown up around this core, material that has inspired individuals, covens, and even other traditions of the Craft to deepen their practices and relationships with a universe populated with a myriad of magical energies, currents, and intelligences.

While its roots are ancient, its branches and fruit offer the modern practitioner a means to cultivate awareness and power, key elements necessary to the refining and strengthening of the *magical will*. As a practice, Faery is less concerned with complex rituals or outer forms than it is with the results provided by a genuine inner experience. It is a bardic path of poetry, of art, of song, and of ecstasy. It embraces both the light and dark aspects of nature and of the human mind. It draws from many different cultural examples in providing a magical worldview and demands a high degree of creativity and personal responsibility.

---

1. While there are many different legitimate spellings for our particular tradition currently in use (most notably *Feri*, though *Faery*, *F(a)eri(e)*, and even rarely *Fairy* sometimes appear), I tend to use the archaic *Faery* as it was the spelling used at the time of my introduction to the tradition, and I also feel it better poetically evokes the relationship between the practitioner and the fae—a detail of mytho-poetic practice that some lines of our tradition do not follow but is central to my own practice and my lineage of BlueRose.

I have been a formal practitioner of the Faery Tradition since 1992. After several years of intensive study, I was initiated into the inner priesthood with a secret rite that passes the unique current of energy that defines our Craft—the Faery Power—and poetically marks the new initiate as a racial descendant of "the little people." In 2007, I was passed the Black Wand of a Faery Master by Cora Anderson, one of the founders of our tradition, and Anaar, the current Grandmaster. This honorific ritually enabled me to found my own lineage of the tradition, which I call BlueRose, through which I offer training in Faery Tradition to my local community in the San Francisco Bay Area, but also internationally through travel and the internet.

The spiritual work that I do is twofold: to empower and inspire people to find their own power and develop it, and to then encourage those people to use their power to work toward the betterment of the world. We find ourselves in a precarious place in terms of politics as well as environmental sustainability. While the governments of the world continue to exploit the land, treating the earth and Her inhabitants as resources to be bought and sold, the spirits of the land have been consistently calling out to us to pay attention—to remember our sacred covenant as caretakers of the land, a tremendous spiritual responsibility of which the human species has been woefully negligent. We must combat this by first restructuring our relationship to the land and realizing that it is *alive* and that it is also conscious. As a species, we used to be able to listen to the voice of the land, of the wind, and of the stars, but as we moved into a technological age, we began to lose the ability as our attentions turned elsewhere. Little by little the magic of the world was seemingly lost. Though we have forgotten much, by contemplating the tales of our ancestors we can use their mysterious wisdom to speak to us now as we relearn these skills anew.

Even in the ancient tales it is said that the fae are receding from the world. Never quite gone, always in our periphery, perhaps offended or even injured by human presence, they are said to have retreated into the wildest of places—in caves, beneath the earth, and under mounds—to gather away from humankind, preserving the ancient life force that is the divine consciousness of the planet. As Witches, we seek to tap into that consciousness, but in order to do so we must first be able to perceive it. Enter here, the tools of magic.

Witchcraft is a dark mirror into which we scry, delving into the unfathomable waters of dream and vision, to peer beyond the veil and the world of things known and into the secret inner workings of nature herself. This is the spiritual nature of reality that we call the Hidden Kingdom, a magical realm in which we see that everything is alive and everything is connected in deep and mysterious ways. We seek to unlock the secrets of the land and those intricate connections that compose and sustain the worlds. We seek to learn the art of manipulating those connections, to perform *magic*, and our study draws us deeper and deeper into a world more largely populated than the conscious mind is usually prepared to accept, let alone effectively explain. We must abandon the restraints of rational thought that tell us that the only things that are "real" are those that we can directly see or experience with our own senses, for that mode of operation can only take us so far. Like the Witches, shamans, and spirit-workers before us, we know that in order to touch the hidden powers of the world we must leave behind the restrictions of logic and have the courage to delve into the wild and irrational abyss, to face our deepest fears and claim whatever power they hold over us. Only then can we truly begin our magical journey.

But we need not make this journey blind. The sorcerers of old left us clues that we can follow. In the form of poetry and folklore, of art and myth, we find fragments of old lore that we can piece together and use as maps to guide the way. Stories of encounters with the Fae, myths of old gods, folk tales that pass down symbolic keys that we use to unlock the secret doors into the otherworld, and to navigate the terrains once we get there. Through meditation, trance, ritual, storytelling, and art we make our way into the deep ancestral memories of the human race, and through those memories we touch *the Other*.

The Faery Tradition preserves this knowledge, called "forbidden" by a church that sought to suppress and demonize avenues to power outside of their control. Possession by spirits, summoning demons, casting curses, oracular divination, necromancy…the Witch seeks out these forbidden fruits and adds them to her diet, rich with spells and lore, myth and secrets, each imparting an understanding of how to approach the world with a different set of eyes, enchanted to see that of which otherwise we would be blissfully unaware. The blinders now removed, we see clearly, a daunting experience for most, as now we find ourselves in another world—alien and unsure—and one in which we are *not alone*. A myriad of spirits and beings populate the many dimensions through which a sorcerer will travel, and through their engagement our work is deepened, empowered by currents of power and influence that have been in existence for as long as there has been a world to observe.

Deepened, yes, but no power comes without price. Some of the spirits we may encounter will not have our best interests at heart. Some will work to deceive or even harm us. Stories of every culture speak of demons or "evil spirits" that infect the lives of those who are unfortunate enough to come across them. Modern psychology speaks of them in terms of complexes, deep-rooted fears that gnaw at us from somewhere deep behind our own conscious minds. But even these twists of the mind can give birth to something more sinister, drawing life force away from its host until it becomes autonomous, a spiritual parasite that can weaken and manipulate its host behind the spotlight of conscious awareness.

Whether these demons be ancient spirits or ones of our own making, we must confront them in order to reclaim the power they have stolen. Toward this end we employ several measures to summon and transform them where possible, and where it is not, we work to repurpose them toward our own goals. Whether human, angel, demon, or god, a Witch bows to no one.

Even those spirits that are genuinely helpful may ask for certain things in return for their knowledge or assistance, and so it becomes especially important to learn how to navigate these relationships before we unknowingly fall victim to our own ignorant exuberance. This is where both tradition and personal experience bear their mark, enabling the veteran practitioner a means to skillfully traverse the other worlds, and to make allies along the way; allies that not only offer us the potential to quicken our journeys, but also to journey to places we could never go, thus expanding the sphere of our magical reach.

A common theme in both shamanism and Witchcraft is the relationship between the spiritual practitioner and the spirit world—in particular, the relationship that the practitioner has with a *specific* spirit, often referred to in Witchcraft as the *familiar*. While popular Neopagan culture most often uses this term to refer to our physical pets (and I can attest that many a cat with whom I have cohabited has exhibited an uncanny sense of magical awareness), traditionally this term refers to a spirit-helper that may appear in many forms that assists the magical practitioner in several ways, such as providing direct knowledge of the spirit world, offering inspiration and power, and even taking flight to other worlds to communicate with other spirits, at times employing them on behalf of the practitioner's magical will.

We find inspiration and magic where it presents itself, whether that is in ancient myths, historic recreations, or completely new innovations based on popular culture. The magic is in the relationship one has to it. In Witchcraft if it speaks, we listen.

This book contains information and magic both old and new, regarding the shadow nature of Faery Tradition. It expands upon that found in my book *Betwixt and Between: Exploring the Faery Tradition of Witchcraft,* but for those unfamiliar with this text I have provided some basic information and exercises in appendix I so that you will be better able to work with the material here. Additionally, I have included a glossary of terms specific to our tradition in the back of this book.

As much of our tradition is passed in trance, so too with this book. A majority of the exercises and rituals presented here are meant to be experienced in the trance state, using specific visual and poetic keys in order to grant a deeper access to the powers and spirits involved. As you read them over, allow yourself to *feel* the sensations described, as if you were going through the trance. Take your time. Reread the trances as you might read a poem. How do the words make you feel? The imagery? In this way, you will prepare yourself to more deeply engage the symbolic material when you later set a formal space and perform the trance in actual. Remember also to record your experiences with the material in your journal, which should contain a record of all of your magical work, providing you not only with much needed documentation of your insights and challenges, but the very act also provides us a means to better develop our own intuitive and psychic skills over time.

This book is intended for the intermediate to advanced Craft practitioner. If you are a practitioner of the Faery Witchcraft tradition then this means you have practiced with material similar to that in *Betwixt and Between* and/or in the appendices of this book for at least two full years. If you are an intermediate to advanced practitioner of a non-Faery form of the Craft (perhaps a third- or even an experienced second-degree initiate in those systems that follow a standardized British Traditional Wicca three-degree format) then, like your Faery-trained counterpart, you may treat this book as a fairly straightforward course of study. After gaining a familiarity with the Faery-specific terms and practices in the appendices, then you may move through this book in the order given, adopting the exercises given here into your own spiritual/magical practice. This practice, in my opinion, should be a fairly consistent minimum of four formal sessions per week, with additional "informal" versions of some of the foundational practices being performed multiple times *daily*. In doing so you will create a practice that creates the necessary momentum by which we may more fully engage the spirits and powers with which we shall be working. As with all endeavors of learning and discovery you should keep a detailed journal of your experiences as you go.

While on this voyage together, we commune with many traditional powers, symbols, spirits, deities, and intelligences along the way. We will summon forth the ancient Wells of Creation, primal undrworld goddesses of the elemental powers, and journey with them into the abyss to face our fears and conquer our demons. We will walk the bone road, opening the Western Gate to commune with the gods of death, and help trapped spirits cross over. We will prepare ourselves as worthy vessels for divine possession, the ecstatic state of being ridden by a god, spirit, or power, and perform as oracles, speaking the wisdom of the gods on earth. And we will consider both the casting and breaking of curses, the dark art of offensive magic.

As with any voyage it all begins with a single step. Come with me as we journey now to Faeryland to visit the shadow of our Craft and make allies of what lives in the darkness there.

PART ONE

THE DARK FAE

The Angels Stand Just There

There is a silent shriek
Electric lightning thunderclaps
Rain against the window glass
Night outside my room

Standing at the edge of dreams
Beneath my feet they shine
eyes cold and beautiful
bathed in storm and moon

Golden skin and golden hair
He looks soft enough to kiss
And she, younger, stands just there
Inhuman eyes that draw me near

I rise
Against my own free will
A pit in my stomach
Aches as if poisoned.

I am drawn,
Against my trembling fear
A sound in my ears
Deafens all reason.

I cannot move
I cannot speak

My soul is snared
My power faltered
Seized by fear and gripped with malice
A trap is set and I am captured

Breathing slow and breathing deep
Arise thy spark!
Arise and conquer!
Fire deep within the soul
Defend the boundaries of thy master!

I find my voice; I find my power
I hum my spell
I sing my tune
The star of nature is my shield
I am firmly rooted in this realm.

Emblazoned sigil in my mind
My throaty drone empowers thee
To cast false angels to the wind
As I WILL, So MOTE IT BE!

The spell is broken
My guests depart
I fall down exhausted
I sleep without dream.

CHAPTER I

WITCHES AND THE FAE:
MADNESS, DEATH, AND PROPHECY

There are more things in heaven and earth, Horatio,
Than are dreamt of in your philosophy.
—SHAKESPEARE,
HAMLET ACT I, SCENE 5

Witchcraft is a dangerous path, though generally not for the reasons postulated by feeble-minded religious fanatics from their bully pulpits. With their fevered insistence of blind adherence to a limited worldview, a veil of terror and fear has been drawn that obscures the true beauty and power of our Craft, leaving many with ridiculous notions as to the nature of our practice, leaving many unprepared for the actual dangers that a magical practice can harbor.

In a society dominated by authoritarian monotheism, we might be forgiven for internalizing some of their dogmatic fears, though this presents us with our first real challenge, for only when we have confronted our fears of "damnation and hellfire" does the work really begin. Only those who are willing and able to look into the abyss are suited for a life in the Craft, and those who would pursue our crooked path without having done so are doomed to failure. Should those fears be buried instead of brought to light and transformed, we will never know the truth of our own potential and will forever be the victim of our own internal demons. Left unchecked and unconquered, they will likely fester, inviting a disease of the mind that will corrupt our foundation, leaving us broken and powerless.

It is a much-cited piece of folklore that says when one encounters the fae, or sleeps overnight on one of their sacred places, one ends up either "dead, mad, or a poet."[2] The first two choices are pretty grim, and the situation is made even more dismal when you consider that Irish folklore places little to no distinction between the last two. With odds like that, who in their right mind would seek out such an encounter? The answer is someone who knows the true value of that third choice.

Poetry might not seem on the surface to be a formidable power, but consider that ancient Irish tradition also drew little distinction between poetic skill and prophetic ability. The "poet" was just as often a "prophet" or otherwise imbued with other-worldly powers.

In the "Ballad of Thomas the Rhymer," we are told the tale of a man who meets the Queen of Faery and is then taken with her into Elfland. After honoring certain prohibitions and serving her faithfully for seven years, he is returned to earth with special gifts: "the tongue that cannot lie" and the ability to speak prophecy.

Prophecy is a power traditionally associated with Witchcraft, and so forming an alliance with a spirit that could impart this ability would certainly be an asset. A Witch will work with many spirits as need arises. They will learn which spirits are good to heal sickness and which others help in drawing love; spirits for granting sight, spirits for blessing, spirits for cursing; and in the middle of all of this, the *familiar spirit*. More than simply a common pet, the familiar was a spirit, demon, or imp that could *take the form of an animal*, but was in actuality a spirit. It offered not just advice, but also *power*. Magical power. It was a guide and source of protection and strength for the Witch.

There is a longstanding tradition of Witches working with the fae to the degree that one simply cannot address one without addressing the other. The Witch would certainly face such grim odds in their pursuit of greater knowledge and power, and a fae being as a familiar spirit would be a particularly powerful alliance. And if they were a well-informed Witch, and had bravely looked into their black heart and gained the power and strength of their shadow, they might not suffer a dark fate, but instead enter into a relationship that would deepen the magic on both sides of the veil.

At the heart of all Witchcraft is the pursuit of knowledge. We seek to better understand the processes of nature, to draw back the veil and peer into the hidden inner

---

2. Robert Graves, *The White Goddess: A Historical Grammar of Poetic Myth* (New York: Noonday Press, 1975, originally published 1948), 91.

mechanisms by which the universe is governed and kept in motion. Over the years we have tread this often-crooked path, we have made certain discoveries along the way, and chief among them is the knowledge that what we can see, touch, hear, feel, smell, or taste is but a fraction of what the universe has to offer.

A basic operating principle of our Craft is that all matter is composed of energy, and all energy has consciousness. With this in mind we understand that the whole of the world—and all the parts and particles that compose the world—are alive and therefore in possession of some level of consciousness. Everything is alive, and everything has a spirit. Additionally, all things are connected. The environment is not a lifeless machine composed of incidentally living parts, but a living (and sentient) holism, with which we can learn to communicate and otherwise engage with on multiple levels. This communication is the very core of magic, the modality by which we are able to enlist the aid of these spirits to assist us in our workings.

These spirits come in many different forms, and rarely do we find normal verbal communication alone to be effective. We have to communicate with them not in our language but in theirs. We must learn the language of symbolism, sensation, and energy. We must shape our consciousness in certain ways to facilitate the connection. Our rituals are designed to evoke certain mindsets, unlocking hidden potentials in the human mind, abilities that may seem small at first, or as unreal as a daydream, but will—over time—grow into a source of inspiration and power. When we engage in communication with a plant or a stone, for example, this is not done through our normal awareness, but through a deliberate shift in perception. We step into an aligned state of *Enchantment* by which our own consciousness is better able to make a direct connection to the consciousness within the plant, stone, or other object. We connect to the spirit of the object in question, and for one who is naturally gifted or trained in magical trance, the communications occur. We may receive messages, and likewise we may impart our own to the spirit, in the hopes of forming an alliance toward our goal.

The road to madness need not come at the hands of dark fae bent on our destruction, as the work we do as Witches can potentially drive us there very nicely quite on its own. This state of Enchantment, so central to the workings of Faery magic, is somewhat of a double-edged sword. To step into an altered state—especially one that brings us closer to the unseen realms and their inhabitants—runs the risk of upsetting the psychological balance of the individual, should they be ill-prepared to face their deepest fears and insecurities. Most people are content to bury their fears and live an unexamined life, allowing the bliss of self-ignorance to act as a pleasant drug, numbing whatever anxieties or pains they carry and softening the edges.

The Craft demands so much more from us. We work to keep open our minds and imaginations … we invoke spirits, angels, deities, fairies, and demons … we engage with the living consciousness of plants, stones, objects, and places. We work to slip into trance at the drop of a hat to commune with our deepest natures, as well as a myriad of other archetypes, symbols, spirits, and beings, and at times even allow them the use of our bodies in the sacred act of *possession*. All of these things, when practiced by an individual who is not mentally balanced, can result in a break in the personality, leading to some degree of insanity.

We seek that balance by first examining what demons lurk within our personal abyss, and to do this we must learn to get comfortable with the uncomfortable. Our own evolution (spiritual, magical, or otherwise) does not happen when we are safe, contented, and unchallenged. Only by delving into our own shadow can we begin to work the magic upon ourselves to transform our fears into power. Many methods can be employed toward this end, some of them decidedly mundane: psychotherapy, counseling, etc. But as practitioners of the Witches' Craft, we are not limited to just the psychological in our approach; we may feel free to "think outside the box" and use the magical as well as the mundane.

Witchcraft is an experiential path. Whether through initiatory lineages that span back to a common spiritual forebear or through mythology or culture that grants a sense of tribal belonging, wisdom is passed from teacher to student, from covener to covener, from lover to lover, or even directly by the spirits to the individual, mostly by means that do not necessarily resemble what we often think of as teaching or learning in the common sense. Ours is not a path that can be fully understood with the mind, but must be lived and felt. Witchcraft must be *experienced*. We *engage* the Craft, not just with our left-brained awareness of logic and language, but also with our right-brain awareness of art, and inspiration, and dream. As activist and priestess Starhawk said in her groundbreaking book *The Spiral Dance*, "Witchcraft has always been a religion of poetry, not theology."[3] It is a practice that is not confined to that which can be fully

---

3. Starhawk, *The Spiral Dance: A Rebirth of the Ancient Religion of the Great Goddess* (New York: HarperCollins, 1979), 32.

grasped by the analytical mind. For this reason, many will discount it as being mere fantasy—a flight of fancy that has no place in the "real world." But what these people fail to understand is that the world is so much larger than what we can directly experience through our physical senses. Were we to speak strictly in terms of science, we might then reference something like infrared light, which cannot be directly seen but can be measured with instruments. In Witchcraft, we are likewise interacting with unseen forces, only those which modern science has yet to explain. In the Craft, we are not asked to ignore the rational, *but to also embrace* the irrational. We live in a world populated by science, technology, and literature, as well as gods, goddesses, faeries, djinn, ancestral spirits, and the like. We recognize that academia and analytical thinking are valuable and necessary—but also that they can only take us so far. Once we have exhausted what linear thinking offers us we are left with the illogical. We are left with poetry, art, music, dance, and the telling of stories.

The Dark Fae of Folklore

If we are to benefit from the wisdom of our ancestors, then we must begin by listening to their stories. When you think of "Faery tales" what images arise? Put from your mind the idea that the faerys are saccharine creatures of fancy, who delight in nothing more than dancing in forests, sprinkling flight-inducing pixie dust on sad and lonely children, or granting wishes. While folklore does indeed present us with such whimsical tales (and in fact, Cora Anderson, the late co-founder of our particular tradition, recalled a childhood story of an encounter with a small winged fairy who informed her where to find a coin under a rock so that she could buy some candy),[4] far more common are the tales of abduction, torture, mental ruin, and even murder at the hands of the Fae.

Several classifications of faerys have been known to cause such misery. *Kelpies* and *will-o-the-wisps* were such dangerous creatures, but they paled in comparison to the dreaded *redcaps* who could kill and eat a person who strayed by their dwellings too long.[5] These more "feral" types of faery beings are contrasted with the "noble" (but no less dangerous) faerys, such as the Tuatha dé Danann, the pre-Christian gods of

---

4. Cora Anderson, *Childhood Memories* (Portland, OR: Acorn Guild Press. 2007), 17–18.

5. Katherine Briggs, *An Encyclopedia of Fairies: Hobgoblins, Brownies, Bogies, and Other Supernatural Creatures* (New York: Pantheon Books, 1976).

Ireland who gave rise to the stories of the *Sidhe*, the divine precursors of those beings we normally think of as the fae.

A common theme in old fairy stories is that of the fae possessing a morality quite different from what is considered conventionally human. The Faery, in general, are not "immoral"; they seem to conduct themselves by a set of rules not immediately obvious to the human observer. Consider stories in which the Fae abducted human children, leaving their own in their place. These "changelings" were often sickly and would soon die, or were actually old faery who would ravenously eat while in the cradle, but never grow, much to the distress of their human hosts.

The general theme of such stories does not condemn the Fae for abandoning their own children, nor for stealing the human ones, even though by some accounts the human children are forced into a life of slavery. Instead, medieval lore often depicts these Fae as being sympathetic and kind, just following etiquette quite alien to our human sensibilities.[6] This on its own gives us a glimpse into the strange world of Faery; it demonstrates that there are certain rules or procedures that must be followed, as opposed to a wholly feral and mindless chaos, though admittedly the rules of Faery may at times appear to us as such. One aspect that is constant in what we might call "the Faery encounter" is that it is *weird*.

The Faery were well respected, but above all else they were *feared*. The amusing titles often given to them—the Good Children, the Kindly Ones, the Fair Folk—were used precisely because a fearful populace wanted to *appease* them, and so giving them compliments (especially where it was "not deserved") was a surefire way to have them look upon our kind favorably. Or at least spare us a terrible fate. Hopefully. This time.

Faery Protection Magic

Much of the folk magic associated with the Faerys was focused on protecting *from* them. One could carry St. John's Wort or wear their clothes inside out in order to secure the protection of one's person, while to safeguard the home, primrose might be placed upon the windowsill to ensure no Faery could gain entry. Horses (in particular danger of being ridden to death by the Faery hosts) might be spared such a fate by

---

6. Mika Loponen, "Faery Folklore in Medieval Tales—An Introduction," 2010, accessed May 9, 2017, https://www.academia.edu/300335/Faery_Folklore_in_Medieval_Tales_an_Introduction.

placing a garland of marigolds above the barn door. However, above all else in terms of efficacy, was cold iron.

Iron has long been recognized as a powerful weapon against *maleficum*, or baneful magic. Cemeteries were often surrounded by iron fencing in order to "contain" the spirits that dwell within. Iron pins sewn, hidden in the hem of the baby's clothes, or a pair of scissors hung over the crib were used to prevent the Fae from abducting or harming the child. Myths often speak of iron dispelling the magic of Faerys or Witches, and in fact folklore seems to approach the two almost interchangeably in this regard. The Witch, however, is also associated with iron tools, such as a knife and a cauldron, and so it would appear that this rule is not one that is universally applied to the human practitioner of magic. In Faery Witchcraft tradition, Victor Anderson, the late Grandmaster of our faith, recommended that practitioners keep a piece of iron on their altars to assist in returning from "between the worlds," i.e., from deep astral or trance experiences. As iron is a major component in our blood, it is an element of grounding and physical life force. To magically use iron in this way it is an anchor to the physical realm, the "middleworld" of existence, dispelling any hold that the otherworlds might have upon the practitioner by reminding our bodies of our physicality, drawing our spirits back and into the world of form. This is another reason why iron is forbidden when journeying in the Faery realm: quite simply, it prevents our full immersion in the nonphysical, and would make such a journey impossible, or at least more difficult.

Faery as Shadow World

What we refer to as the Faery realm is a particular layer of planetary consciousness that can be said to reside in the underworld. While many would consider the underworld to be exclusively the land of the dead, we might view the underworld as an energetic vibration that underlies our own normal perception of the world, and as such it is much larger than what is generally thought. In the Faery Tradition, we see the underworld as being dual in nature: the land of ancestors (death), and the realm of the Fae (life). Both of these expressions are said to mirror our own world (often called the middleworld) and so working with them can be quite useful in coming to a better understanding of ourselves. "As above, so below," so the old Hermetic principle goes, a reminder that whatever we seek in the other realms has a direct correlation to what we are dealing with internally, and vice versa. Because of this, we must be prepared to face whatever lurks in our own shadow.

Consider that every fear you possess, every weakness, every negative quality is existing within you, right now, as a coalescence of energy within your *fetch,7* the primal part of your soul structure. Because this energy has coalesced, it is no longer freely available to you, and as such you are depleted and unable to reach (and therefore expand) your potential.

Further, these energy forms are largely unnoticed. Of course, you may be aware of some of them, in the sense that we each may know that we have a tendency to yell when we are angry, or say inappropriate things when we are scared, or overeat or use drugs to numb our pain. But they can be small things that slip by our awareness and this is where things start to get tricky. These smaller weaknesses are insidious and will dictate from their unseen places within us, and we can be powerless to stop them, even if we are somehow made aware of their existence. We might never know that we are presented with certain choices, because our own shadow will have carefully tugged on inner strings to steer us in certain directions to avoid confrontation with the conscious mind (or *talker*), which is a necessary component of stealing back our power.

Once we have begun the journey to take back our personal power we start to see how this is really just one step upon a larger journey: that of reaching beyond the firelight of human perception and into the *outer darkness*—the poetic term for that which exists outside of existence itself—and from here, more than anywhere else, is where a Witch steals their power.

We must all be prepared to look into the face of the abyss. This dark mirror shows us a reflection of who we really are, granting us an opportunity to really see beyond our normal ego-perceptions and perceive the world through the eyes of the Witch. The Witch sees the interconnections that compose the world. They know how to navigate them, how to tug here and to coax there, in order to achieve the desired result. They engage the intricate web of connections that is the secret workings of nature: the world behind the world, and in so doing they learn much about themselves.

---

7. The Faery Tradition postulates the existence of three souls (or three parts of the soul) of the human being. These are *fetch*, the primal, subconscious, animal part of our nature; the *talker*, which is roughly analogous to the conscious mind; and the *(holy) daemon*, which is the "higher self," "personal god," or "spark of divinity" within each person. We strive to align them and keep them in good health. I have included a basic soul alignment exercise in appendix I.

There are deeper layers to ourselves than we realize. There are entire worlds to be explored. Within each of us is a hidden gateway into the realm of the fantastical but most of us are too ignorant, too prideful, or too afraid to even notice. We have been lulled into a dreamless sleep in which we go about the lives that have been laid out for us by the culture in which we participate. It is the artist, the poet, the shaman, and the Witch that transcend the confines that our culture would impose upon our study of the relationship between our own consciousness and the rest of the universe. Or, to put it more simply, our study of *magic*.

Meeting the Challenge

The ultimate goal of Faery is nothing short of the re-sacralization of the world. This isn't simply a metaphor for how we treat (or don't treat) the planet with respect, but a deep and ongoing conscious relationship with the land—not as resource—but as ally. The land itself is alive and demands to be seen as such, or rather our own need for survival demands that we shift our relationship from one of exploitation and into guardianship. But to truly enter into this relationship, we must be pure of heart, without fear or reservation.

In folklore, some sort of challenge often accompanies encounters with the fae. Usually this is an assessment of the heart of the human, perhaps to determine their worthiness of the Faery gifts, and often occurring in the context of a moral test. We are all probably familiar with the archetypal story: in the course of one's normal routine, one comes upon a beggar, usually an old man or woman. If the person is kind to the beggar then they are granted some boon. If not, then a terrible curse is placed upon them. Many versions of this story exist in the folkloric tales from cultures all over the world; an archetypal pattern playing out, the stakes of which are nothing less than the cultivation of the individual's own soul.

When we are confronted with such a challenge while engaging our spiritual work, we are often more likely to "take the high road," offering our assistance to whatever spirits may present themselves to us in need. But these challenges do not only present themselves to us in the comfortable confines of our magic circles and temple spaces. More often we will be presented with such a challenge "in real life": the homeless person asking for change, the elderly person who is in need of assistance. The spirit and magic of the world plays out *through* the world, not outside of it. Consider this the next time you are called upon to perform a charitable act. For a true Witch, there is no such thing as "a day off."

JOURNALING: Ethics and Morals

Ethics is a code of right and wrong as deemed by society. Morals are what *you* believe is right and wrong. This exercise helps us clarify where our own ethics and morals may resonate as well as where they may differ from societal expectations.

Items needed:

A pen

Your journal

Contemplate both ethics and morality. How are they different for you? Where do you transcend the cultural norms? How are they the same? How have societal ethics influenced your personal morality? Do your own ethics differ at all from those with which you were raised? If so, how? If not, have you examined why you think certain things are right or wrong? Just or unjust? Journal on these questions—and whatever related subjects may arise for you—for at least five to ten minutes. When finished, reflect on what you wrote. Does it feel "right" to you? Are you surprised by some of your thoughts on the subject?

The point of the above exercise is not to try to instill a particular ethical code in the reader, quite the contrary. Ethical codes only really work in so far as the personal morality of the individual is in resonance. And while we know that the morality of the fae is not the same as those of humanity, we *do* know what kind of moral displays they will reward and which they will punish. If we are to work closely with the fae, then we will need to make certain that we are living our lives in a manner that promotes this kinship with all life, rather than that of a miserly narcissist. Ask yourself, "What small change can I make *right now* that will encourage this kinship?" Perhaps it's volunteering at a soup kitchen or a homeless shelter. Or maybe it will be donations made to charitable causes. Or even perhaps it will be simple acts of kindness, perhaps anonymously given, with the intent to affect the web of connections that governs all life. We are all called upon to be healers in some way or form. What will you heal today?

The Second Sight

A recurring theme surrounding the Faery encounter is—barring insanity and death, of course—that the experiencer is granted certain conditions or gifts, most notably among them being "the Second Sight." This poetic term for an "extrasensory" perception refers to a type of visionary ability of being able to see into the otherworlds that intersect our "normal" one. Historically, this ability was often involuntary (as opposed to some other cultures, such as those of ancient Greece or Rome, in which ingesting some type of hallucinogenic substance precipitated the ability.[8] In Scotland, however, this ability was widespread, perhaps due to the fact that it was culturally accepted and therefore openly discussed. Even in Scotland, however, this ability was often seen as more of a curse than a blessing.[9]

While it might be tempting to simply equate this Sight with a modern idea of psychicism and clairvoyance, this would ignore the poetic implications of the culture that gave rise to it. Just as often the visions experienced were *symbolic* (such as seeing a person wrapped in a death shroud, as opposed to witnessing their funeral procession)[10] and as such were open to some interpretation. According to Druidic tradition, the talents for poetry and prophecy were not as clearly separated and defined as they most often are to a modern sensibility, and following in the tradition of ancient Irish lore, the Faery Tradition explores their shared liminality: the poetic and the prophetic are one and the same, or at the very least, two sides of the same coin.

One characteristic of this Sight is that it would grant the ability to see the Faerys, those mysterious beings of power that are intimately connected to the land and the hidden spiritual processes of nature. One particular tale much beloved in our tradition is that of the midwife who one night is suddenly called upon to attend a birth in a strange location (sometimes described as being a simple cottage or other times a grand castle). She is instructed to rub a certain ointment on the eyes of the newborn but is admonished to take care not to get any on her own. As she feverishly works to successfully deliver the child, she absent-mindedly wipes the sweat from her brow and

---

8. Elizabeth McQuillan, "From First person to the Second Sight," Caledonian Mercury, 2010, accessed May 10, 2017, http://caledonianmercury.com/2010/06/12/from-first-person-to-the-second-sight/008473.

9. Ibid.

10. Shari Ann Cohn, "Scottish tradition of second sight and other psychic experiences in families," Edinburgh Research Archive, 1996, accessed May 10, 2017, https://www.era.lib.ed.ac.uk/handle/1842/9674.

accidentally rubs a small amount of the ointment into her eye. The baby is born, she is paid for her services, and she is returned to her home.

Sometime later, while she is at market she recognizes some of the other people who attended the birth, including a man who is brazenly stealing, and apparently doing so completely unseen by the merchants. The midwife greets him, and he is surprised that she can see him. "By which eye do you see me?" he asks. She responds by pointing to the eye into which this one had rubbed the ointment. And with that he blew on her eye, blinding her for the rest of her life. In this we see that the fae can not only bestow the Sight, they can also take it away.

Navigating the Faery Encounter

There are many examples within folklore that describe the Faery encounter, but among the most clear and detailed are those of Thomas the Rhymer, Tam Lin, and Rev. Robert Kirk. In each of these accounts we are presented with specific poetic keys that are especially potent when engaged in the act of aligning our consciousness to the Fae realm, and for navigating our way once we are there.

In *The Secret Commonwealth of Elves, Fauns, and Fairies*, Rev. Robert Kirk, famed scholar and folklorist, describes a world populated by Faerys, spirits, wraiths, and sprites in a series of stories collected in his travels of the Scottish Highlands before his death in 1692. What makes him unique is that it is said that instead of dying he was actually abducted into the Faery realm, reportedly appearing after his "death" to his neighbors who—due to a state of shock—failed to follow the necessary magical procedures to free him from the spell and thus return him to human life.

The "Ballad of Thomas the Rhymer" is a traditional Scottish "border ballad" that describes an encounter between the titular character and the Queen of Faery. What makes this particular story so important to a study of the Faery Tradition is the level of symbolic detail in which is described the Faery encounter, and that when taken together the narrative can be understood as mapping out an initiatory journey from novice to adept within the folkloric tradition.[11]

Another interesting detail of this story—like in the stories of Rev. Robert Kirk—is that it is about an actual person. Thomas Learmont was born in 1220 in Erceldoune

---

11. RJ Stewart, *Earth Light: The Ancient Path to Transformation Rediscovering the Wisdom of Celtic & Faery Lore*, (Rockport, MA: Element Books Limited, 1992), 125–136.

(now Earlston), Scotland, in the area bordering England.[12] He was considered a great prophet, and a good number of prophecies are attributed to him.

As with all ballads there are many different versions, each of which are considered to be traditional. In bardic tradition, it is not only common but expected that a story-teller embellish or otherwise alter the minor details of a story in order to "breathe new life" into it. In each retelling, we are perhaps able to look at the story from another perspective, every nuance revealing something new that might otherwise go unexamined. Each new version will still draw from a common underlying theme, but may add additional details to the story to augment the meaning. There is a fine line to be walked in this, for just as one aspect of bardic tradition is concerned with preserving history by transmitting old stories, another purpose is providing the ability to problem-solve by inspiring visionary access to the imagination and creativity. Creativity, vision, and inspiration are valued traits in a bardic society. This type of culture can be seen somewhat like a tree—a living thing with a strong foundation in history (roots) providing the basis and knowledge for living in the real world (trunk) and granting access to creativity and spirit/higher-mind/divinity (branches, flowers, and/or fruit).

With all this taken into consideration, I have included my own reworking of the traditional ballad in appendix II. I have made every attempt to closely follow the particular traditional versions upon which this is based, paying attention to symbol, rhyme, and meter, while changing the language to make it more accessible to the modern ear and the overall narrative clearer.

In this traditional telling we are given certain keys to the Faery encounter. The tale begins with Thomas sleeping underneath a tree where he has a vision of a beautiful woman riding toward him on a white horse. The original refers to this tree as the "Eildon Tree," which stood at Eildon Hill in Scotland. This tree died before a written historic record, knowledge of it passed down in oral tradition alone until a memorial stone was erected to mark the spot where it once stood. The species of the tree is never identified in the original tales, though some writers have assumed it was the magical hawthorn (or simply, "thorn"), which is said to be a portal into the Faery realm. This is unlikely, however, as references to the hawthorn as an entrance to the

---

12. RJ Stewart, *The Underworld Initiation: A Journey Towards Psychic Transformation*, (Lake Toxaway, NC: Mercury Publishing, 1990), 189.

fair realm seem not to exist before the early twentieth century,[13] so we may assume that these are modern inventions. Another speculation (and one with which I am inclined to agree, hence its use in my version) is that this tree was the oak.[14] This tree fits the various descriptions from the original versions of the ballad; being a "greenwood," a tree that grew in the area of Scotland referenced, as well as being tall enough for the Queen to ride underneath its canopy, as per the story. It also carries the significance of being one of the three magical trees associated with the Faery, the others being ash and the previously mentioned thorn.

While underneath this magical tree, Thomas kisses the Queen, even though she forewarns him that to do so would mean that she would be in charge of his body. By doing so he has entered into a Faery contract, and now must abide by the rules of it, even though he might not yet fully know its full extent. She explains to him that if he were to speak while in her realm he would never be able to return to earth. There is some speculation concerning this passage as to the possibility that the Queen actually took his voice from him, leaving him mute so as to not accidentally break the prohibition. She also warns him not to eat the fruit there, for they are filled with all the curses of hell. This is a variant of the more common prohibition against eating or drinking in general while in their realm, for to do so would be to become bound there.

She instructs him to mount her horse with her, and—perhaps by some magic connected to the silver bells mentioned—the steed flies "faster than the wind." They are then described as reaching a "desert," the fuller text stating, "living land was left behind." This also—to my mind—lends credence to the idea of Faery being an aspect of the underworld, which is most often associated with the dead.

Once there, the Faery Queen shows Thomas three visions in the form of roads. I have always interpreted this setting as being at a traditional four-way crossroads, with the road they were traveling from being the road to/from earth, while the three described in the ballad are the road to hell (often mistaken for heaven), the road to heaven (though it being such a difficult terrain it is most often ignored) and the "bonny" road to Faery being in between them. This described Faery as being a liminal space "in be-

---

13. Lee Raye, *The Eildon Tree in 'The Romance of Thomas of Erceldoune' (Thomas the Rhymer)*. Natural History blog. 2014. https://historyandnature.wordpress.com/2014/05/18/the-eildon-tree-in-thomas-of-erceldoune/ (Accessed June 16, 2017).

14. Ibid.

tween" the conventional concepts of "good" and "evil" and prepares us for the reality of the Fae's morality as being different than our own.

As they continue their travels in this strange land, they see "neither sun nor moon," but they hear "the roaring of the sea." Here we may catch another glimpse of what identifies this as being an underworld encounter and we may use them for our own sojourns into the fair realm. The setting described is lacking any celestial details, which can imply a symbolic subterranean environment. Often, we will hear of the sky in Faery being similar to twilight on earth, but without a sun or moon. Paradoxically, we may find references to stars in the sky in Faery; these "stars within the earth" are the "Faery stars," the hidden spirit within matter or the presence of the magical within the mundane.

While traveling with the Faery Queen, they encounter a river of blood, which they must wade through, which is said to be from "all the blood that's shed on earth." Blood is a poetic rendering for genetic wisdom, that which is passed "through the blood." It is significant that in this telling it is specifically connected to warfare and violence. These examples of the darker side of human nature represent both a power and a poison at the heart of humanity and must be confronted head on (i.e., "waded through") in order to claim whatever power and wisdom we may wish to gain from our experiences. We cannot deny the dark aspects of ourselves, or our species. We must embrace them, lest they have power *over* us.

The "River of Blood" is at once both personal; relating to one's (generally biological) ancestors, as well as transpersonal, embodying the collective wisdom of humanity. To wade through it is symbolic of consciously facing our shadow, as well as delving through that ancestral wisdom, allowing it to inform and guide us.

Some accounts of the Faery journey also include a "River of Tears," which is said to be those shed by mothers, weeping for the loss of their sons in battle. This too is a call to confront our own collective pain; that darkness within the heart of the human soul that would allow us to inflict pain upon others or even just to justify cruelty when we see it being inflicted. These tears are cleansing; we become purified by facing our darkness and then resolving through our actions to address it.

The River of Tears is also symbolic of stellar consciousness, contrasting with the earthly consciousness of the River of Blood. Together they are two sides of the same coin, red and white; the double rose, the two dragons. They are complementary forces working together, or at least working toward a common goal. We might also see them represented in the Iron and Pearl pentacles, two of the most beloved magical tools of the Faery Witchcraft tradition. The rivers—like the pentacles—share a common theme: that of the confrontation of weakness—both personal and transpersonal—and their subsequent transformation and reintegration into the self. We must be purified if we are to survive the Faery encounter with our sanity intact.

At this point in the narrative, we skip to what might be Thomas's return, here describing a green garden. The Queen then plucks a fruit (sometimes described as an apple, so popular in fairy tales) and offers it to Thomas with the knowledge that it will grant "the tongue that cannot lie," which he first protests but is effectively cowed into obeisance by the Queen's decree. In some accounts, he selects an additional fruit at the Queen's request, which grants him the additional gift of prophecy, which he chooses over mastery of the harp.

Finally, we are told that Thomas was given a "coat of the even cloth" and a pair of green velvet shoes. We know that the traditional Faery color is green, and so the shoes are to mark him as being "fae-touched," and "even cloth" can be read simply as "fine cloth"; that of the highest quality. In my version, it has been changed to "elven" cloth, to further illustrate Thomas as being marked by the fae, as well as to avoid the archaic tenor of the original.

The Underworld Journey

The imagery described in this ballad constitutes a symbolic map of initiatic progress through the inner planes. By identifying with Thomas, we are able to use this narrative as a guide in our own workings with the Faery realm. This particular journey is one specifically aligned to the confrontation of the human shadow and as such we may describe this type of working as belonging to the "dark side" of Faery, sometimes called the "night realm."

Take note that this—while being a relatively simple exercise—is actually a deep work of soul transformation and constitutes a type of "initiation" on its own. Do NOT attempt this if you are new to meditation or ritual workings and have not already formed a personal relationship with the Faery realm using visionary experiences, as this working in its unaltered form constitutes engaging in a type of "Faery contract," which will likely bring a lifetime of responsibility in its wake. You have been warned.

EXERCISE: Journey through the Faery Shadow

Open the Way.[15] If you work with a particular "inner temple," then align to it as normal. When you are ready, imagine yourself in a beautiful countryside with a serene view. See the grassy hills, the vast open blue sky, and whatever other details arise, making sure to keep the environment calm, beautiful, and completely one of nature. Use all of your senses to make it feel more "real" to you.

Imagine a large oak tree growing on a grassy hill and feel yourself drawn to it. Imagine standing underneath its canopy so that you are surrounded by a pleasant shade.

Lie down and relax, imagining the dappled sunlight flickering through the canopy of leaves overhead. Allow yourself to fully relax and drift in this serene vision. Imagine now a beautiful woman riding a white horse emerging from the surrounding countryside and trotting up toward you. The horse has a beautifully ornate saddle and bridle, and on the horse's mane are numerous little silver bells. With a sense of respect and compassion in your heart, greet the Queen of Faery and await her signal to join her on this journey.

If you do receive such a signal, you may mount the steed. If you do not, then simply give the Queen a heartfelt sense of love and gratitude and end your session for now, resolving to try again on another day.

Once you have successfully mounted the steed, reach forward to stroke its mane—causing the bells to chime—and the horse takes off, moving faster than the wind!

Imagine the whole world blurring and streaking around you until you come to a desolate place, devoid of all life. Contemplate this place, reaching out with your awareness and engaging your senses. Journeying onward, you come to a green garden, full of lush plants, flowers, and inviting fruits. Take care not to touch any of the fruits, for the food here is poison. Here the Queen may offer you bread and wine, the metaphoric flesh and blood of the earthen god, and thus reaffirming your human divinity and your anchor in the middleworld. You may do this either physically as in a ceremony, or simply as a visionary experience, according to your preference or ritual skill.

---

15. This is a shorthand term that refers to a series of basic preliminary meditative exercises that are strung together in the BlueRose work as a container for all other work we do, which includes relaxation, grounding, and alignment. I have provided a simplified version of this work for you to use in appendix I.

After you have rested, you may journey onward, imagining now that you are at a great crossroads where you see the treacherous road to "heaven" … the beautiful and inviting road to "hell" … and the good fine road to Faery in between them both. Imagine travelling down this Faery road, winding about the ferns and the trees, until you come to the edge of a wide river that blocks your forward movement. This is the River of Tears. Ask yourself what pains you have suffered. What pains (knowingly or unknowingly) have you inflicted upon others? Allow these memories and their associated emotions to rise up as you face them. When you feel ready, imagine riding forward through the river … the waters coming up to your knees. Feel the strong current. Imagine the river "washing you clean" and aligning you to its stellar consciousness.

You continue to wade through on horseback, the sky becoming like twilight, but with no sun or moon. Imagine that you can hear the "roaring of the sea," and allow this sound to lull you deeper into trance. "Feel" yourself wading further out through this river until you reach the other side and continue your journey forward.

The sky darkens into the black of a moonless night. Now you come to the River of Blood. This is what you share with all other humans—connected by blood. Through this river runs ancestral wisdom. You wade through to make your way across—again, up to your knees. Imagine this river also flowing in your own veins. You are a part of this river … part of an unbroken lineage of life that stems back to the earliest humans and will continue onward until the very last of our species has drawn their last breath. Be open to receiving ancestral guidance—from your personal ancestors, as well as that of earthly consciousness that we share with all forms of life on this planet. Take note of whatever images and insights may arise during this phase.

As you finish crossing the river, you find yourself in a magnificent wooded place full of marvels and wonders. Allow yourself the silent space to commune with the Faery Queen, taking care to speak *only to her* should any other faery or spirit present themselves.[16] Take note of whatever images or insights may arise for you, but try not

---

16. In this initiatic pattern we must remember to obey the traditional keys, and the ballad clearly prohibits Thomas (the seeker) from speaking while in the Faery realm (though some tellings specify that he may speak only to *her*. As the embodiment of the land, the Queen is the goddess of sovereignty, and it is through a marriage/commitment to her that the seeker is able to progress along the path, allow him or herself to be guided by the voice of the land itself, and become a priest/ess of the chthonic powers. It is through *silence* that the student is able to learn the deeper mysteries. By quieting the mind and voice and becoming *empty* the student is able to commune with the powers that be and allow themselves to become changed in the exchange.

to interpret them at this juncture. Just note them, whether you understand what they mean or not.

When you are ready to move on, the Queen will prompt you to continue your journey and she *may* pluck a fruit from a high branch as a gift of power and blessing. This you may freely take and eat, as you have been properly "attuned" to the energetic vibration of the Fae realm through observing the initiatic pattern. Notice what you feel this "gift" is and eat reverently.

Our journey nearly done, cultivate a sense of love and gratitude for the Queen and her gifts and imagine this feeling shining outward from the center of your brain, your heart center, and your sex. Feel yourself relaxing even further … and imagine yourself awaking underneath the oak tree on the grassy hill. Return to normal awareness. Remember to record your experiences in your journal.

Once we have aligned our consciousness toward that of the Fae realm, we may then begin the arduous work of awakening to our own true self—not just as a human practitioner in the middleworld, but as a spiritual consciousness that spans *multiple* worlds. We must break the spell that has fed the illusion of our separateness and kept our divine nature hidden. And this means that we must look deeply—and unflinchingly—at who we really are.

This is the real danger of Witchcraft, for to recover that power we must face the deepest, darkest parts of ourselves. We will scry into our own abyss, and we will see our own faces, changed into the most appalling and frightening of forms. We must look into that dark mirror, meeting our terrible reflections in the eye and holding fast, no matter what we may see. Only then will the spell be broken.

In the story of Tam Lin, another traditional Scottish border ballad, the headstrong Janet defies the order for maidens to avoid Carterhaugh (a wooded area of land owned by her lord and father) because Tam Lin, a young faery man, resides there and demands payment, often in the form of a maiden's virginity. She plucks a "double rose" and is then challenged by Tam Lin, who seduces her. Upon returning home she is confronted by her father, who fears she is now pregnant and asks which of his gentlemen is the father. Janet replies that it is none of them and she returns to Carterhaugh in the effort to gather abortive herbs. When she plucks the poisonous plant, Tam Lin again appears and asks her why she intends to harm the unborn child. She replies that were he a human gentleman she would bear his child, but since he is "elfin grey" she cannot. He informs her that he was indeed a faery, but that he was not always so, captured and changed by the Faery Queen herself and forced to be her servant for the past seven years. He goes on to tell her that each seven years on Halloween the Faery pay a tithe to hell, and this time he fears that it will be himself. He tells Janet exactly how she might rescue him from such a fate, and steal him back from Faeryland to return home with her.

The next night is Halloween and Janet is in the forest hiding out of sight, waiting for the Faery procession as instructed. A black horse and rider passes first, followed by a brown, but when the milk-white steed comes next, Janet leaps up and pulls the rider down, who is Tam Lin and who then changes into several frightening creatures—a snake, a bear, and a lion—before changing into a red-hot bar of iron. Janet knows to be steady and hang on tight no matter what, until he becomes a glowing coal, which she then throws into the well where he finally transforms into a naked man. She then wraps him in her green cloak and hides him from sight as the Faery Queen rages. The spell now broken, Janet takes Tam Lin home, who has now been restored to his humanity, so he can marry her and be the father of her child.

In the oldest versions of this traditional ballad, it is strongly implied that Janet may not be a consenting partner to the sexual act, which quite disturbingly makes this ballad potentially one of rape. While not all versions depict it in this way (and my own reworking, given in appendix II, has consciously chosen to depict Janet with full possession of her own agency), we would do well to face this unpleasant history head-on to see what might be learned from the narrative.

There are many reasons why it would have been symbolically significant to depict Janet with her agency removed in this way. Janet first defies human custom by going to Carterhaugh, and then Faery custom when she plucks the double rose. This last act is a symbolic "de-flowerment" for which she suffers in the actual. She further insults the Fae by defying Tam Lin when she says that she will come and go as she pleases and she will not ask him for his leave (permission). In turn, he does not ask permission from her.

I feel compelled to point out that regardless of how we might view the story, a ballad involving the kidnaping of human children into otherworldly dimensions and the payment of souls to hell is probably not the best source upon which to build a morality or viable worldview. This most certainly does not constitute a justification for rape in the real world, and any who might suggest otherwise should be sternly and unequivocally corrected.

The physical transformations that occur in this ballad are a common theme in folktales around the world. We are being shown that things are not always as they first appear, and that if we are able to face our fears—and hold to our highest ideals—then we will be able to overcome adversity. This take in particular is important to our study, as the Witch must be able to confront her fears if she is to steal her power from them.

One way to read this type of tale is in the context of dream interpretation. In this way, we might view all the characters in the story as being aspects of the self. Janet, as the protagonist of this story, is aligned to our own talker, while Tam Lin would be aligned to our fetch. We are here poised to "rescue" the "other"—our own hidden power from the shadow of our personal abyss, aka our "Shadow Twin."

EXERCISE: Rescuing the Other

In this exercise, we will follow the symbolic pattern set forth in the ballad in order to call forth the guardian of the Faery woods, initiating a process of challenge and transformation. Perform this exercise only once you feel you have become proficient with the previous one.

Items needed:
A black "scrying" mirror
A candle

Position the mirror in front of you and the candle behind you so that—when lit—it will *not* be directly reflected in the mirror, but instead give an ambient light to the room. For best results perform this exercise with your eyes open, softly gazing into the mirror. Alternatively, you may wish to move in between, having your eyes open and closed.

Open the Way. When you achieve a deep trance, make your journey to the Faery realm. (You may use either the previous exercise, or another method with which you are already familiar.) Allow yourself to settle in to this place, using your senses to make it feel more "real" to you. Once this has been achieved, imagine moving into a densely wooded area in which you come to a small clearing. Here you find an ancient well, covered in rose vines. Look at the roses. Notice the soft texture of their petals and their sweet scent. Here we will call the Faery guardian of this place using the symbolic pattern set forth in the ballad. Search for a "double rose," a single rose that appears to be a "bloom within a bloom." Allow yourself to really look at it, taking it all in. Know that this rose is sacred to the Faery folk. Reach out and pluck it, breaking the stem. Hold this rose close to your heart and inhale its scent.

The guardian of this place appears before you. Notice what form they take. Be aware of any emotional response you may have as well as any physical sensations. Take some time to commune with this being and notice whatever images or insights may arise.

After some time, this guardian will either dismiss you or lead you to the next phase of our journey: a nearby clearing where there is a crossroads. Once here you will position yourself in the forest trees and await the Faery procession to arrive.

When they appear, you see them on horseback. First appears the night-black steed. Allow this to pass you by. Then will appear a brown one. This too you shall let pass. When the white horse appears, leap from your hiding place and pull the rider off their saddle and onto the ground. Gazing into the mirror, imagine the rider—who is yourself—changing forms before your eyes. You may see images appearing physically in the mirror, or you may just have a mental vision. Either way, do not look away, even though you may be surprised and/or frightened by what you see. Allow the transformations to continue as you hold fast, not breaking your gaze. Eventually, the frightening images will fade away and into an image of your divine self. Notice what form this takes and imagine wrapping this form in your green cloak to hide it from sight. Embrace this form as you would a lover, and imagine both of you transforming into a beautiful shining light. Like two candle flames flowing effortlessly into one, you merge together; the marriage of your human and faery nature. Once complete, make your way back the way you came and return to normal awareness. Extinguish the candle.

Having rescued our Shadow Twin, we can begin the next phase of the work: integration.

CHAPTER 2
THE DARK MIRROR:
REFLECTIONS OF LIGHT AND SHADOW

For I am divided for love's sake, for the chance of union.
—ALEISTER CROWLEY, *THE BOOK OF THE LAW*

In *Aradia, or the Gospel of the Witches*, the primary deity is known as Diana, Queen of the Witches and Faerys. In this myth, it is She who is the undifferentiated universe who—out of Her own desire—divides Herself into darkness and light. She retains the darkness for herself and the light is named Lucifer. They are twin powers—each complementing and defining the other—and through their union is born Aradia, first of the Witches, who was sent to earth to teach humankind the art of the Craft.

This myth is pertinent to a study of Faery in that it follows the same basic pattern of creation as described in our tradition, owing most certainly to the high esteem our tradition's founder held it. Victor Anderson reportedly used this myth at times to illustrate his own cosmological thoughts to his students, and there is a substantial written record that supports this in the form of personal books of shadows widely circulated in initiate circles. There is a primal truth to be found here and in the words of Victor when he said, "Darkness is older than light."

It is said in Faery that the universe was created out of darkness in an act of self-love. When God Herself looked into the black mirror of curved space and saw her own reflection, she was filled with the desire for union. Cosmologically this is the origin of "the other": where previously there was only the undifferentiated *one*, through the process of reflective individuation there were then *two*. When the universal singularity became a duality, only then was the concept of union a possibility. And from that union was born something *new*.

In this we see the mirror as a tool of creation, revealing not just aspects of ourselves but entire worlds. The mirror allows the Star Goddess to experience Herself in a new way, not merely as subject but as object. It is this expansion of Her consciousness that is the expansion of the universe. When Her vision is opened to new possibilities, those possibilities become reality. This is the very first act of *magic*.

The Divine Twins

Twin deities are central to the mythos of the Faery Tradition where they appear as the dual offspring/consort/other-half of the Star Goddess. These Divine Twins appear in our tradition in many different forms and in various genders. Even their mytho-poetic relationships to each other change from telling to telling, each offering a different perspective that the practitioner will contemplate and engage in their magical workings. This can be confusing to seekers who want clear answers to what I'm sure to them seem like simple enough questions. If you were to ask several initiates of our tradition, "Who are the Divine Twins?" you would likely get very different answers, depending on the particular lineage into which they had been trained.

Most practitioners of modern Witchcraft will recognize the Twins as the polar opposite Oak and Holly kings of British Wicca, representing the light and dark halves of the year, respectively. But while in popular Wicca they are treated as separate entities (each vying for the affections of the Goddess, doing battle as the tides of power shift during the year), in the Faery Tradition each is seen as the counterpart to the other. In many of their stories they are depicted as lovers, but may appear as siblings or with some other relational bond. Sometimes they appear as enemies. Sometimes they are something else entirely. One piece of lore of particular interest to those in the LGBT community is that of the Gray Dove and the Gray Wolf, each of them being symbolic of one of the Twins as the patroness of gay men and the patron of lesbian women, respectively.[17]

The Twins may appear at times as "opposites," but on a deeper level they are understood to be part of the same being, much as the left and right hemispheres of the human brain serve different functions, and operate together as a whole. "Either one

---

17. Tom Johnson, aka Niklas Gander, "The Divine Twins: A Mystery of the Feri Faith," *Witch Eye* #2 (2000): 12–17.

or both of the Divine Twins can fulfill the function separately or together like two candle flames blended into one."[18]

It is perhaps because of their nebulous nature that in some lineages of our tradition the Twins are passed not as ordinary knowledge but instead as a type of ritual-transmission of mystery.[19] Though the names and practices around these Twins may differ by lineage or by coven, they are essentially the same; they each present a form of the Twins as powers in relation to each other, and each of the potential combinations of relational possibilities can give us much upon which we may contemplate and use as foundational work for our own magic.

In the BlueRose lineage of the Faery Tradition, these Twins are usually first encountered in the forms of a red serpent (which, among other things, is the embodiment of earth and fire) and a blue dove (which embodies water and air). Like all deities in the Faery worldview they are gender fluid and their forms are likely to shift and change. Each of them is representative of a type of polarity, but not in the forms that we might normally encounter. They are not "light and dark" or "good and evil" or even "male and female." They are not "opposites" in the classical sense, but are complementary. The serpent embodies the terrestrial powers, while the dove is the celestial.

The paradoxical nature of the Twins sometimes poses a challenge for the student to know them, as they cannot be fully understood by the logical mind. They must be experienced. We must develop nothing less than the aforementioned Second Sight, and to begin this work we need to learn how to look at the world in a different way.

EXERCISE: Twins of Space and Form

This exercise is to allow us to begin to see what Faery Grandmaster Anaar has called the "radical holism" of the Divine Twins, by using the tools of visual arts training.[20]

I have rewritten her exercise and presented it here with her permission.

Items needed:

A pen or pencil

A sketchpad

---

18. Cora Anderson, *Fifty Years in the Feri Tradition* (San Leandro, privately published, 1994), 7–8.

19. Johnson, "The Divine Twins."

20. Anaar, "The Winged Serpent: Seeing the Divine Twins," *Witch Eye* #10 (2005): 14–15. http://www.feritradition.org/grimoire/deities/essay_winged_serpent.html (Accessed 6/28/2017).

Go outside and perform this physically, if possible—weather permitting.

Lie down beneath a tree and look up at the sky through the branches. Focus on the branches and mentally trace the edges of each branch and leaf, taking care to notice each curve and angle. On your sketchpad, draw those lines, focusing only on the edges of the branches and leaves. You need only spend a couple minutes doing this, but do it reverently and in complete silence. Really pay attention to what you are doing. Now close your eyes and clear your mind. Open your eyes and choose a fresh sheet of paper. Now look at the "pieces" of sky that appear in between the branches. Repeat the exercise as before, only now tracing the curves and angles *of the space in between the branches*; i.e., the "negative space." When you are done, compare the lines you drew from the first part of the exercise to those of the second. Theoretically they should be identical. But they are not. Notice how these new lines differ from those you traced previously, and yet the tree and the sky remain the same. In essence, *they are the same lines*, and yet they are not.

This exercise should be repeated at semi-regular intervals, perhaps once per week for three to four weeks, and then revisit it months or even years later to see what—if anything—has changed. It is through the repetition of this exercise that will eventually cause your own inner sight to shift and you will begin to see the multitudes and paradoxes that exist all around you. But, like with most things, it takes time and practice.

Victor Anderson sometimes described the Twins in terms of modern science, invoking the imagery of an atom of the first element, hydrogen, which he called "the breath of the Goddess."[21] Composed of a single proton and electron, this model demonstrates how the Twins are individual parts of a greater whole, and it is this holism that is sometimes symbolized in our tradition as a winged serpent. Known to the ancient Aztec as Quetzalcoatl and as Kukulkan to the Maya, the imagery of this deity demonstrates the union of both earthly and celestial powers, symbolized individually by the snake and the bird. In Faery Tradition, this being is also known as Dian y Glas, "the Blue God," and is the symbolic representation of the fully realized human being—one who has integrated their duality and achieved a state of "embodied transcendence."

---

21. Oral tradition.

EXERCISE: The Twins of Three

This visual meditation is also from Anaar and uses optical illusion as a method for experiencing the shifting and paradoxical nature of the Twins—specifically, how they embody both duality and unity at once.[22] This is my version of her exercise. The whole endeavor should only take you a few minutes. You will want to perform this exercise several times over the course of your studies or until you are able to achieve the final results nearly instantly.

Figure 1: "My Wife and My Mother-in-Law."

---

22. Anaar, "The Winged Serpent."

Ground and center. Look at the Figure 1, "My Wife and My Mother-in-Law," drawn by artist William Ely Hill in 1915. You are quite likely already familiar with it as it has been used as a classic example of an optical illusion for many years. Depending on how you view it, you may see either of two women: one young and the other old. For the sake of this exercise, each of these individually represents one of our Twins, revealing the dual power they possess. Relax your gaze and allow your focus to softly shift from one to the other, and gently back again. She is young... she is old... she is young again. Imagine how this subtle shift is the passing of power between them both as they shift in... and out.

After a couple minutes of this, take a deep breath and then allow *both* images to arise gently and equally into your conscious focus. When you can see both the old and the young woman *at the same time* and maintain the stability of said image, then you will have had an experience of the profound unity that lies at the heart of the Divine Twins. Individually, they are two. Taken together they are *three*; their unique identities shared with their combined presence is greater than the sum of their two individual parts, creating in effect a third entity. *1+1=3.*

As the Star Goddess looks into the curved black mirror of space, she sees her own reflection. In this act, She Herself becomes twinned: her reflection becoming the "sacred other." This reflection is sometimes said to be Nimuë,[23] the Faery maiden goddess of joy, desire, and innocence. She makes love with the Star Goddess, resulting in the orgasmic creation of the universe. From duality, we are now presented with *multiplicity*. In this simple narrative, we see the act of self-individuation as well as union, an ecstatic annihilation of the self through which the universe is better able to know itself. "In the act of creation, it remains unclear whether Nimuë is Other, or one with the Star Goddess, which is as it should be. And, ultimately, it matters little in the Divine Scheme of Things."[24]

Just as we did with the ballads, we can take the imagery of our creation myth and use it to direct our magical work. In this case we are being taught—quite literally—to look into the mirror and notice what stares back at us. We need to discover our shadow self, our own "other" who resides within. We need to find our Shadow Twin.

---

23. Johnson, "The Divine Twins."
24. Ibid.

JOURNALING: Polarities of Being

For this exercise, you will spend a few minutes journaling about your strengths and weaknesses. We will be using the traditional poetic polarity of "beauty" and "darkness."

Items needed:
A pen and your magical journal

Choose two pages in your journal so that they face each other. On the left, you will journal your weaknesses. Label this page "darkness." On the right, you will journal your strengths. Label this page "beauty."

Begin with beauty. Contemplate your positive qualities … your strengths and values. Spend five full minutes writing down whatever comes to mind. How are you strong? What actions have you performed that exemplify your positive qualities? What parts of yourself do you try to share with the world? Be honest with yourself.

(If you absolutely cannot think of anything then you will need to do this exercise after having spoken to friends and family, getting their input. Be open to what they have to say, and then revisit this exercise.)

Once complete, switch to the darkness page on the left and spend another five minutes journaling about your fears and weaknesses. What parts of your personality bring you shame? What do you try to hide from the world?

Repeat this exercise once a week for at least two weeks. You may add to the original pages at your discretion. Once this has been done, perform this exercise again, only now, on a fresh sheet of paper, journal about how some of your darkness has given you greater insights, and also perhaps how sometimes things in your beauty category have led to you ignoring other things in your life. In essence, try to see how each of them have their own lights and shadows. Journal on this for at least five to ten minutes.

This exercise gives us an opportunity to confront our relationships to the concepts of beauty and darkness, leading us to be able to see the seeds of either in both. Once this has been done at least once a week for two weeks, then you will be ready to move on to the next exercise, a ritual of reflection and integration.

RITUAL: Light Mirror/Dark Mirror

This particular rite is about finding beauty within your darkness and vice versa. Each of them contain a gateway into their "twin."

Perform this ritual at night or in a light-controlled environment, such as a closet or another room with no windows.

Items needed:
A black mirror (preferably concave)
A silver (normal) mirror
A white candle
A black candle
Your journal

Position the silver mirror in front of you to your right and the black mirror in front to your left at such a height that you can easily see your reflection. Position the white candle behind you to your left, ensuring that it is not directly reflected when viewing the silver mirror from your vantage point. Do the same with the black candle, behind you to your right, and not reflected in the black mirror. Open your journal to the pages from the previous exercise. Give yourself a few minutes to silently read over what you wrote about your strengths and weaknesses. Allow these words and any attached emotions to wash over and through you.

Open the Way. After you have enjoyed the sensation of being in a light trance for a couple of minutes, begin to focus on your strengths, your inner beauty. Feel this as a divine white fire within you. Light the white candle and say:

Flame of beauty in my soul,
Illuminate the darkness whole.

Softly gaze into the silver mirror. Imagine the light of your inner beauty illuminating the darkness within you, revealing to you the even greater depths of that darkness. Down deep … in the empty space between your molecules … composing the majority of your physical body's mass is … nothing. Emptiness. Blackness. *Darkness.*

Darkness is older than light.

Allow spirit to lead you. Empowered by your strengths, scry now into the black mirror and allow images to arise. Take note of them. After a few minutes of this, take some time to jot down your experiences on a fresh page of your journal before moving forward to the next part.

Now, focusing on that darkness within, light the black candle and say:

> *Shadow dark, here called by flame,*
> *My strengths hard-won you now proclaim.*

Softly gaze into the black mirror and focus on how your weaknesses have inspired growth and eventual strength. Where there was fear, your power grew. Focus on those challenges that you were able to address. We only become strong when we have difficulties through which to work. When we find ourselves in difficult or seemingly impossible situations, we either adapt or we die. No one ever evolves while staying safe in their comfort zone.

Focus on those new-found positive qualities, those forged in the fires of your adversity. Be aware of whatever images may arise within the mirror. Shift your gaze from the black to the silver. What changes? What arises? Again, after a few minutes take some time to write down your experiences on a fresh page in your journal.

When you are done you may snuff out the candles and use them to repeat this exercise later. Return to normal awareness. Write down anything else in your journal that you feel is pertinent.

These exercises begin to reveal to us our own twinned nature, for we all have seemingly contradictory aspects of our personality that are in conflict with each other. But working with them helps us to bring them together into a harmonious state as we seek that radical holism for ourselves.

Divine Multiplicity

There are many different ways in which to view the Divine Twins of the Faery Tradition. While the lore of "Old Faery"[25] describes specifically the Twins as being the dual male consort of the Star Goddess, we can see how even she becomes her own "twin,"

---

25. I am using this term to refer specifically to the lore that Victor and Cora Anderson imparted to their students, and *not* as any current lineage or practice being done today. It is safe to say that NO ONE is practicing the tradition in exactly the same way as the Andersons did (and rightly so, as a large focus of our tradition is about the individual's relationship with the worlds). The authenticity of our tradition is in the working of the practice and the power, not in the dubious claims of supposed antiquity of any of its current lineages.

and how those forms, which are said to have been birthed from her cosmic womb, can also be twins for each other.

This brings us to a somewhat well-known Faery Tradition concept, that of the seven-fold cosmology. This teaching model was popularized by the coven Bloodrose, and is what in BlueRose is called "the *Infinitum*," or "the Gods of Infinity." This is a particular grouping of seven deities comprising a triple goddess and a triple god, arranged on a symbol such as the lemniscate or a vesica piscis. In this model, the Star Goddess is positioned at the center of both glyphs, while the six remaining deities are arranged on each of the two lobes or circles according to their gender. On the "female side" we have the maiden, Nimuë; the lover/mother, Mari; and the hag, Ana. On the "male side" we have the youthful Dian y Glas; the lover/father, Krom; and "old Scratch" himself, the Arddu.

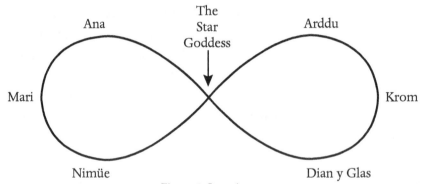

Figure 2: Lemniscate

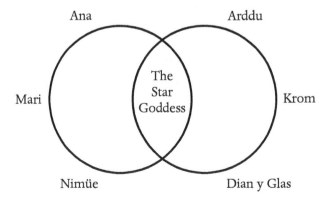

Figure 3: Vesica Piscis

On the surface, this may appear to be in contradiction to the Old Faery concept of a triple goddess and a dual god (a concept that was almost certainly borrowed from the 1949 novel *Seven Days in New Crete* by Robert Graves) but a closer examination will demonstrate that this is just another poetic extension of the wisdom that the old lore offered us. For each of the two lobes represents one of the Twins, this model offering us a balanced view of a gender binary, complete with an examination of a gender spectrum on each and also what might be called transhuman elements for good measure. For example, on the "male side" we see a clear shifting of gender in the gods from the effeminate and youthful (and "enlightened") Dian y Glas, to the archetypically masculine Krom, and then to the androgynous (and animalistic) Arddu. While true that on the "female side" the androgynous elements are less overtly pronounced, they can still be found, if somewhat veiled in subtlety, in Nimuë's "tom-boyish nature" and in Ana's often post-sexual characterization. Each of these goddesses are also embodiments of lunar, stellar, and/or earthly powers, again causing us to move beyond the local foci of just ourselves and into a global, stellar, or universal consciousness, in which everything is part of everything else. It is *here* that our magic really begins.

Faery's approach to deity is nebulous in nature; we see a kaleidoscopic cacophony of mythic stories, symbols, and relationships that each offer up something unique and then flow back into the formless void only to be birthed again in a new form. And in all of them we look for patterns. In ritual, we work to align our consciousness to their stories that we may come to understand the world in new and different ways.

Taken together the triple goddess and the triple god of the Infinitum are just varying aspects of the Twins to each other; they are dual forces emerging from the singularity of the Star Goddess, and then emerging into a multiplicity of forms. Even the variant forms within each Twin can be further examined and be a sort of twin to each other. In this we might be forgiven if we were to invoke an observation of holograms, in which the part contains the whole. By contemplating our cosmological pattern, we can see patterns emerge that reveal the Twins in different ways. It is easy to see the mother goddess Mari twinned with the horned god Krom, or even Ana with the Arddu. But these extend further when we see Dian y Glas reflected in either of those two, or Krom twinned with aspects of himself, such as the Red Man and the Green Man, who are depicted as lovers and offer themselves to each other in rapturous ecstasy.

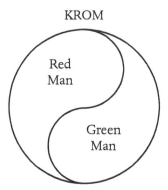

KROM

Red
Man

Green
Man

Figure 4: Krom, Red and Green

The fractal nature of the gods becomes evident when we remember that each deity is a reflection or emanation of the mysterious Star Goddess. Just as she created through union with Herself and gave birth to her "son, lover, and other half,"[26] all things are of Her, and so all things contain Her divinity. There is nothing that is outside of Her. She is the form and the formlessness; she is the dreamer and the dream.

In terms of exploring deity through the lens of Faery Tradition, this examination barely scratches the surface. It is a core teaching in Faery that the gods will present themselves as male, female, neither, or both, all depending on the needs of the moment. The forms they take while they engage with us are dependent on that which *we* might need, or, at times, what they feel they need in order to get their message across.

The thing to remember is that—in Faery Tradition—*all* of these observations are correct. None of them may be held above another as being more or less true. Poetry is valued over dogma. This demonstrates the paradox of Faery Tradition; contradictory concepts and definitions can sometimes be equally true.

While we could examine the psychedelic and celestial nature of the universe for some time, we will now narrow our foci and choose specific patterns upon which we will place the locus of our magical consciousness that are more down to earth. Or that is to say, more *within* it.

---

26. Oral tradition.

The Faery Queen and King

The Divine Twins manifest in many ways, and one of the strangest amongst them is the Queen and King of Faery. For those lineages of our tradition that work directly with the faery beings[27] these are often among the first inner contacts that are imparted to the student when working in that realm.

Often depicted as sister and brother in traditional Faery Witch lore, the Queen and King can be understood as being specific focal points of *intra*terrestrial consciousness, aligned to the mysterious hidden side of the land and nature. As presences in the underworld, they are the chthonic powers of the earth itself; they are the wraith force of the land and everything that lives in relation to it, the very consciousness of the "faery fire" of magic and mystery.

In the previous chapter, we met with a helpful aspect of the Faery Queen aligned to the traditional ballad of Thomas the Rhymer, and we also read about a wrathful aspect presented in Tam Lin. In this we can see examples of both the Seelie and the Unseelie Courts, traditional terms used to distinguish between helpful and harmful fae (though both are understood to be dangerous). So far, we would be forgiven if we were to approach them as wholly separate beings, each with their own personalities, energies, and consciousness. Each will have their own preferences in terms of their offerings, devotional practices, and the like. And yet, they are also of the same being; they are a singular consciousness. Approached separately, they are each *a* faery queen. Together, they are *the* Faery Queen.

In my personal work with the Faery realm, I have encountered many different types of beings and have perceived that some exhibit a type of hive consciousness that seems to manifest with some regularity, especially amongst certain types of the noble fae. There seems to be a collective consciousness at work, and individual queens may focus that consciousness in particular ways that are beneficial to the practitioner, *if* we are able to properly align our consciousness to them. In addition to basic trance work, we might engage the fae through the observation of culturally specific practices or customs, by visiting particular physical locations associated with them (such as certain sacred sites), or by making offerings, especially as part of larger rituals of devotion. The wrathful end of the spectrum of that consciousness can be invoked through the

---

27. I feel obliged to remind the reader that our tradition is sufficiently diverse so that this type of work is not compulsory, thematically relevant though it may appear.

interruption of certain natural and folkloric rhythms, such as with the slow ebbing of a practice that once fed them, the abrupt withholding of devotion once set in motion, or more drastically with the destruction of a sacred mound, tree, or site. They can also be offended by our being disrespectful or any other reason, however ostensibly arbitrary. Because it is sometimes quite easy to mindlessly offend certain types of fae, regular observances can help to mitigate the damage. There's a good reason people made and still make regular offerings to the fae. Better safe than sorry.

Regular offerings are a foundational practice to aligning with the fae, and if you have not already made such offerings a regular part of your practice then you are not ready to move on with this work. Once this practice has been cultivated then the next step would be to make a connection with a faery being and begin to develop a deep personal relationship with that particular being, taking care to observe the traditional prohibitions and taking the necessary precautions. After this relationship has been developed and deemed trustworthy, then—and only then—may we proceed to making a personal connection with the royal court of Faery.

The Queen and King are presented here in a way that will be useful to the uninitiated, and in keeping with the tradition of transmission by poetic vehicle, I present this devotional poem from my book *The Stars Within the Earth:*

The Stars Within the Earth
In darkness underneath the moon
The quiet forest sleeps
And hides the ancient mystery
Of that which lies beneath.

Down below the solid ground
The realm of all things known
By way of cave, or well, or mound
We journey toward the throne.

Past root and muck
And bone and shade
And place of crystal's birth
We seek the light within the dark
The stars within the earth.

They shine like jewels on velvet dark
And call us to our place
The stellar sphere
Is now drawn near
The paradox of space.

By foreign constellations led
To the palace of Her majesty.
Cthonic powers sleep below
Awaiting rediscovery.

The Faery mound that shrouds the gate
From prying eyes remains unseen
Except to those whose hearts yearn for
The kiss of Faery's Queen.

The King and Queen of Faeryland
Protect the secret power
Of divine spark within the land
Bringing consciousness to flower.

The bridge is us, that lies between
below and of above
And joining worlds unknown and seen
Our birthright formed in love.

The Faery Queen and King are most often depicted as being brother and sister, twin potencies of the land in perfect stewardship, and in Faery circles are often linked with the Norse deities Freya and Freyr. Though certainly not identical, we can get a feel for these twin powers of Faery by looking into their Vanic cousins.

That both Freya and Freyr are of the Norse deity group known as the Vanir is of particular interest to our study. Compared to the conquering Æsir (arguably the gods of civilization) they are an older class of deities that are closer to the earth and her primal mysteries. The Vanir are more aligned to fertility, sexuality, and primal magic, and are known to enjoy music and carousing, so they are obvious examples of what we have come to know of the Fae. In one tale, Freyr was even given the realm of Álfheim (aka the realm of the elves and Faerys) as a teething present, so the association is far from incidental.

Freya is associated with love, sex, beauty, fertility, war, and a specific type of magic known as *seiðr*, which was most often practiced by women. This most likely contained shamanic elements of visionary trance and oracular divination and may also be related to the traditional Witchcraft practice of "seething," which is the controlled rhythmic convulsing and releasing of muscles in order to induce a trance state. The god Odin learned this special magic from her and as a result took on the accusation of *ergi*, a connotation of unmanliness due to its indirect and manipulative nature. It is likely that the practice of *seiðr* also involved sexual acts, and combined with the knowledge that Odin's practice of it was in conflict with the societal gender roles of that culture and period, we can deduce that this practice was at least somewhat rebellious in nature. This likens it to the practice of Witchcraft, which—if we subscribe to the mythos in *Aradia*—is similarly subversive.

In Faery Tradition, the Faery Queen is the Lady of the Gray Dove and is also symbolized by pomegranates, a reminder of her station in the underworld. She is the mistress of women's mysteries as well as patroness of gay men. She is the shamaness who sees in between the worlds and is the living presence of magic itself. Hers is the fertility of the land, and so we may see her in the depictions of what might be thought of as more conventional goddesses of nature, like Demeter, Gaia, but she is not just the land and the processes of nature, but also the mystery behind what we perceive as nature. She is nonlinear. She is otherworldly. She is *weird*. As Green Mari, the Queen of the Faerys reminds us that she too is a face of the Star Goddess, here presented through the modality of the underworld and the magic of the deep mysterious earth.

She appears to those who work with her in a myriad of ways: a pale, elfin queen in regal gowns, fair of face and sharp in tooth, or a strange woman with numerous tendrils, tentacles, or antennae, alien or insectoid in nature. In some cases, she is described as vibrating or buzzing like a hive of bees. My personal experiences with her almost all exclusively appear reminiscent of the way that some have described as extraterrestrial: completely hairless, with an exceedingly slight build; large, dark, almond-shaped eyes, etc. She possesses a beauty that is both regal and disturbingly *otherworldly*: nearly nude, clad only in a multitude of jewels with silver-blue skin and pointed "elfin" ears. She exudes sexuality but also a refined nobility that is in no way conflicting.

Freya's brother, Freyr, is also associated with sexuality, often with phallic iconography. He is a sacred king, which is to say that he is a sacrificial steward for the land, the god of sovereignty. A god of prosperity, peace, and pleasure, Freyr bestows his blessings upon humankind with good times and fair weather.

He is the Lord of the Gray Wolf (or Gray Hound) and is the master of men's mysteries as well as patron of lesbian women. Like the Faery Queen, the King can and does appear in many different ways. Where she comes to me in a near-constant form, he tends to reveal himself in a myriad of ways, depending on the situation or his whim; he is certainly the most changeable in both form and feeling. I have seen him as a larger-than-life and boisterous-feeling man with a large, unkempt beard, wearing large animal skins and furs, as well as a slight, almost effeminate, well-spoken, elfin man, wearing delicately embroidered fineries. These are very different experiences, and yet I know that I am in the presence of the same being. Here is revealed something of the "twin within the twin" nature of this particular deific pattern—the Divine Twins embodying a functional dichotomy.

What is consistently reported from those who have had ritual contact with him is that the King is most often *completely silent*. While a few of my students have reported opposite findings in their personal work, most often the King never speaks, the role of royal voice belonging almost exclusively to the Queen. The King seems to provide silent support in these situations like a type of psychic battery. He also sometimes seems to be playing the role of a type of focusing lens through which her will is directed but most often taking a sort of "supporting role" in his interactions with her.

While there are specific (and often secret) practices that individuals and lineages may attribute to these beings, the beings themselves are not secret so much as *private*. At best, they simply will not reveal themselves to those who have not first been aligned to them through a regular practice of visits and offerings. At worst, they may decide to help draw your darkest personal demons to the front of your psyche … and then leave you there to sink or to swim in your own terrifying madness. It is for this reason that I highly recommend that, prior to attempting the workings of this ritual, you first become proficient with those given in appendix I (or something of similar scope) for a period of at least six months.

Figure 5: Royal Court Sigil

RITUAL: Petitioning the Faery Court

For this ritual, you will need to find some place out of doors where you will be able to sit quietly and meditate undisturbed at dusk and into darkness. This place must have trees or other live plants as we will be using them as a portal. This ritual will take place over seven nights, and *ideally* the seventh night should be the full moon.

Items needed:
A piece of parchment paper
A pen
Their sigil (Figure 5)
A Second Sight oil that contains rue
Some honey and whole milk
7 whole oranges or tangerines
A knife and cutting board
A spoon
A paper bag for refuse
Gloves (optional)

For the first six nights, prepare your offering by cutting the orange or tangerine in half so that the sections are showing. With one half of the fruit, use the spoon and scoop out the insides, leaving the peel intact. We will use this as a biodegradable container for your offering of milk and honey. You may either eat this fruit, or discard it in some fashion. Wrap up the intact peel, the half an orange, and your milk and honey and make your way to your outdoor location.

Anoint yourself on your third eye with the Second Sight oil. Open the Way. Do this as an internal practice, without using any tools.

Feeling aligned, open your awareness to the underworld…to the land below. Be aware of the pulsing life within the land. Though your fetch you connect to that realm. Guided by your holy daemon (aka your "higher self"; see appendix I), you can touch its magic. When you are ready, place your offering by pouring the milk and honey into the intact peel and placing this along with the half an orange underneath a living, green plant or tree. Feel how the roots of this plant flow into the underworld, from where it draws power. This plant is a connection…a doorway into the underworld below. Say a prayer to the fae, such as:

> *Hail to the Shining Ones*
> *Who live on earth unseen*
> *Except to those who've gained their favor*
> *And that is what I seek.*
> *Take this, my humble offering*
> *Of milk and honey 'neath the green*
> *And I'll return on seventh night*
> *To petition Faery's Queen.*

Take a deep breath of power, feeling how you are drawing in wraith force from the environment. Kiss the palm of your hand and, with your exhale, "blow a kiss" to the fae as you send a beam of love and gratitude from your heart and into the offering you make. You may stay for a few moments if you wish, but then leave quietly, and if you see any trash on the ground make an effort to leave the place nicer than how you found it. Journal your experiences and thoughts.

Do all of this for six nights, each successive night first cleaning up the previous night's offering if it still remains. Place this into your paper bag, using gloves if necessary, before placing your new offering. When you return home you may either dump the contents of the bag in some wild place, as they are biodegradable, or you may simply throw them away in a compost or in the trash.

On the seventh night, return to your spot and clean up the previous offering. Place your new offering, which now includes the addition of their royal sigil drawn onto parchment paper. Sit down facing where you have placed your offering. Anoint your third eye with the oil and Open the Way. Say:

> *Hail to the Shining Ones*
> *Who live on earth unseen*
> *Take this, my humble offering*
> *Of milk and honey 'neath the green.*
> *On this the holy seventh night*
> *By their sign on parchment drawn*
> *I seek the company of the Queen*
> *And her King, until the dawn.*

Close your eyes and imagine that this plant before you is actually a great tree, and you feel quite small underneath it. Its roots sink down into the underworld, and its branches—covered in many different roses of many colors—stretch high into the overworld. This is the anchor between the worlds through which we travel to which we return.

As you contemplate this Faery Rose Tree, a white horse trots up to you. If it shows you a sign that it is willing to be mounted, do so. If not, then continue to wait (you may need to wait for some time) and if it still doesn't give you a sign, then call it a night. You will need to start the seven-night process all over again, in which case it would be even more advisable to incorporate the full moon into your working.

Once you have successfully mounted the steed, reach forward to stroke its mane—causing the bells to chime—and the horse takes off, moving faster than the wind!

The whole world blurs and streaks around you until you come to the desolate, life-less place. Journeying onward, you come to the green garden of plants, flowers, and fruits.

You come to the great crossroads where you see the three roads. Imagine travelling down the Faery road, winding about the ferns and the trees, until you come to the edge of the River of Tears. What pains have you suffered? What pains have you inflicted upon others? When you are ready, ride forward through the river…up to your knees. Imagine the river "washing you clean" and aligning you to its stellar consciousness.

You continue to wade through on horseback, the sky becoming like twilight but with no sun or moon. You can hear the roaring of the sea. Wade further out through this river until you reach the other side and continue your journey forward.

The sky darkens into the blackness. Now you come to the River of Blood. You wade through to make your way across—again, up to your knees. Imagine this river flowing in your veins.

As you finish crossing the river you find yourself in a magnificent wooded place where the horse brings you to a small clearing. The thick canopy of the surrounding trees gives this place a feeling of privacy and intimacy. You dismount and see before you a great well, made of white stone and covered in vines. There are roses carved into the stone, and there are roses growing all around in a multitude of colors, some you had not considered before now. Call the sigil of the royal court to you by imagining it in your hands. As you contemplate the symbol, imagine that you are able to fold this paper into the form of a rose. Hold the intention in your heart to have an audience with the Faery Queen and King, and breathe out on the paper rose.

It "comes to life" in your hands, becoming a fresh, bloodred rose. As an offering, toss this into the well with a prayer of connection and respect.

Just on the other side of the well, there is a figure you had not noticed before. They stand silently on the other side of the well, watching you. They may change forms, even drastically. Allow them to settle on a form. This is a guardian spirit and they challenge you from going forward.

Take a moment to reaffirm your soul alignment and then hold the mental intention that you wish to seek audience with the Queen and King of Faery—to help you deepen your relationship to the Fae realm and to help form a bridge between our worlds. Imagine this intention forming into a symbol, an image, and send that image into your fetch. Breathe wraith force into it and send it up with your breath into your holy daemon. From there it ignites into holy fire, which shines through you and out through your heart center, illuminating the well and this clearing.

The guardian stands on the opposite side of the well from you and gestures for you to look inside.

You look down into this well and you see the reflective surface of the water, and your rose offering floating lazily below. You see your own reflection, as well as that of the guardian.

The guardian reaches down into the well and stirs the waters ... they become a luminous whirlpool, filled with stars, and you find yourself drawn inside ... the guardian guiding you through this portal.

You emerge in a room that defies your senses. It appears at once to be both indoors and outdoors as if the structure you are in were grown like a tree instead of built. Branches and tree trunks form the walls, and the ceiling—if it even exists—is obscured by fluffy, fog-like clouds overhead. The quality of the light here is silvery, muted, as if in constant twilight, and comes from no apparent source.

The "room" in which you stand is enormous, filled with several long banquet tables set into rows, seated at which are a congregation of beings, humanoid as well as not, laughing, talking, and feasting together. This is a banquet hall. On the far side of the room are steps leading up to a raised area, atop which are two seated figures, crowned, and sitting upon elaborate thrones. There is an enormous silver mirror mounted on the wall directly in between and behind their thrones, which makes this room seem even larger than it really is.

The guardian escorts you up the stairs to stand before the Queen and King. They are both strikingly beautiful. How do they appear to you? They too may change their forms. Take some time to commune with them. One or both of them may speak to you. Notice whatever transpires.

At some point the Queen and King will invite you to look into their mirror. Gazing into the silver reflection you see the face of your own power. What do you see? You might see a bright image—a valiant representation of your courage and strength. Or you may see a dark image—revealing a hidden power within a perhaps long-forgotten pain. Just notice whatever arises for you. Feel the emotions that are attached to it. Revel in this newfound knowledge.

After some time, the imagery will fade and you may ask a question of the Queen and King. Notice how they answer. When you feel you are ready, bow in reverence to the Queen and King and send them a genuine sense of gratitude and respect. The guardian comes to escort you back… back through the portal and to the well in the clearing where the white steed awaits. Climbing on it takes off and the world streaks around you once more. Breathing deep… you awake underneath the Faery Tree, covered in roses. As you breathe, the Faery Tree becomes the mundane plant once more, and you open your eyes to see the plant and your offering underneath. Without saying a word, gather your belongings and make your way back home. Record your experiences in your journal and pay particular attention to your dreams, as you invited the presence of the Queen and King to remain with you until sunrise.

As this ritual is repeated, you will likely find that you are eventually inspired to make additional offerings or even those that are altogether different. It is not uncommon to make an offering of poetry, art, dance, incense, live plants and flowers (cut—and therefore dead—flowers are frowned upon), or even just beautiful objects and jewelry. As your relationship with the fae grows, they will tell you what they want.

PART TWO

BEYOND THIS LIFE

Fear and the Knife

Fear of death creeps over me
Time and time again
Black slicing madness of eternity
A tremor in my brain.

The end of reason
The end of thought
The end of feeling
The end of form
Calling from across the Void
Calling me home.

Greeted at the gate by He
Who over darkness rules
I shed the garments of my life
My soul a shining jewel.

My fear I give
I now release
its grip upon my throat
and offered up to She who is
mysterious and remote.

Clad in black, Her silk fine hair
in strands of pearl and white

a silver sickle stained with blood
Reflects the full-moon's light.

The gate is opened wide and then
I see beyond my life
and know beyond the shades of doubt
the gift of Ana's knife.

CHAPTER 3
WALKING THE BONE ROAD:
NECROMANCY AND THE DEAD

The boundaries which divide Life from Death, are at best shadowy and vague.
Who shall say where one ends, and where the other begins?
—EDGAR ALLAN POE, *THE PREMATURE BURIAL*

While a significant characteristic of the Second Sight is the capacity to perceive the Fae, another equally vital aspect is the ability to see and/or speak to the dead.

Who among us has not had an experience with the dead? Perhaps we have seen a loved one who had passed on or have had an encounter with an actual haunting. It may be easy to assume such encounters are the result of a delusional mind, but the sheer number of reports suggests otherwise. It is culturally taboo to believe in such things, much less talk about them, making them the topic of quiet conversations in hushed tones, even in places where one might think such topics would be par for the course. Along with my partners in coven, I own a brick-and-mortar metaphysical and spiritual supply store in the greater San Francisco Bay Area where I have worked and taught for many years. I have come to think of my time there as "frontline priesting," a term I first heard in relation to my work there from Faery initiate and teacher Francesca DeGrandis. This accurately describes the practice in which many who work in shops such as these engage: meeting with the public, hearing their stories, honestly assessing their situation, reassuring them that they are not alone, suggesting spiritual/magical or other methods to address their particular needs (taking care not to give medical, financial, psychological, or legal advice), providing them with whatever resources are needed to help, and then likely moving on to do the same for another, usually in fairly quick succession. "Magical triage" might also be a good term in some more extreme cases. Even there—surrounded by all manner of crystals, herbs, candles, books, tarot cards, occult jewelry, and ritual tools—the client or customer will suddenly get quiet and begin describing their personal experience with a spirit, usually beginning with the words "OK...I don't want you to think I'm crazy, but..."

For those individuals who have any type of relationship with spirits after they have passed from this physical life, we know that there is much more to life than just *living*. What we think of as "life" is just the visible portion of a fuller existence, and whose reach extends far beyond what our waking consciousness normally allows. Since our current technological understanding of the universe does not allow for the continuation of consciousness after physical death, those of us who are scientifically minded need not reject science, but instead embrace spirituality, poetry, art, and even religion in order to help describe our "extraordinary" experiences. We recognize that these are all just different languages used to help us describe the universe.

Even still, Witchcraft offers no universal claim as to what happens to our consciousness after physical death. Some traditions do have teachings regarding this and as such might promote reincarnation, especially the notion that initiated members will be reborn in the Craft amongst their loved ones once more. Other traditions may suggest any number of shifts in consciousness after physical death, whether that is becoming "one with the Goddess," becoming a faery being or spirit guide, taking on some new form, or even just outright oblivion. Even among Witches who share the same tradition, there are lively debates about what happens after we die. Death, like the gods with whom we work, is a *mystery*.

This, of course, doesn't mean *unknowable*. While we will likely never learn all his secrets, we can come to know a great many things about our dear friend, Death, even as he remains mysterious. For those that have ever been in the presence of a dead human body, one common observation is the energetic or spiritual sense of *emptiness* that seems to permeate the once living flesh. This alone implies that this body was once *full*. We do not necessarily recognize life force because it is all around us and always has been. Only when we attune ourselves toward Death do we begin to see the world through a new set of eyes, and ones that do not filter out the obvious.

The dead have an enormous role to play in the world of Witchcraft, and on this point Faery is no exception. While much of the emphasis in our tradition often focuses on the sexual nature of our Craft (Cora Anderson herself referred to Faery as a "sex cult"),[28] we can be said to be just as much one of ancestral reverence as anything else. Our path deals in a two-headed mystery: the knowledge that sex and death are in a sense *one*... or at least sides of the same coin.

Ancestor work in Faery is twofold. The first level is personal, as is the case with the ancestors of one's blood. We carry these spirits with us wherever we go. This is not a metaphor. We literally carry our biological ancestors with us in our blood. Just as every herb, every stone, every tree, and every lake has a spirit, so too do the strands of DNA within you. Your ancestors are alive within you *right now*.

They are invested in helping their lineage to thrive, for it is through our work in life that assists them with theirs. We work to elevate them. We work to heal them. And, in turn, they do the same for us.

We are not limited to working with just the ancestors of our blood, though they *do* tend to be the "closest" to us, so generally a better choice for a spirit ally than nearly any other. Besides our biological connections, we also have those formed by marriages on the astral, which may or may not coincide with similar unions formally celebrated in the physical.

A true marriage isn't a physical union or even necessarily a romantic one but instead is a union of spirit. These bonds are formed in many different ways, the most natural and pleasant of which is when two or more beings fall deeply in love. We are spiritually connected to those that we deeply love. Our love for them—and the love they mirror back to us—changes us on a deep and personal level. We become permeable. We exchange a part of ourselves. We carry a little bit of them with us, just as they carry a part of us.

The intensity of the shared emotion creates a type of unification—a marriage—on a soul level for the parties involved. But where there is light there must also be shadow. Bonds can be formed of anger, hatred, and obsession just as readily as with love. In fact, any sufficiently deep or strong emotion has the potential of forming such a bond.

These marriages of spirit can come in the form of adoption, as well. When a child is adopted into a family, there is a spiritual bond that grows that is akin to that of a blood-bond.

---

28. Oral tradition, from a private conversation with Cora before her passing.

The magic of marriage and adoption also applies to initiation. To be initiated into a tradition of Witchcraft is to be made part of the spiritual family, the bonds of which run just as deep as any forged in blood. Every initiate of the Faery Tradition is of the Faery Blood, which is to say that we are literally related to the fae, and to each other.

These bonds are created through powerful initiatory experiences. They have been empowered not only by the emotions of those who participate in them, but by spirits, rituals, and egregores. These bonds have tremendous momentum behind them; these are the connections that can potentially propel us into new directions, give us access to specific spirit contact or currents of mystical power, offer us magical protection, or even just allow us to draw more wraith force from the universe.

In the case of initiatory lineages, those of us who have received such initiations are now able to work with the ancestors of our traditions in ways that are close and personal. These might be nonhuman spirits that are attached to the particular energetic currents that are passed, or the sprits of previous members who now act as tutelary spirits from the other side. Once we have been initiated, these spirits are able to recognize us as family not just by our use of the proper signs and rites, but also by our energetic signature. This is the mark of the true initiate—one who has passed through the dread door and been changed by the experience, a change that is recognizable in the spiritual realms and which opens the door for a much larger world of spirit travel and connection.

In Faery Tradition we honor those teachers who have gone before us. In our individual lineages and also beyond. For example, the late Gwydion Pendderwen is not in my personal lineage, but I honor him as one of our Mighty Dead, offering inspiration and magic from beyond the veil.

The Mighty Dead is a Craft term that refers to those spirits of Witches who have passed through the veil and are now offering magical assistance from the other side. It is observed that in life, certain people with strong personalities (and especially those empowered by a magical practice) generate an "astral pattern." This preserves their personality and knowledge and will linger—sometimes for thousands of years—after their physical death. This is not a static, dead recording such as often found in a haunting, but a living, dynamic expression of that person's life force. The individual's consciousness will continue its journey of growth and evolution, but this pattern will remain as a spirit with which we may interact to the betterment of our Craft. The lineage of the Mighty Dead includes those Witches we have known in life and stretches back into antiquity, to the very first shamans and Witches of the Neolithic era. Their symbol is the skull and crossbones, and may be represented in our rites as an X with a circle placed in the upper chevron.

The process of calling upon the dead is called necromancy and is done for many purposes, such as divination or lending their power to a rite or other observance. If the Mighty Dead in question was an expert in a certain area of magic, then they might be called upon when living practitioners wish to increase their skill or knowledge of said area. They are also summoned to bear witness to certain rites, such as initiations, the passing of lore, and the like.

Other individuals, besides those on a magical path, may have also generated these astral patterns. Certain historic individuals who have "left their mark" likewise possess these patterns and may be called upon in much the same way. Artists, writers, philosophers, and other great thinkers may generate these astral patterns which—as with their magical counterparts—may or may not bear a resemblance to their actual living personalities.

Some of our Mighty Dead do not require one to be initiated into (or to even practice) our tradition in order to qualify for an astral visitation. Victor Anderson is said to show up to circles—any circles—at the drop of a hat, as long as he is invited, and it has been my personal experience that this is true. He fully lives up to the title of "Mighty Dead" in that he is eagerly offering advice and teaching from beyond the grave. Hail, Victor!

Even without initiatory connections there are practices that anyone can do to honor their ancestors and the Mighty Dead. Establishing an ancestral altar is a great first step. But once this has been done, what can we do to deepen those connections? For starters, we must really begin to confront our own fears of death.

As human beings, we are acutely aware of the eventual finality of our own physical existence. I sit here writing these words and my thoughts turn to the myriad of possible ways in which I will eventually perish. Will I have a heart attack? Will I die in a car accident or in a plane crash? Will I be murdered? Will I trip over my own shoelace and fall headfirst into a pit of vipers? No matter the method, I know that one day *I am going to die.* As will everyone who is reading these words right now. One day *you* are going to die. It's inevitable. It's basically already happened. No exceptions.

In Witchcraft, we do not attempt to placate ourselves with gentle platitudes in a feeble effort to eradicate our fear of finality. Instead, we face it head-on. To us, Death is a person. The Great Teacher and Final Lover. We seek to study Death, to learn from his dark presence so that we may one day fathom its mysteries. To us, Death is a *god*.

The Dark God

Strong and silent, robed in black
With head of goat and wings of bat
A flaming torch between his horns
The god of all who's dead and mourned.

The Dark God manifests in many different forms in our Craft. Most often we call him the *Arddu*, an Old Welsh word meaning "royal darkness," but he comes to us with many names and in many guises. He is the darkness beyond what our eyes can see and our minds can conceive. It is he who challenges us to face our fears, that we may be free enough to move unhindered between the worlds. He stands where two roads cross, the red and the black—life and death—and to him we must make our petition if we are to move beyond the realm of the living to commune with the spirits of the dead.

As the Breton *Ankou*, he is a type of "grim reaper" figure, a collector of souls, and protector of graveyards. In Faery Tradition, he is the primal and lust-filled dark. He is both primal, animal desire, as well as an enlightened intellect.

He is the necromancer, the Old Wizard who knows the deep secrets of nature; he is a master of the secrets of life and death. He is also a sexual god. His primal power rises from below and manifests in the mind-searing bliss of orgasm, the annihilation of the self that, however temporary, mimics that achieved at death. He is the *Thanateros*; the combined presence of the twin powers of the Eros (Sex) and Thanatos (Death).

A common visualization for our Dark God is that of the Baphomet; the half-beast/half-human, half-man/half-woman deity, sometimes called the Goat of Mendes. Here shown in the now famous drawing by occultist Éliphas Lévi in 1854, Baphomet is the paradoxical harmonization of seeming opposites, polarities being overtly expressed through the Latin words on the forearms of the image, which evoke the alchemical maxim: *"solve et coagula,"* "dissolve and coagulate," twin powers of destruction and creation.

Figure 6: Baphomet

We find ourselves once again in very nebulous territory; when we approach the Dark God in this way, we begin to see how he is not exactly separate from the Star Goddess. The Baphomet can be thought of as being post-gender and is the extension of the Star Goddess's presence through the spectrum of manifestation. The unknowable (and pre-gendered) God Herself becomes the Star Goddess when formlessness becomes form, and that form expresses itself as her son/consort, the dualistic or twin powers that the Baphomet expresses as a holism.

To begin or to deepen our work with the Dark God, we must engage in practices that will evoke the presence of archetypal Death. This can prove to be troubling at first, as some people find that working with death energies can produce undesirable side effects, such as mild illness, fatigue, and even depression. This is usually only a temporary condition, as the work that we do leads us through such rough emotional terrains with the goal of reaching the other side. That said, if you have been diagnosed with depression or you feel that you might be depressed, then you may wish to consult a counselor before engaging in the exercises given in this section. Once our consciousness has been appropriately shifted, we will find ourselves better able to work with these energies without taking on the potential negative side effects.

EXERCISE: Drawing in the Darkness

This aims to align one's consciousness to the death mystery. It should be performed in the middle of the night, in near-total darkness. It is ideal to do this outside in some wild place, but even doing it in your own home with the lights turned off will yield useful results.

Open the Way. With your eyes open, reach out with your awareness and into the surrounding darkness. Even if you are in a familiar place, notice how here in the dark things look less familiar than they do during the day. If you feel any sense of uneasiness, notice where and how in your physical body that is manifesting. Slowly move about your area. Imagine that your gaze is a soft caress upon the objects around you. Imagine that your own energy body is like a thin, billowing veil that gently glides over (and even through) these objects, and you can feel a subtle sensation when it does so. Enjoy these sensations and allow them to deepen your trance state.

Staying aligned with your holy daemon, attune to the death presence by thinking about those people you knew and who have since died. Family members. Friends. Coworkers or schoolmates. Even beloved celebrities. Of those whom you may have loved or admired, recall how you felt when they died, and how those feelings may have changed in the time since. Again, tune in to how your physical body is responding to this. Do all of this, while quietly chanting:

I summon Death from darkness.

Continue to quietly repeat this phrase over and over, finding a rhythm. After some time, imagine that the darkness around you is *alive*. The actual *darkness*, a living, sentient presence. You may or may not receive a visual image for this being, but if you do, remember that this is a *symbol* and that they embody the darkness that is all around you. Everywhere you look, there they are.

This darkness is not only all around you, it is all over you … within you. There is darkness everywhere. It is the rule, not the exception. Darkness is the default. It is the womb; everything comes from the darkness. And it is the tomb; to the darkness all things must return.

Breathe in this darkness. Imagine that your inhale brings this darkness into your consciousness and now you are keenly aware of your own mortality; the processes of your body a seemingly tenuous happenstance of almost unimaginable *good luck*, because if just *one little thing went wrong* you could simply be gone. A heart that stops. A brain that suffers an aneurysm. A flawed human body that comes with no guarantees, just … ceases to be alive. Everything that you are attached to … severed. Your likes, your loves, your hates … everything with which you were in a relationship, now … gone. Consider all this … your potential death could come at any moment. And it is *stalking* you … from within this very darkness.

Darkness calls to darkness. You breathe it in, and this external darkness flows into the darkness within you … down deep … in between your molecules in the dark, empty space. Here it is *transformed*. Within you … death becomes *life*. You breathe it out … your offer of *life* unto the darkness of death. Give and take. Two sides of the same coin.

Spend some time breathing in and out, feeling the connection to Death, and feeling your offering of life force with every exhale. When you are ready, return to normal awareness, turn on the lights, and record your thoughts in your journal.

Once you are familiar with the state encouraged by the above exercise you can "tap into" it simply by recalling the relevant bodily sensation. For many of the remaining exercises in this chapter you will be asked to connect to the death force. You need not do so formally unless you feel it is necessary.

Witchcraft is a path that recognizes the subtle shifts of energy that occur in the natural world; there are certain times and places in which different energies, spirits, powers, and the like can be "tapped into" in order to help us toward our particular goals. When dealing with necromancy, the best times are at Samhain and Beltane. In terms of the natural tides of power, we may be forgiven if we were to celebrate on the fixed days usually labeled as such, but in BlueRose the general practice is to honor the astrological dates, which for these sabbats (in the northern hemisphere) would be the sun at 15° Scorpio (usually Nov 5–8) and 15° Taurus (May 5–8). (Check an ephemeris for exact dates each year.) Other temporal observances appropriate to necromantic work include the last quarter of the waning moon. The time between Samhain and Yule is considered the "dead time" and it is traditional for those Witches of the Bone Wand to leave open the Western Gate the whole time while they tend to the spirits. A dark moon during this period is considered especially potent for this type of work.

For this next rite, you will need to embark on a series of preparatory observances for thirteen nights prior to this working. Each night, using some sort of visual link (such as a photo, drawing, piece of jewelry, or some other physical object), consider the particular spirit that you wish to call to you. They can be anyone: a personal ancestor, one of the Mighty Dead of the Craft (such as Doreen Valiente or Dr. Leo Martello), a "Craft martyr" such as those executed for the "crime" of Witchcraft (like Isobel Gowdie or Bridget Bishop), or even an historic figure, perhaps one associated with magic or artistry such as Austin Osman Spare or Oscar Wilde. The process of meditating on the spirit while holding or touching the physical object will gradually attune you, the object, and the spirit toward each other, paving the way for the spirit encounter encouraged by this rite.

RITE: Summoning the Dead

This is my reworking of a rite from the coven Korythalia, dated 1984.

The rite, as given here, is a sort of a suggestion that can be embellished with elements to make it more personal to the spirit with which you are working. Writing your own invocation is advised. If you are not working with a specific spirit, but merely wish to open the way for the Mighty Dead, then making them an offering in the west will suffice.

Items needed:
3 black candles
1 red candle
An image of the Hag and the Dark God

An object to use as a link to the spirit

A piece of silk, either white, red, or black, large enough to wrap your visual link object

Small white stones, salt, chalk, tape, or other means to mark on the floor

A skull (human or animal; may also be an image of a skull or skull and crossbones)

An incense burner

Anointing oil

Your blade or wand

A mirror

This should be performed only at night. The original text specifies that the Watchers (i.e., the "fallen" angels or Elder Gods from which the Witch Blood is said to have originated) are *not* invoked for this rite.

Begin by using the stones, salt, chalk, tape, etc. to mark out a circle in the floor large enough to contain yourself and your altar in the north, with some extra room for a triangle, placed inside the western edge of the circle, with its apex pointing west. We will deal with the magical nature of the triangle more in-depth later on, but for now we will just be using it as a ritual point of focus. Inside this triangle place the skull and on either side of it place a black and a red candle.

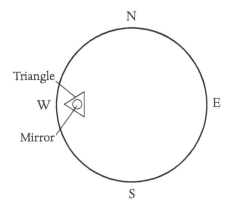

Figure 7: Summoning the Dead Circle/Triangle

The altar should have central images of the Hag and Dark God. These can be statues, symbols, drawings, inspirational photos culled from the internet, etc. Use whatever you feel is inspirational. These images are then flanked by two black candles. You may add further embellishments to suit your sense of style.

Take a ritual bath and anoint with an appropriate oil. My personal preferences for this work are blends that contain anise, but follow your own preference and herbal relationships. Returning to the ritual area, light the incense and cast the circle counterclockwise,[29] empowering the marked circle on the floor to come to life.

Go to the north. Connect to the death force. Using your blade or your wand, invoke the dead:

> *Oh, you of the Mighty Dead!*
> *We call you from between the worlds!*
> *Ancient Ones!*
> *Mothers and Fathers of the Craft!*
> *Who watched the stars,*
> *Who read the signs,*
> *Who worked the herbs,*
> *Who made the magic.*
> *I am your child,*
> *Come to me!*

As you speak this aloud, with your blade or wand draw a large circle in the air before you with Blue Fire, then make the sign of the X through it. See this image blazing before you. Repeat these steps for west, south, and east before doing it again over the altar in the center.

Return your tools to the altar and extinguish all the candles so that you are in near to total darkness. Take hold of the wand in one hand and the visual link in the other and go to the west. Stand before the triangle. Close your eyes and cross your arms over your chest, left over right. Bow in reverence, and then silently recite the incantation to yourself, imagining that you are hearing it boom in a thunderous voice:

> *I invoke the Mother of the Stars*
> *Who was and is and ever shall be*
> *Androgynous source of all creation.*
> *All seeing. All knowing. All pervading. All powerful.*
> *Shine in me your holy flame!*

---

29. For the northern hemisphere. Southern practitioners will want to cast clockwise.

> *By the Hag and by the Dark God,*
> *I call you forth!*

With the recitation of the last line, draw a pentacle in the air before you with your wand to invoke all five elements, each line of the star being a different elemental color. See it shine before you and then "pierce" it with your wand and *will* the pentacle to change into white fire. Focusing through your visual link, call to the spirit by name, three times silently, and then again three times out loud.

Now, just be open to whatever messages you may receive. If you are new to this work this may take some time. Don't be impatient!

In the case of working with specific spirits long term (such as with ancestors or the Mighty Dead) you may wish to create a permanent link, which will make "dismissing" them at the end of your rite unnecessary. In these cases, the physical object should be placed in the triangle and the spirit invited to inhabit it. To make such an invitation, you may use something along the lines of:

> *NAME OF SPIRIT (3x)*
> *Life and death, this space between*
> *An open gate through which I call*
> *And offer this by name and sign,*
> *Within this object you may dwell.*

To end the rite, simply give them thanks and offerings and wrap their link object in the silk and put away from view, then rekindle the candles. End your circle as you would normally. This object should be used frequently, especially when first establishing the link.

For other spirits, perhaps those only sought for a "one time job," there is no need to use a physical object and you will want to dismiss them properly when you are done, which is to say perform a cleansing/banishing of the area, after you have given them an offering and rekindled the candles. (For a full Banishing rite see chapter 6). Remove the triangle and open the circle.

EXERCISE: The Little Death

This simple exercise utilizes solitary sex magic and is intended to allow you to experience the duality and unity of the Twins in their forms as the lovers Life and Death, and how they are intimately connected to sex.

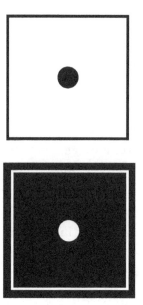

Figure 8: Points of Light/Dark

Familiarize yourself with the above images. Be able to recall them in your memory and be able to hold them in your internal vision for the span of *at least* several breaths without losing focus. Depending on your visualization or meditative skill you may wish to allocate some time to practice the technique before combining it with the rest of the exercise.

Open the Way. Connect to the death force. Feel how it is connected to *sex* ... how sex is *life*, and life and death are twins. Part of the same thing. Lovers.

Feeling the internal darkness, begin to make love to yourself. As your pleasure rises, you are transforming the darkness of death into the light of life ... let it rise within you.

Darkness and Light, merging and separating and then merging again. Life and Death are making love within you. You see the point of light in the darkness, like a single star in the cold and lonely void ... overlaid with the point of darkness—absolute—in an exuberant sea of bright celestial light. Complete and total opposites. Each struggling for supremacy. They shift back and forth ... darkness in light ... light in darkness ... Which vision remains? In your mind, they are brought together as one. Flash on this image before and/or immediately after your orgasm. *La petite mort.* Let the little death overtake you. Let your mind be blank. Let light and dark be as one.

Record your experiences.

EXERCISE: The Bone Pentacle

This exercise is based on a model conceived by my husband Chas Bogan. This pentacle, like the others more commonly used in the Faery Tradition, offers us a means to map out our relationships to certain key concepts, in this case with those that are specifically in tune with those that are aligned to working with the death force. Having an emotional connection to each concept, being able to discern the emotional and physical sensations brought on by each, and then bringing all five of those energies together as one, the Bone Pentacle will allow us to concentrate our magical awareness so that we can tap into the death force, and better utilize this awareness in our own work with the spirits of the dead.

Figure 9: Bone Pentacle

Items needed:

A piece of paper

A pen or pencil

A cell phone or timer (optional)

Begin by Opening the Way. Draw a pentacle with a single point upward at the top of the paper. Above the top point write the word "Death." Attune your thoughts to the dead. Call up a mournful sense of loss. Underneath the pentacle, begin writing whatever comes to mind about death. Any images, memories, emotions, weird half-sentences, whatever comes to mind. Check in with your body: when you think of death how does your body respond? How does your back feel? Your stomach? Your chest? Do this for two minutes.

Now, on the bottom right point of the pentacle, write the word "Honor." Bring yourself into a space of reverence for the dead. They are no longer bound to the physical and so are closer to the mystery. Underneath your previous writings, begin to write whatever now comes to mind as you contemplate Honor.

Next, on the upper left point, write the word "Memory." Call up a memory of the particular dead with which you wish to work and make a pledge to keep their memory alive. Now down below, write what comes up for you. It need not be "pleasant" or even "fair," only genuine. What memories about this dead do you have? Be honest.

When you are finished with Memory, focus on the upper right point and next to it write, "Release." This is especially important for those with an emotional connection to the particular dead: Let. Them. Go. You must grieve, but not wallow in grief. We must feel ourselves letting them go, as if letting go of a balloon; effortless, painless, calm. Write down all the things that connected you to them, but now view those connections as being severed. They no longer connect you to the person. That person—at least in that form—is gone. As you write, tell that person goodbye.

Finally, near the bottom left point of the pentacle, write the word "Repose." Call up a state of calm, peaceful, reverential memoriam. While contemplating this state, finish your journaling project by recording what comes to you.

Once you are familiar with these points and the presences they carry you will likely wish to abandon the formal journaling aspect of this exercise in favor of a more free-form contemplative meditational style as a means to more regularly engage this pentacle as a whole. Once an energetic momentum has been established, the Bone Pentacle will become a tool to be used in certain rites or workings that involve communing with the dead.

To shift our conscious toward the dead we must attune to those environments in which they are present, or which cause our own thoughts to turn toward them. The easiest among these environments (and usually most potent) are cemeteries. These places are steeped in the death force in that they not only house the remains of the dead, but also—due to the many living who visit them—the veil between the worlds begins to thin to the point that historical graveyards often present particularly potent portals into the world beyond.

For this next lesson, written by my husband Chas Bogan and borrowing from his work in Conjure and Hoodoo (a magical influencer of our own Faery Tradition), you will be required to physically go to a graveyard to collect some dirt as a physical link with a spirit with whom you may work.

GOING TO THE GRAVEYARD
by Chas Bogan

The person who takes something from a cemetery
will return more than he took.
Folk-lore From Adams County Illinois; #10358
——HARRY M. HYATT

Various traditions acknowledge various spirits who govern graveyards, and when doing cemetery work practitioners will respectively acknowledge, avoid, or appease such spirit. For our work, we will petition Black Ana and the Arddu, asking them to favor our journey into the cemetery and to assure that whatever other spirits may have dominion in this graveyard will in turn be appeased.

To be respectful and safeguard against trouble, we will be working with our Queen of Death, Black Ana, and the Arddu, who serves as a psychopomp between the living and the dead. It's the same as if you are entering an apartment complex, best to be invited by someone who lives there, someone who is expecting you and who knows how to deal with the strange and cantankerous neighbors.

Traditionally offerings for the spirit(s) of the graveyard are left at the front gate before entering; however, it is often the case that you must first travel through the gates in order to park. When this is the case you can simply pick the start of any path, just be sure to make your petition prior to stepping among the graves. Rather than play favorites, we will be giving both deities the same offering of Spirit Water, the recipe for which is as follows...

Spirit water is made of equal parts water and Anisette. To make Anisette you need:

1 cup of vodka

8 drops of essential anise or star anise

1 tablespoon of Simple syrup; made from 3 parts sugar dissolved into 1 part boiling water

Now you will either set two bottles of the Spirit water on the ground or pour the Spirit Water into a pair of shot glasses, baby food jars, or what have you.

For this I have two bottles filled with Spirit Water, each of which also includes three pieces of Pyrite. Pyrite is often used in mojo bags to draw money and good fortune. Some may use coins as a form of payment, as we will do to pay for our dirt later. Although symbolically meaningful, the dead don't really need coins, and pennies and dimes, though traditional, really can't buy much in today's economy anyway. Keep in mind though that by burying coins you are returning treasure to the land below, the underworld, from which it was originally mined. Part of the idea here is to give back. Seen in this context Pyrite is appropriate, or if they reject the offering you will learn of it soon enough when they strike you dead.

We will place the bottle of Spirit Water on the ground to our left and invoke Black Ana with this chant by Storm:

> *Ancient Queen of Death's Repose,*
> *Sharp your scythe and true your sight,*
> *Revealing secrets no one else knows*
> *Grandmother! Queen of Night!*

Now, place the other bottle on the ground at your right, far enough apart so that you can step between them eventually. We will invoke the Arddu with this chant, again from Storm:

> *Primal Lord of Darkened land,*
> *Sex and Death at your command*
> *Scent of musk and sight of bone,*
> *Guards the gate to the Unknown.*

Sense now how Black Ana and the Arddu stand before you now on opposite sides, and we bid them now by saying:

Walk with us,

Guide us,

Protect us,

As we journey into the breathless realms.

Get to it. Step between the two bottles and begin your journey to find a grave from which to collect some dirt.

You may choose the grave according to:

• Personal Relationship

 – Grave of relative/friend/coworker

 – Grave of pet/familiar

• The Mighty Dead, Sinners, and the Weak Willed

 – Mighty Dead: Royalty, Soldiers, Healers, etc.
 Individuals of great accomplishment and power in life are often able to provide assistance from "the other side." Working healing magic? Look to the grave of a doctor. Looking for protection? A police officer or priest might fit the bill.

 – "Sinners": Murderers, Thieves, Gamblers, Prostitutes, etc.
 People who went against the rules of a society or indulged heavily in earthly pleasures. The spirit of a thief might help to get a stolen item back, while that of a gambler might assist with one's own gambling luck. The grave of a prostitute might yield an ingredient for a lust spell.

 – "Weak Willed": Unbaptized Babies, Addicts, Suicides, etc.
 Thought of as suited for any work, as reportedly they submit more easily to the stronger will of the practitioner. These are generally considered "lower level" spirits and are mostly creatures of deep emotion and not much else. Some might even be what we would consider to be "feral." Individually they might not be much of a boost to the practitioner's own power, but in numbers they can prove to be very potent; provided they are properly fed and maintained, of course.

- Auspicious Location
  - Direction
    - East for knowledge and conception
    - South for sex and vengeance
    - West for love and peace
    - North for wealth and healing
  - Divination
    - Numerology: Numbers can be determined by need (such as lucky seven or thirteen for gambling luck), or chosen by lot. Site is then determined based on numbers on gravestone; or steps or graves counted from gate or monument
    - Throw a coin such as a silver dollar into the graveyard and dig at the site it lands, leaving the coin as payment
  - Spirit Led
    - Follow a moving animal or insect, leaf, or request written on paper or onion skin
    - Let the spirit call to you and guide you

Paying for the Dirt

There are many ways of leaving coins for payment of dirt, many of which utilize an odd number of coins left in positions above the body. My method is to place three coins, dimes, or silver dollars in a triangle and dig dirt from the center. You can place them above certain areas of the body that correspond with your need, such as above the head for knowledge or strategy, the heart of love or emotional healing, the sex for vigor, the feet for success in new endeavors.

Other offerings may include alcohol and tobacco, although it is wise to know the relationship the deceased had with such substances, they may have struggled to overcome alcoholism, or they may have quit smoking for health reasons that they no longer need to care about. Flowers also make a nice offering. According to Greek mythology, the dead much prefer offerings of blood. Allegedly Victor Anderson spoke against blood offerings, saying that they drew the presence of unwanted entities, and it has been suggested that red ink be used in place of blood, such as can easily be made by dissolving Dragon's Blood resin in alcohol. Blood, or its surrogate, is rarely left as a 'thank you' gift to spirits of the dead, however it can be utilized to create a strong connection between the deceased and the living, such as can strengthen bonds of mediumship.

The Bone Pentacle

Facing the grave, place five dimes over the deceased's head, hands, and feet. We then draw an invoking pentacle connecting the five dimes, declaring the energy of each point.

Death

Honor

Memory

Release

Repose

This is done five times to awaken the spirit within the grave; then, from the center of the pentacle we remove the graveyard dirt.

For this lesson, we will simply take home some of this dirt to place on our ancestor altar to strengthen and honor this spirit.

Though Faery Tradition does not have a singular theory or teaching for what happens to us after we die, there are a few commonalities. It is generally believed that the consciousness of the deceased will remain in some form around the body and/or the home for a period of three days after physical death. There is also the general belief that initiated Witches will have some level of controlled reincarnation, and so will find themselves among their loved ones once more, in another life. Cora Anderson spoke of souls returning to the cauldron of the Goddess and remaining there for a period of eighty years before coming back to the earth plane. Other initiates adhere to the Tibetan concept of the "Bardo state," which is an intermediary plane in between life and death.

One interesting bit of Faery lore concerning death concerns the Doctrine of the Three Souls.[30] Each soul has its own journey after death, though nothing is written in stone. Generally, it is said that a fetch returns to the earth, enriching the planetary consciousness that we might call the Earth Mother. Here the fetch either stays and is recycled or, due to some events in life, is nurtured and given some additional stretch to their evolutionary journey. It is believed that a fetch can eventually evolve (some say by merging together) into a talker, and a talker into a daemon. This last revelation also explains one way in which our ancestors are with us; multiple talkers in our bloodline—over many lifetimes—have formed together and become your holy daemon. It/ they are a part of you. This is reminiscent of the Huna idea of the *aumakua*, which is a type of family god, or an ancestor who has risen to the level of divinity.

It is said that under certain circumstances, such as a violent death, these souls can split apart causing certain types of paranormal phenomena. When a fetch has been disconnected from its soul structure, it may remain on the physical plane but have no talker to give it the ability to communicate. As a result, this creature of primal consciousness, sensation, and memory may lash out at the living. If the person in life suffered from severe mental illness or addiction, then the disconnected fetch can continue that aetheric pattern, potentially affecting the living in that area. In extreme cases, this can account for most of what has been labeled "demonic activity"; in that the disconnected, frightened, angry (and possibly feral) fetch is lashing out like a wounded animal.

---

30. A basic exercise for experiencing and aligning the Three Souls can be found in appendix I.

In these cases, we may wish to assist this fetch in finding peace, much as we might help a trapped animal or child. Likewise, in the cases where a talker has been displaced and is earthbound, we may find ourselves in the position of needing to assist these souls to move onward, to whatever the next phase of their personal mystery may be.

EXERCISE: Journey through the Western Gate [31]

This trance exercise will allow us the means to travel into the intermediary state between life and death so as to assist those souls who may be trapped there. It is presented here in a simple form, but may be expanded with other ritual elements if desired. This exercise should be repeated periodically, especially around Samhain or whenever you are personally called to do this work.

Ground and center. Open the Western Gate. Imagine moving through this gate and into an "in-between space" in the form of a beautiful and serene grassy meadow. The time of day appears to be twilight, but you can see neither the sun nor the moon in the sky. As you walk farther out toward the horizon, you come to the edge of a great river. There is no way to get across this river that you can immediately see. On "this" side of the river are those souls who have not yet fully "passed over." The other side is the great mystery that lies beyond. Some souls may still be on this side because they have unfinished business on earth, or they may be lost and confused and unable to get across. Remember your three souls in alignment and reach out with your awareness. Imagine that you either find or create a bridge that connects this side of the river with the other. *We* will stay on this side, but now pay attention to any of the beings that you may perceive here. You may show them this bridge and even suggest that they cross over, but never force them. They must choose to cross of their own free will. Imagine assisting these spirits over the bridge and just allow your trance to unfold naturally. After several minutes come back to normal awareness and record your experiences in your journal.

The Dark Goddess

Wind shriek howl and raspy whispers
Ink black madness, three dark sisters

---

31. To perform this exercise, you should already be familiar with the Western Gate as a portal between the worlds of the living and the dead. If you are not yet proficient at opening this energetic gate, you will need to practice with that before attempting this and I have given a simple method for doing so in appendix I. For a more in-depth look at this concept, see my book *Betwixt and Between*.

Bone thin hand, which grasps the night
Ancient Queen of death and fright.

The Dark Goddess has many faces to the Faery Witch. She is a goddess of ancient wisdom and, in particular, the "forbidden mysteries" of Witchcraft. She is a poisoner, a healer, a priestess, and an oracle; she is the very archetype of a Witch. It is she who holds the threads of fate, and who uses her silver scythe to cut those threads when their time has come.

She is the thrice-formed Hecate, titan-goddess of Witchcraft and the crossroads. She is the Morrigan, battle goddess and sovereign queen. She is Baba Yaga … she is Lilith … she is the Cailleach. The Faery Witch knows that she is *all* of these goddesses and so much more. She is the mystery; the ever-changing Star Goddess, and as Ana, we see that in the iconography that is handed down for her, where she is crowned with nine stars, making this connection as clear as a cloudless night sky.

Ana is related to that figure known as *Black Annis*, a sort of bogeyman figure from English folklore. She was widely known to eat human flesh, tearing it off of her victims with her iron claws. In this we see her shadow aspect. Ana can be the matronly grandmother, telling stories and tending wounds. Or she can be the horrific stark terror of the Cailleach, the unforgiving winter land that slowly drains life and hope away into the white void.

EXERCISE: Journey to Her Cauldron

Here we will journey to meet with the Dark Goddess, seeking her powers of transformation. This trance should be performed in actual at least three to four times before moving on to the next work.

Ground and center. Imagine an opening in the earth that leads into a cavernous place below. Imagine yourself climbing down into this cavern, feeling the air grow cool and damp, and hearing the echoing drips of water in the distance. Down deep, you explore this cavern noticing that the stalactites and stalagmites form a series of columns that seem to draw your attention deeper into the heart of the cavern. Follow, and you come to a large clearing. The only source of light seems to come from a large fire in the center, on top of which is placed an enormous black iron cauldron. There is a wooden ladder that leads up the side of the cauldron, and you are compelled to climb up and to peer over its edge.

Looking inside you see your face reflected in the dark liquid. As the fire continues to heat this brew, you begin to see bubbles form, and begin to swirl, obscuring your reflection so that something new arises. What do you see? Let go...

Suddenly you are pushed over the edge and you fall into the cauldron. The hot liquid washes over you and you accidentally take it into your lungs. Your body fights against it, but your limbs soon become heavy and you surrender to your fate.

Just relax and allow yourself to float. Notice what thoughts begin to arise and how your body feels in this state. Imagine your body melting away ... becoming part of the boiling brew. You swirl and churn within the cauldron ... float and sway ... in the peaceful blackness ... amongst the stars ... the stars of her crown. She is standing over you ... her starry crown illuminates you. She shows you the curved edge of black space ... it is a mirror. What do you see?

After some time allow yourself to come back into normal awareness. Reaffirm the alignment of your three souls. You may wish to also perform a grounding exercise and the Waters of Purity.

In the same vein as the Greek Moirai or the Fates, the Dark Goddess is She Who Cuts the Thread—that precious cord of life that weaves into the Pattern. In addition to the lives of individuals, these cords are also the wraith threads that connect us to other people, places, and situations to which we are bound emotionally. Energy and consciousness can travel along these threads and there are times in which we may wish to sever them, as in the case with negative relationships or traumatic events in our past that we find we cannot move beyond. Using this modality we can use our magic to help us sever those threads and break the chains that bind us.

SPELL: Cutting the Cord

Cutting the cord is breaking a connection to a person or to a power that has some level of negative control over you and your life.

This is best performed outside in a place not where you live. Alternatively, you can perform the majority of the rite at home and then travel to a new location to complete the spell.

Items needed:
Two small beads: one white, the other black

A length of black thread roughly 13 inches

A pair of sharp scissors

Begin by Opening the Way. In your Enchanted state, name and empower each bead by holding them close and saying:

I am the bead of white,
I keep this charm to guide my sight.
[NAME OF PERSON OR NEGATIVE POWER] is the bead of black
I keep my power and send them back.

Thread the beads in such a way so that one bead is tied at one end while the other bead is tied at the opposite end. Inwardly focusing on the connections you have with the person or power while outwardly focusing on the black thread, begin to rhythmically chant, building to a frenzy:

This is the cord that binds me to you.
This is the cord that binds me to you.
This is the cord that binds me to you.
I cut the cord, I break the chain.

When you reach the peak of power, use the scissors and cut the thread. Imagine the energetic and spiritual ties connecting the two of you have now been severed.

To complete the spell, recite the following, or similar:

Bead of black,
[NAME OF PERSON OR NEGATIVE POWER]
Our connection has been severed.
And far away from me you fly!

Using all of your strength, throw the black bead as far away from you as you can, imagining this person or power as moving far, far away. Return home and take a cleansing bath. Perform the Waters of Purity rite.[32] Keep the white bead as a charm to keep your power.

---

32. See appendix I.

EXERCISE: Drawing Down the Dark Moon

This is a variation on the "Drawing Down the Moon" exercise normally given earlier on in Faery Witchcraft training. It utilizes some imagery from the poetry of Victor Anderson and combines an oral teaching from him that indicated that "drawing down the moon" was in fact drawing down one's own God Soul, i.e., the holy daemon. It should be performed on the night of the dark moon.

Items needed:

A black altar cloth

A black candle

A silver or earthenware bowl, filled with water

Nine blue stones

Incense that you associate with the Dark Goddess, such as those containing anise or
   black copal

An incense burner

Charcoal

An offering of food, whiskey, etc.

Go outside, preferably a place that is not overly polluted with artificial light. (You can, of course, do this in your own home with the lights turned off, but in this case, it would be good to at least open a window so that you can breathe the night air.) Arrange your altar space to your liking by placing all of your items on your black cloth. Light the charcoal.

Open the Way. Feel the night air. Imagine yourself tuning in to the darkness around you, but this time not as Death…but as *Mystery*…Affirm your soul alignment and place some of the incense on the charcoal. Imagine reaching out through your daemon and into the darkness all around you. Imagine that this darkness is part of the presence of the moon…hidden…but present…lurking unseen in the sky. The land is cast in shadow.

Light the black candle, and drop the nine blue stones into the water—one by one—as you make your prayer:

> *To the darkness of the moon*
> *I send my voice and now call down*

Three times three, the stars of blue
That brightly gild her starry crown.

Take a deep breath and open yourself to the darkness. Feel this potent darkness … the dark womb, pregnant with possibility. Now is the time to delve into the Dark. Feel the darkness permeating the stone-filled water. Take a deep breath and breathe wraith force into the water, imagining the nine blue stones beginning to shine with celestial light. Do this for eight more breaths, seeing the stones glow brighter with each successive breath. On the ninth breath imagine the stones igniting into star-fire, radiating into the water with an invisible light. Take a sip of the water and feel this invisible light flowing into you. Open yourself to the dark moon. Open yourself to the mystery. What comes to you? Express it! Let it move through you! Sing, or dance, or laugh, or cry … sway to and fro … let your body move … fast or slow … loud or silent. What comes to you?

Imagine the nine blue stars upon your own head as a crown. Imagine their light shining through the veil and into the realm of the dead. What spirits come to you? Who do you call? Let the ancestors speak to you.

Make your offering.

After some time return to normal awareness and write down your experiences in your journal.

———————————

No matter what we believe happens to us after we die, the fact remains that we just don't *know*. Death is the final mystery. And as practitioners of the Witches' Craft, our job is to dive headfirst into the unknown. We are the edge-riders, the mysterious freaks who go against the grain of societally sanctioned practices and beliefs, and we revel in it. We might be drawn to the dark because we hear the calling of our own power and knowledge from deep within the pit of that darkness. We are called to face our inner darkness, and perhaps even to help others face their own.

CHAPTER 4
QUENCHING THE FIRES OF HELL:
THE RITE OF THE SEVEN JARS

I believe I am in Hell, therefore I am.
—ARTHUR RIMBAUD, *A SEASON IN HELL*

One of the most important aspects of the Faery Tradition, in my opinion, is the idea that evil is something that can be *healed*.

Instead of throwing people away in some sort of moralistic trash heap, we operate under the fundamental principle that even those who commit evil are deserving of compassion and, in most cases, can potentially be "redeemed." Not just in the eyes of a mythical Creator God (or Goddess), but in the eyes of their own daemon—their own God Soul.

In our capacity as "Faery Doctors" we are sometimes asked to provide magic and spiritual assistance to those who do not do magic for themselves, often from religions with values that may be in conflict with our own. In her book *Fifty Years in the Feri Tradition*, Grandmaster Cora Anderson recalls a story in which Victor was administering the Kala rite[33] to someone, presumably a non-Witch who was seeking help. This person had seen or committed atrocities during the Vietnam war and was haunted by what he experienced there as a young soldier in an impossible and nightmarish situation. They felt as if they were broken, unlovable, even evil, like they didn't deserve happiness or forgiveness. Victor told this person that God had forgiven them a long time ago, but now they must forgive themselves in a way that included their God Soul

---

33. This is the more traditional Hawaiian name for a simple purification ritual that in BlueRose is called "the Waters of Purity." See appendix I.

(their holy daemon). Victor charged the water, took a sip, and gave the rest to them to drink. When they did, they received a slight electric shock[34] and were paralyzed for several minutes before returning to normal. After that, they were at peace.

Some might have seen the actions taken by the ex-soldier to have been "evil" and then perhaps decided to not help them find the peace that they sought; thinking that to deny them such equates to some sort of justice. But this type of thinking does nothing to actually help the world. It might feel good for our ego in the short term to lash out at someone who has been hurtful to ourselves or others. But in the end such actions and emotions merely bind us further to them, and rob us of the golden opportunity to practice fierce compassion.

I personally have ministered to many individuals from various faiths and have been asked several times by many of these people if I believed that certain of their actions were "against God" and would damn them to hell. Here I know to tread carefully, as I do not wish to appear to be usurping their religious systems and values and inserting my own, while at the same time needing to provide a balanced view that alleviates their stress and fear.

"Hell is something we make for ourselves on earth," I often tell them. "It is the absence of God Herself. And if you are honestly pursuing your highest ideal, then you are already on the path to God."

Hell. It's not something that many Neopagans like to talk about. Considering that most of us at one time or another have been told in no uncertain terms by some pious monotheist that we are going to spend eternity there, it is usually not high on the list of topics to which we as a group devote our attention. It's a piece of Christian mythos, used as a tool of fear and oppression against the masses to ensure blind obedience. And it's a total downer. Pain. Suffering. Torment. For all of eternity. It seems like such a *waste*.

The Devil is at least a little more interesting. We can see him in our Horned God, primal and lusty and full of sensual pleasures, the likes of which would easily scandalize the sexually repressed Christian. But a lord of absolute evil? Not exactly plausible.

---

34. This is a common detail often reported by those around Victor when he would perform this rite for others. This is explained as the charge of the water dramatically interacting with the energy body of the recipient. In my own work performing this rite for others I have not experienced such a dramatic charge, but have seen distinct and undeniable benefits of the workings nonetheless.

We might not believe in these things as a point of any particular religion, philosophy, or dogma. But a lot of people *do*. And belief is a type of devotion. And devotion brings … energy … movement … changes … powers … spirits. Witches know the power of focused belief. We know how to mold and shape it into something that can help us reach our goals. We know how the human mind can create *magic*.

In this case, a spirit. An *egregore*, or "thought-form," to be exact, a type of artificially created entity or energetic form that is given its astral existence by the belief, will, and life force of an individual or group.

Usually this is done with concentrated effort, often with ritual focus, but also these forms can be created by the will of those who are unusually strong or through the communal belief of a group. Even if we hold fast to the indefensible prejudice that somehow our pantheons are real while insisting that their God somehow *isn't*, with all this in mind, is it so far off to assume that by the collective belief of so many in a largely Christian dominated society that hell itself would exist in this manner as well?

Whether or not we personally believe in the infernal dimension, we must accept that there are many more who have lived and died by the belief, and for those who have passed on believing that for whatever reason they were going to hell, it is the power of their own belief that ultimately condemns them. This is another example of what can cause a spirit to be restless.

We might say that both heaven and hell are of our own making. They are states of mind in which have shaped the lives of many generations of believers and non-believers alike. Someone who lives their life under an oppressive religious system that teaches them to fear and distrust themselves is very likely to be psychologically and spiritually wounded. By being raised in such a toxic environment these wounds will have been impressed deeply onto the fetch, where they will remain to be a problem for the individual until they are able to face their fear and shame and steal their power back from it.

But what happens if someone does not face their fear? What if there is no moment in which the truth is faced? If one lives their whole life under the damaging lies of the false god,[35] and dies believing that they are damned … what then? What of those who

---

35. Victor often referred to the "false god" not as a blanket reference for the god of Christianity, but for any supposed monotheistic deity that would deny the existence of any others while also denying the basic decency and sovereignty of the human being, i.e., the "angry, jealous god" who would deny us our own divinity. I am using this term in this same fashion.

committed suicide even though they believed it was an unforgivable sin? What about LGBT people who knew the truth of who they were, but also believed the lie that they were morally inferior because of it? What of anyone who failed to live up to the standards of a Church whose main interest has historically been the accumulation of wealth over the spiritual lives of its parishioners.

In the Faery Tradition, we *identify* with deity. Since we are all children of the Goddess we especially identify with the Blue God, the firstborn of the Star Goddess who is also her consort and other half. In his aspect as Melek Ta'us, the Peacock Angel of Middle Eastern myth, he is said to be related (or in some cases equated) to Lucifer, that Promethean light-bringer who in modern times has been erroneously conflated with the Christian prince of darkness, but who is rightfully the rebellious spark of individuality and divine freewill within us all. The Blue God, Melek Ta'us, is said to rule over humankind as the *holy daemon* of the world.

To some this might seem paradoxical; how can our collective higher nature be the same being described as the prince of evil? Further insight may be derived by looking deeper into another piece of Faery lore which states that while underneath the hand of the Goddess he is beneficial and loving, but removed from Her influence he is wrathful and terrible. In this we can see the touch of a patriarchal culture; when the Goddess is removed from the picture, then our lord becomes the jealous and wrathful god that is mentioned in the Biblical texts.

In one myth, it is said that he was cast out of heaven for the sin of pride, which is a story with which most are more familiar in its Christian form as the famous "fall from grace," giving us the concept of the "fallen angels." After the Fall, Melek Ta'us was said to repent for his sins, weeping for over seven thousand years and filling seven jars with his tears, which he then used to extinguish the fires of hell, thus establishing him as a savior figure.

This is also a myth about free will. In older versions of this myth cycle, Lucifer (along with all the angels) is ordered by God to never bow before anyone or anything, save for God himself. It is only later, after God creates Adam, that they are asked to bow before God's humanly creation. As the rest of the angels dutifully bow before the first human, it is Lucifer (Melek Ta'us) alone who refuses ("I am made from light and he from dirt! I will not bow before him!"), thus establishing Melek Ta'us as a figure with a will of his own, a characteristic associated in Islamic tradition with the *djinn*, as opposed to angels who have *no choice* but to obey the will of God. It is the establishment of free will that makes our beloved Melek an important—and accessible—figure for us. He contains multitudes; he is the first emanation of God Herself, and thus represents God on the earthly plane. His image is the peacock; a heavenly bird that is linked mythologically to earthly serpents, as it was believed that they got their radiant iridescent colors from a snake's venom, to which they were believed to be impervious. He is the unified Divine Twins, the serpent of primal, earthly powers melded with the dove (or other bird) of transcendent spirit.

That he embodies both good and evil, spirit and matter, and beauty and darkness makes it easier to identify with him; he has the same potentials and limitations that we all do. He is inextricably linked to us; as we evolve, so does he.

Having firmly established Melek Ta'us as a savior deity, we can turn to him in that capacity in order to heal our own pain and suffering; to "save" us from our own undoing. We all have secret pain. We might not be aware of it (though we often are), but aware or not, it is there. It is that part of us that secretly believes that we are not good enough … not worthy. It is the presence of our inner demons that perhaps were originally invoked in order to protect us from further pain, but now—with a life and will of their own—have begun to dictate to us the boundaries of our existence, constricting us and preventing our fullest potential.

Often, we judge ourselves harshly for having these feelings, which simply compounds their negative impact upon us. We tell ourselves that if we were truly spiritual, enlightened, etc., then we wouldn't feel powerless, shameful, or desperate. We often respond by attacking ourselves for our weakness, and when this happens we are very likely to attack others in the same way.

In another myth of Melek Ta'us—attributed to the Yazidi[36]—a poor shepherd awakens one day to find a wounded peacock lying on the ground outside his home. Seeing that the bird was very close to death, the farmer decides—at great burden to himself—to forgo his daily chores and instead care for the wounded creature. All night the shepherd devotedly attends to the sickly bird, feeding it and giving it water … giving it his bed to sleep in and warming it by the fire. The next day the shepherd awakes to find the peacock restored to full health and is shocked to hear the bird speak:

---

36. It is my belief that this is not an authentic Yazidi myth, but is instead attributed to them by Islamic dogmatists in an effort to "prove" that the Yazidi are "devil worshipers," which is a false accusation. Nevertheless, the symbolic message of the myth stands on its own merits and serves to illustrate an important spiritual truth.

"Noble shepherd! Thank you for mending my wounds and restoring my spirit! For I am the spirit of evil and shall reward you and your family for your kindness."

With that the peacock placed a blessing upon the shepherd and his family and with a cry, flew up into the heavens.

———

This myth centers around deep compassion, not just for the sickly or those less fortunate *but even for evil itself.* If we accept the definition of "evil" as "life force that has been twisted" then we are perhaps less likely to delve into the realm of moralistic absolutes that plague much of monotheistic thinking. When we see evil as something that can be *healed,* then we perhaps are in a better position to do that healing; to open our hearts in compassion for our own weakness and that of others, instead of reproaching it. We are being called to do what is perhaps the most difficult thing ever: we are asked to have compassion for *all* parts of ourselves, which includes the weakness, the sickness, and the pain.

"We do not coddle weakness," the familiar Faery tenet begins, "nor do we condemn it in others."

Our beloved Peacock Lord wants us to be happy. He wants us to share in his universal dance of ecstasy and desire, and we can only truly do so when we have healed our guilt, shame, and inhibitions. Once healed, we can begin the work of helping to heal others as well.

> *If you're going through hell, keep going.*
> —WINSTON S. CHURCHILL

RITE: The Rite of the Seven Jars

This ritual was inspired by the trance experiences of my husband Chas, from which he created a meditative exercise.[37] I have taken his idea and expanded it into a ritual that can be used by an individual or a group. This ritual develops on our previous work with helping souls cross over, but now involves the savior figure, Melek Ta'us, as a magical catalyst. This rite is considered to be somewhat "heavy." You will want to engage in some self-care activities afterward, such as the Waters of Purity rite, as well

---

37. See Chas Bogan, "Our Faith Has No Hell," *Witch Eye* #10, http://feritradition.org/grimoire/deities/essay_no_hell.html

as getting rest and eating healthy food. This ritual should be done *sparingly*. Perhaps even as a once- or twice-yearly observance, if even that. Follow your intuition. When in doubt, refer to your divinatory tools.

Items needed:
A black scrying mirror
A few peacock eye feathers in a small vase
A skull or image of a skull (preferably human)
Seven small jars
A chalice (each participant should have their own)
A small pitcher of water
Anointing or blessing oil
A black candle
A blue candle
A red candle
A violet candle
A bell

In the center of your working area, prepare an altar to the Blue God on which are placed the candles, the seven jars, the water pitcher, and the vase of peacock feathers. In the western edge of the circle place the skull.

Open the Way. Create a ritual space (such as casting a circle). Perform the Waters of Purity rite.

Invoke the spirit of the serpent by lighting the red candle, saying:

> *Earthly serpent,*
> *Coiled deep and down below,*
> *With scarlet flame rise to us*
> *And fill us with Passion and Power!*

On the last line, imagine those points of the Iron Pentacle mentioned in the charm being activated in your body, the connecting lines between the two, glowing clear and strong.

Invoke the spirit of the dove by lighting the blue candle, saying:

> *Celestial dove,*
> *Stretched across the heavens,*
> *With blue flame descend to us*
> *And fill us with Pride and Self!*

Again, imagine those Iron points and the pathways between them glowing bright.

Taking both the red and blue candles, use their flames to light the violet, thus bringing the powers of the Twins together:

> *Winged Serpent! Melek Ta'us!*
> *Firstborn rainbow light of God*
> *Spread amongst the earth and heavens*
> *And merge with us in the name of Sex!*

Allow the energy of all the activated points of the Iron Pentacle to flow upward and into the point of Sex, which shines with a crystalline rainbow flame.

Allow your energy body to open up as you would open to a lover. Tender. Passionate. Erotic. Imagine his rainbow light shining deep within you … charging you with the power and purpose to face your true self.

When you feel sufficiently charged, look into the scrying mirror so that you can see your own reflection. Allow yourself to remain open and calm … Look deep into your life and your power. Be aware of any insights that may arise.

Make a prayer that he assist you in discovering and facing your own hidden shame:

> *Peacock Angel! Peacock Lord!*
> *Shining light into the dark*
> *Descend you now the rainbow flame,*
> *Revealing here our secret shame,*
> *Into hell you now embark!*

Allow his rainbow light to flow down deep into those areas which are buried and dark. Allow this light to illuminate an area of your life that you have kept buried—that which you do not want to think about. Allow yourself to recall something in your life that you feel has brought you guilt or shame. It can be something you did to someone else, something that happened to you, perhaps recently, or in childhood, etc. If it becomes too uncomfortable, just relax and remember your soul alignment.

Imagine that these feelings are part of a secret, toxic fire that has been silently burning within you. Feel how this fire is like a small sphere of toxic flame that burns somewhere in your fetch beneath your navel. Feel how it calls into itself every bit of your own power that has been turned against you: every feeling of unworthiness, of shame, guilt…each time you have felt powerless…scared…alone…and especially those feelings that you have kept to yourself…perhaps fantasies of hurting someone…of hurting yourself…of coercing someone, or otherwise subjugating their will. No matter what it is…even if you do not understand what it is…allow yourself to feel it…to face it…and allow its power to burn in that sphere of toxic flame within you. This is the presence of your own personal hell.

Hold those emotions within you and allow them to shine. Emotions are nothing more than energy running through your psyche, so let that energy build and shine. See how it is actually power, and though it has up until now been turned against you, you can control it, tame it, transform it. When you feel the energy is at its peak, breathe three times into your *hellsphere*, allowing this power to be sealed into it.

Feel how Melek Ta'us feels your pain; how he feels the pain of all who suffer. Imagine him larger than life standing before you, his radiant light filling the room, the sky, the world. Imagine (and feel) that he begins to weep, his etheric tears raining down upon you. Recite the Prayer of the Tears:

> *You shed your tears to end our suffering,*
> *Into seven jars they flow*
> *Washing clean our pain and sorrow*
> *Quench the fires down below.*

Focusing on this etheric rain, slowly pour some water into each of the seven jars, feeling how they not only represent Melek's tears, but that they *are* his tears. See his rainbow light descend into each of the jars and from them into your chakras.

See the power of red flowing through the first jar and into your base chakra. Feel how it is filled with vitality, potential, and life force. Feel your fetch. Chant or tone power into the jar and the chakra. Continue chanting or toning for each.

Still in the realm of the fetch, feel orange flowing through the next jar and into your second chakra, which glows with unbridled creativity and pleasure.

Now, feel how your fetch merges into your talker at about your solar plexus where you see yellow shine through the third jar and into your solar plexus chakra, filling it with the qualities of confidence and power.

In your talker, green shines through the fourth jar and into your heart center, filling it with connection, community, and love.

The vibration of the talker is elevated as you ascend up into your fifth chakra in your throat. Blue shines through the fifth jar and into your chakra, filling it with the qualities of communication.

Talker merges with the holy daemon (God Soul) in your sixth chakra—your "Third Eye." Violet light shines through the sixth jar and into the chakra, filling it with intellect, vision, and dreams.

Feeling the presence of your daemon at your crown, white crystalline light shines though you and into the seventh jar, filling it with understanding, knowing, and divine inspiration.

Anoint yourself on your chakra areas with the water from each of the corresponding seven jars, feeling how the tears of Melek Ta'us are cleansing and soothing you, like a healing salve for your soul. Feel how you are being healed.

All of these power centers in your body are alive and active. Feel and see the light of each of them shine outward into your chalice, which now shines with multicolored, crystalline rainbow light.

Chant whatever sounds you are inspired to make and see how your chalice explodes with a torrent of rainbow-pearlescent liquid energy in which Melek Ta'us now appears as a pure white peacock. Drink deep from your cup and feel how this charged water—his etheric tears—are filling, empowering, and healing you. As you drink, feel how he flies above you into the heavens, weeping his healing tears down upon you, flowing down into that space within you that has burned with the toxic fire. Hear the fires sizzle as the tears begin to douse the flame. Feel these fires being quenched and soothed until there is only wet ash and soot.

Call Melek Ta'us down into you. Feel him descend from the heavens and flow down through your crown and into your body, moving erotically through you as he scrubs and brushes you clean, finally exiting through your perineum with a flow of erotic energy. Notice how he takes on the drab colors of all that toxic muck. He lies on the ground before you, wet … drab and dirty … next to lifeless …

Feel how you have been cleansed and empowered. Feeling yourself shine with rainbow light, open your heart to him *and to the dark powers that he now holds within.* Open yourself to compassion…*feel* compassion not just for the God…but for his weakness; *your* weakness. Feel compassion for sin, wrongdoing, and even evil—not as a justification for it, but as a means to move beyond judgment and therefore become free of it. Let this compassion shine from your heart and into the Peacock Angel.

When he has taken all of it in, he slowly rises, turns, and then beats his tail feathers upon the ground three times—filling all seven heavens with thunder! As you ring the bell three times, he transforms himself into a radiant peacock of many colors, filling your body with his rainbow luminescence once more. Bask in this presence for a while.

Facing the skull, open the Western Gate in whatever manner you are accustomed to and perform the Journey through the Western Gate exercise. You stand on this side of a riverbank amongst those souls who have not yet passed on and into the next phase of life after this one.

Now your journey truly begins. Allow Melek to guide you to a place in the ground where you find an opening. Notice what it looks (and feels) like, and taking a deep breath of power, descend down into the underworld. Down into a cavernous place…down…down…cool at first, the air now begins to heat up the farther you descend. You finally emerge into a place of fire and light…of torment and of pain. This is the transpersonal dimension of hell, and you are able to perceive souls here who are trapped and who believe that they deserve to be here.

After you have taken in as much detail as you can stand, allow Melek's presence within you to shine outward through you. You may experience great sadness at the suffering of so many. So be it. Allow it to inspire great compassion that moves out in waves from you. If you begin to weep, so much the better…allow your tears to be those of Melek Ta'us, and see his ethereal tears splash down upon the fiery ground, quenching those flames here as they did within you. Hear the flames sizzle and sputter as they are extinguished. You may wish to chant the Prayer of the Tears as you do this.

Feel how Melek's tears are so awesome that they actually begin a torrent of etheric water that soaks this place, completely dousing the flames leaving, once more, the ash and soot of pain and suffering. Feel how those suffering here are being soothed and freed; the light of consciousness being fed to them so that they become aware of their state—and of their power.

Once more Melek shines with a pearlescent flame and he moves outward and into this place, taking all the suffering and muck into himself, once more becoming drab and dirty. Again, shine compassion into him … and with three beats of his tail feathers upon the ground (and three rings of the bell), he again transforms his appearance and is radiant and beautiful once more. With a lively shriek, he rises up out of this place.

With your will, you reach out to those souls here and invite them to follow him up … imagine a crystalline stairway emerge that spirals up through the opening into which you came into this infernal place. Chanting or singing if you wish, begin to ascend, being aware of those who chose to follow you. Rise up and back into the place of the river where you assist them to cross into the next phase of existence by projecting the mental image of a bridge that crosses the river. (Remember not to force anyone to follow or to cross the bridge. We can only show them the way, but the path is their own.)

When you are ready, return to the realm of the living and close the Western Gate. Anoint yourself with the oil with a blessing. Give thanks to Melek Ta'us … to the Dove … to the Serpent. Give thanks to the Star Goddess and open your circle.

Drink some water. Have a bit of chocolate. Eat real food. Take a bath. Take a nap. Lighten up. Change your vibe. Enjoy it while you can.

The hard work is still ahead.

PART THREE
THE DEMON WORK

The Shadow Demon

Twisted shade, thy wraith of fear
of shame, of guilt, of anger's wrath
who darkens still my silver mirror
who poisons soft behind my mind

For years you've lurked beyond my knowing
at times, you'd rise like flames and then
to hide in ashes, cold and slumbering
and then as quick to rise again.

Shadow demon, it's you I conjure
From dark abyss within my soul
To show your face, by word of honor
And I will know it's not my truth.

Shadow, this I offer to you
By magic power of your true name
Shadow, be my demon lover
And merge as one into my flame.

CHAPTER 5

THE WELLS OF CREATION: GODDESSES OF THE PRIMAL ELEMENTS

Creation which cannot express itself becomes madness.

—ANAÏS NIN

On the journey of demonic discovery and reclamation, it becomes necessary to find allies along the way. While much work can and will be done on our own (for an effective Witch must first and foremost be a solitary practitioner, before all else), there are certain situations that may require we reach out for help. There are many alliances into which a Witch or shaman will enter during their tenure in the spirit realms. While most will be unique—personal to the individual practitioner— there are also those that are aligned to a specific place, practice, or tradition. Many traditions of the Craft, for example, work with specific gods, spirits, or powers that are allied to their tribe or their goals. I have previously written about many of the spirits and deities with whom we work in Faery Tradition, such as the Infinitum and the Watchers,[38] and now that we are on our quest to confront our own demons, we are ready to engage another class of beings: the Faery Goddesses of the Elements.

There are a few ways to which this particular grouping of Goddesses are collectively referred, depending on the lineage or coven of our tradition. The "Goddesses of the Quarters" or the "Goddesses of the (Primal) Elements" might be the most common,

---

38. See appendix I.

but my personal preference is the poetic term "The Wells at the Ends of the World,"[39] or what BlueRose refers to as the "Wells of Creation."

These beings are the raw power of the elements as they originate in the underworld, first and foremost in a state of *pre*-manifestation and as such are understood to exist in the underworld. The "Wells" are the poetic and visual keys by which these underworld powers mediate upward and into the middleworld of manifestation and form.

They are also "wells" because we can draw from them. They are entry points into vast storehouses of primal elemental power. The Wells, generally speaking, are the Goddesses themselves, but more specifically they are the nexus points between the two worlds through which the presences of these elemental Goddesses flow. In this each Goddess has three aspects: their underworld presence, their manifestation in the middle-world, and the nexus between the two.

Toward a greater understanding of the nebulous nature in which these Goddesses exist, let us turn for just a moment into the realm of art, poetry, and storytelling. I refer here specifically to Neil Gaiman's *Sandman,* an exceptional story about ancient powers, gods, Faerys, Witches, and the awesome nature of the universe with some family dynamics thrown in for good measure. While to some it may sound strange to bring into a serious discussion of magic and spirituality the likes of a comic book, I will remind the reader of the poetic and creative nature of our Faery Tradition in which the practitioner must listen to all potential sources of magic and inspiration. The Hidden Kingdom speaks to those with the ears to hear their message (artists, poets, visionaries, and other creatives) and transmits this message to the masses through said art, even sometimes in the most seemingly mundane of places.

To summarize the relevance here, in this story the title character (Dream/ Morpheus/"the Sandman") is one of seven powers called "the Endless," who are the foundational powers and principles of the universe. Each inhabits and "rules" a realm (Death, Destiny, Delirium, etc.), but they are not separate from that realm. For example, Dream is not only the ruler of his realm ("the Dreaming") he is an inextricable part of it, the very intelligence of it—the realm being simply an extension of his body or soul. You can't have one without the other. So too is it with the Wells of Creation. They are at once both the very realms of the elemental presences, the processes that they carry out, as well as the conscious, intelligent forces that direct them.

---

39. Faery oral tradition.

Beyond this, it should also be noted that the Wells of Creation are *actually only one Goddess*. Collectively, they are the Star Goddess, the primary deity of our Witchcraft, here understood in multiple forms as expressed through the classical elemental powers. Much how light is broken into the spectrum when projected through a prism, each of the Wells is a specific reflection of the singular Star Goddess, as seen from a different vantage point in the curved black mirror of space and time.

With one notable exception, the names of the Faery Goddesses of the Elements were first revealed to the public in the pages of Starhawk's book *The Spiral Dance*. Because of this I had actually been working with them for many years before I stumbled upon training in Faery Tradition, even using these names in public classes and workshops. Later, when I would encounter then in the context of Faery, their presence would be given a greater depth.

Following in the tradition in which I was originally taught, when invoking the presences of these primal goddesses, we are instructed to first invoke the Watcher associated with that direction/element. The reason for this is twofold. One is the Watchers are able to "invoke that which we cannot,"[40] meaning that they have a much larger reach in terms of access and thus are able to make a much deeper connection than we could on our own. The second is that these Goddesses are *raw, primal powers*. They are not neat, simple, mental constructs that merely represent psychological ideas of how the elements relate to our psyches. They are much bigger than we are, and so the mediating presence of the Watcher serves the purpose of translating the consciousness/energy/presence of the Goddess into a form that is more easily (and safely) digestible or understood. In this we are reminded that another name for the Watchers is the Guardians. And as the Guardians of the Wells they serve their purpose by protecting us from experiencing the full presences of the Goddesses' power, which otherwise could potentially have undesirable results.

If you have not yet worked with the Hidden Temples of the Elements or the Faery Watchers, I have provided a very simple structure for doing so in the appendices, but would recommend that you refer to my book *Betwixt and Between*, which goes into greater detail about working with these concepts and beings and how to develop a deep, personal relationship with them.

---

40. Faery oral tradition.

You will probably wish to work with them individually for at least two to four weeks each, with a minimum of four times per week. Remember to record your experiences in your journal.

Air: Arida, the Well of the Rising Sun

Arida is the Goddess of the east and is synonymous with the primal powers of elemental air. Like all the deities in Faery, she may appear in a multitude of forms. Some notable forms are a tornado with a woman's body or a hawk's head, a feathered serpent, or the silhouette of a hawk made from morning sunlight. She is sometimes called "the Bright Lady," as well as "She-Who-Comes-with-the-Dawn." She brings the winds of change and new beginnings. She is also "the Hawk of the Day," a title that perhaps reflects her primal animal core. Her essence is uplifting, inspirational, and powerful. Invoke her when you feel the need to shed light on a subject or an aspect of yourself, or when you feel that you need clarity, inspiration, or assistance with communicating your deepest thoughts. Don't let her oftentimes "airy" appearance fool you; she is a powerful and primal force and, like the hurricane, she can sweep you away with a breath if she so desires. Treat her with respect and she will teach you much about yourself.

EXERCISE: Opening the Well of the Rising Sun

This exercise can be performed at any time of the day, but is most especially aligned to performing in the morning at sunrise. Experiment with different timing to better suit your needs.

Items needed:
A golden yellow candle adorned with the following sigil:

Figure 10: Arida Sigil

Face east, Open the Way, and invoke the Hidden Temple of Air: a meadow in the spring at the first light of dawn. Feel the rising sun become a golden dome, which projects into your throat, becoming a golden half-circle. Feel the powers of *resonance* and *clarity* flowing through you, radiating from and through that glyph in your throat. After some time invoke the Watcher *Star Finder* and take some time to feel his presence as you breathe. Maintain awareness of Star Finder as you open yourself deeper to the elemental air...

Imagine an enormous silver gateway appear in the sky in the east, through which you see the vast open sky, fast swirling clouds, and the majesty of the rising run. Imagine the gate shimmering. Star Finder moves out through the gate and draws you forward to follow. He leads you deeper into the east and to a low stone altar, upon the top of which is painted a yellow half-circle with the curvature facing upward on a square background of golden brown. Kneel down before this altar and gaze at the symbol and the colors. Feel your consciousness projecting into this symbol as you open your eyes in the mundane world. Maintain the connection of both places existing simultaneously. Light the candle and say:

I conjure open the Well of Sunrise!
And peer into the Whirlwind!
Hail Arida! Rising Sun! Hawk of the Day!
You who shine with the breath of light
In the palaces of pleasure
Birthing day from night!
We salute thee, IAO!41

The top of the stone altar slides open, revealing a great well underneath, up from which a fast swirling wind flows—a great whirlwind—carrying golden morning sunlight along with the clean scent of rain, and earth, and *life*.

Imagine her emerging from below like the dawn, filling the sky with her presence. She appears surrounded by birds and clouds, and the elemental beings of air: Sylphs. She is the primal air... a breath from the underworld that flows up into ours to become

---

41. A magical cry from ancient Greek often used in the Craft. Pronounced EE-AHH-OH and usually expressed in one long, fluid exhalation.

a thought…an idea…the very air we breathe…a breeze…a wind…a cyclone. Her power is both life and death.

Allow her presence to move into you with your breath. Just notice how she appears to you and more importantly how her presence *feels* to you. Maintain this for at least a few minutes.

When you are finished, give her thanks and say:

> *Arida, Well of the Rising Sun,*
> *I thank you for your power and your presence.*
> *Hail and Farewell.*

Extinguish the candle. Imagine returning back with Star Finder through the silver gateway, which shimmers, and then is gone. Commune with him for a moment and then release the Watcher in the usual way. Return to normal awareness.

Fire: Tana, the Well of Plasma (or Liquid Flame)

As one of the Wells of Creation, Tana is the Goddess of the south and is synonymous with the primal powers of elemental fire. She can appear as a being made entirely of star-fire, white-hot luminescence. She may appear clad in red and is seen dancing in a desert underneath the blazing stars. She is "the Bringer of Passion" bringing the fires of energy, change, and ecstasy. She is also "Lady of the Scarlet Lust," a title that reflects her primal sexuality. Her power is vitalizing, energizing, and powerful. Invoke her when you feel the need to increase your energy or personal power, when you feel down or sluggish, when you need to direct more energy into a situation in your life or an aspect of yourself, when you need the fiery powers of transformation, or even when the powers of destruction are called for. Her fires build as well as destroy.

Tana is the name that Victor Anderson reportedly first received in his childhood initiation as a name for the goddess. Tana is an Etruscan name for the goddess Diana, who is the central deity in the collected folklore of Charles Godfrey Leland in his work *Aradia, or the Gospel of the Witches*. According to Raven Grimassi in his book *Hereditary Witchcraft*, Tana is the name for the universal aspect of the Goddess. In Faery terms this denotes her as an aspect of "the Star Goddess" and it is from this embodiment of stellar flame that we can begin to see how she is related in our tradition to the element of fire. She is the fiery womb that gives birth to and transforms all matter.

EXERCISE: Opening the Well of the Liquid Flame

This exercise can be performed at any time, but is most aligned to performing at noon. Allow yourself to experiment with timing.

Items needed:
A red candle adorned with the following sigil:

Figure 11: Tana Sigil

Face south, Open the Way, and invoke the Hidden Temple of Fire: a vast, open desert at noon in the peak of summer. Feel the sun become a ruby-red upward-pointing tetra-hedron (three-sided pyramid), which projects into your lower belly beneath your navel as a red triangle. Feel the powers of *strength* and *potency of action* flowing through you, radiating from and through the triangle in your belly. After some time invoke the Watcher *Shining Flame* and take some time to feel his presence as you breathe. Maintain your awareness of Shining Flame as you open yourself deeper to the elemental fire …

Imagine an enormous golden gateway appear in the sky in the south through which you see the vast open desert and the summer sun. See the gate shimmering in the heat of the day. Shining Flame moves outward through the gate and draws you forward to follow. He leads you deeper into the south and to a low stone altar upon which is painted a red upward-pointing triangle on a square background of golden yellow. Kneel down before this altar and gaze at the symbol and the colors. Feel your consciousness projecting into this symbol as you open your eyes in the mundane world.

Maintain the connection of both places existing simultaneously. Light the candle and say:

> *I conjure open the Well of Plasma!*
> *And peer into the Eternal Flames!*
> *Hail Tana! Liquid Flame! Scarlet Lust!*
> *You who burn with growth and destruction*
> *In the Passion of Life and Death*
> *Reveal now your grand seduction!*
> *We salute thee, IAO!*

Imagine the stone altar opening to reveal a deep well underneath. From this well rises a great heat … and then molten magma, as if the well were a volcano. Feel the presence of Tana explode upward from the well, filling the sky and the desert with her presence. She appears surrounded by sparks, flames, and ever-churning fires, as well as the elemental beings of fire: salamanders. Allow her presence to move into you with your breath. Take note of how she appears to you, and most importantly how her presence *feels*. Maintain this for at least a few minutes.

When you are finished, give her thanks and say:

> *Tana, Well of the Liquid Flame,*
> *I thank you for your power and your presence.*
> *Hail and Farewell.*

Extinguish the candle. Imagine returning back with Shining Flame through the golden gateway, which shimmers, and then is gone. Commune with him for a moment and then release the Watcher in the usual way. Return to normal awareness.

Water: Tiamat, the Well of the Watery Abyss

The full appellation for this Goddess is "Heva Leviathan Tiamat." This speaks to the fuller nature of this deity. The name "Heva" is related to "Eve," as in the first woman, "Leviathan" is the great primal serpent of antiquity and symbol of the primitive world of chaos. "Tiamat" is the ancient Sumerian/Babylonian goddess of the primordial ocean.

In Faery Tradition She is the Goddess of the west and is the primal powers of elemental water. She may appear as a beautiful mermaid with blue-green skin or as a giant octopus or kraken. Often her tentacles will sway in the water like a mermaid's hair, the rhythmic undulations lulling the viewer deeper into trance.

She is the chaos of pre-creation bringing the fullest potential of all possibility. She is also "the Womb of the World" a title that reflects her primal creative core. She is the Great Mother as all life emerged from the sea. Her power is chaotic, creative, fierce, adaptive, dangerous, and powerful. Invoke her when you feel the need to tap into your own creative powers, when delving into the deep unknown, or when working with astral projection and dreams.

EXERCISE: Opening the Well of the Watery Abyss

This exercise can be performed at any time of the day, but is most especially aligned to being performed at dusk. As before, experiment with different timing.

Items needed:
A blue candle adorned with the following sigil:

Figure 12: Tiamat Sigil

Face west, Open the Way, and invoke Hidden Temple of Water: the ocean and beach at dusk in autumn. Imagine the sun setting below the horizon and becoming a sapphire-blue sphere, which projects into your heart center as a blue circle. Feel the powers of *fluidity* and *adaptability* flowing through you, radiating from the circle in your chest. After some time invoke the Watcher *Water Maker* and take some time to feel her presence as you breathe.

Maintain your awareness of Water Maker as you open yourself deeper to the elemental water … Imagine an enormous algae-green metallic gateway appear in the sky in the west through which you see the vast open ocean and the setting sun. See how the gate shimmers in the dim sunlight with every breath. Water Maker moves outward through the gate and draws you forward to follow. She leads you deeper into the west, beneath the waves to the bottom of the sea, and finally to the ocean's dark floor. By the light of your own holy fire you can see a low stone altar upon which is painted a blue circle on a square background of rose pink. Kneel down before this altar and gaze at the symbol and the colors. Feel your consciousness projecting into this symbol as you open your eyes in the mundane world. Maintain the connection of both places existing simultaneously. Light the candle and say:

> *I conjure open the Well of the Watery Abyss!*
> *And peer into the Whirlpool!*
> *Heva Leviathan Tiamat! Ancient Serpent! World-Birther!*
> *You who flow with primal waters*
> *As the kraken rises from below*
> *From the Deep come your sons and daughters!*
> *We salute thee, IAO!*

Imagine the top of the altar sliding away, revealing a great well underneath from which flows the origin of all waters, spiraling up in a whirlpool. Feel Tiamat flow up from the well—she who is the ancient serpent—ascending from the depths below the waves, she carries you with her, and fills the ocean with her presence. She rises from the sea and appears surrounded by mist, waves, seaweed, and a plethora of fish, dolphins, whales, and squid, as well as the elemental beings: undines. Allow her presence to move into you with your breath. Maintain this for at least a few minutes.

When you are finished, give her thanks and say:

> *Tiamat, Well of the Watery Abyss,*
> *I thank you for your power and your presence.*
> *Hail and Farewell.*

Extinguish the candle. Imagine returning back with Water Maker through the algae-green metallic gateway, which ripples, and then is gone. Commune with her for a moment and then release the Watcher in the usual way. Return to normal awareness.

Earth: Verr-Avna, the (Deep) Well of Space

The name "Verr-Avna" is most likely unique to Faery Tradition by way of Victor Anderson's personal astral dealings. Some lineages use the name "Belili" to represent this Well, a name for the ancient Mesopotamian moon goddess. She is the goddess of the north and is synonymous with the primal powers of elemental earth. She may appear as a woman covered in mud and clad with living vines and foliage, stars in her hair like jewels. Alternatively she can appear as an animated corpse wearing a black wedding dress. She carries the scent of earth and soil.

She is "the Bringer of Joy" as well as the personification of both "passion" and "terror." She is the embodiment of stability, structure, form, as well as growth and change; the fullness of the cycles of life, death, and rebirth. She is also the "Black Virgin of the Outer Darkness," a title that speaks of her pure and untamed power. Her essence is that of both growth and decay—creating forms, then breaking them down, reabsorbing them and creating new forms from the old. More than just form, she is also the inherent consciousness within *all* form, an idea underscored when Victor described her name as meaning "molecules of universal consciousness."[42] Invoke her when you have practical needs, such as money, shelter, or health concerns, as well as when you feel trapped in old patterns or have the need to cleanse outmoded thoughts, relationships, or habits.

EXERCISE: Opening the Well of Space

As with the others, this exercise can be performed at any time, but is most aligned to being performed at midnight. Experiment!

Items needed:
A black and/or green candle adorned with the following sigil:

---

42. Victor Anderson in a talk given at PantheaCon in San Jose, CA, 1996.

Figure 13: Verr-Avna Sigil

Face north, Open the Way, and invoke the Hidden Temple of Earth: a dark forest in the dead of winter, at the stroke of midnight. See the dark cave before you in which you can just see the black cube, glowing green, which projects into midsection at your solar plexus as a black square. Feel the powers of *structure* and *stability* flowing through you, radiating from the glyph. After some time invoke the Watcher *Black Mother* and take some time to feel her presence as you breathe.

Maintain your awareness of Black Mother as you open yourself deeper to the elemental earth… Imagine an enormous moss-covered gateway of black stone appear in the north, through which you see the dark mountains, the deep forest, and in the sky the north star. See how the gate darkly shimmers in the dim moonlight with every breath. Black Mother moves outward through the gate and draws you forward to follow. She leads you deeper into the north and into her cave… all the way to the back and to a low stone altar upon which is painted a black square, on a square background of dark blue. Kneel down before this altar and gaze at the symbol and the colors. Feel your consciousness projecting into this symbol as you open your eyes in the mundane world. Maintain the connection of both places existing simultaneously. Light the candle and say:

I conjure open the Well of Space!
And peer into the Outer Dark!
Hail, Verr-Avna! Black Veiled bride of death and renewal!
Cavernous tomb and womb in one!
You who stand with the strength of stone

Shining dark in The Crown of the North!
Reveal the truth of flesh and bone!
We salute thee, IAO!

The stone altar opens, revealing a great well underneath from which flows an almost tangible darkness, as if formlessness were somehow given form. She is here in the north, filling the land with her presence. The beasts of the earth are one with her will. She appears surrounded by mountains, trees, foliage, horses, cows, bison, elk, deer, and the elemental beings: gnomes. Allow her presence to move into you with your breath. Maintain this for at least a few minutes.

When you are finished, give her thanks and say:

Verr-Avna of the Well of Space,
I thank you for your power and your presence.
Hail and Farewell.

Extinguish the candle. Return back with Black Mother through the moss-covered black stone gateway, which flickers like a fleeting shadow, then is gone. Commune with her for a moment and then release the Watcher in the usual way. Return to normal awareness.

———

This element of aether is treated somewhat differently than the others. By its very nature it is nonphysical, nonlocal. It is consciousness itself, rather than form. If the four physical elements are seen to form a crossroads or circle, aether then forms the central axis, transforming our two-dimensional circle into a three-dimensional sphere. For this reason aether is often assigned three directions: above, below, and center, each possessing their own unique nuanced expressions of the elemental power. While some lineages pass only the four Goddesses of the physical elements, in some lines of the Faery Tradition it is taught that the Goddess of aether is the Star Goddess, who is possessed of many names. According to our central myth, when the Goddess looked into the curvature of space-time, she saw her own reflection and everything changed: where there had been only *one* now there were *two*. In BlueRose we recognize twin aspects of the Star Goddess that correspond with the different manifestations of aether: images of the Goddess that each reveal something more, above as well as below.

Aether Above: Quakoralina, the Well of Stars

Quakoralina is much larger than simply the Goddess of aether in the overworld. She is the Star Goddess as the embodiment of the infinite light of consciousness, symbolized by the stars in the heavens, which makes her the obvious choice when approaching aether above. This is the aether of *transcendence*, of infinite expansion. This is the Star Goddess as the womb of the universe, as each star in the cosmos is a womb of fire: creating the elements of matter in a fiery forge of creation and then spreading the seeds of potential out into an otherwise lifeless and unfathomable expanse.

She is also a goddess of infinite connection, a visual key being to imagine every star in the heavens being connected to *every other star* through fine, silvery webs, which collectively form her divine garment. She is the queen of heaven, and the revolutions of the galaxies are her grand procession.

As an overworld figure she is associated with all deities and angels of the upper realms: the refined or "civilized" forces of order and logic. Devotions involving high ceremony and ritual would be especially aligned to her work.

EXERCISE: Opening the Well of Stars

Since there is no specific time associated with aether (save the symbolic and potent "right now"), you may perform this whenever you wish.

Items needed:

A violet candle adorned with the following sigil:

Figure 14: Quakoralina Sigil

Open the Way and invoke the celestial sphere above. Imagine the starlit expanse extending from the horizon all around you and upwards into the heavens. Directly above you in the zenith you see a shining violet pentacle, which projects into your crown. Feel the powers of *radiance* and *awareness* flowing through you, radiating from and through the pentacle. After some time invoke the Watcher *Heaven Shiner* and take some time to feel this presence as you breathe. Maintain this for at least several breaths.

Maintain your awareness of Heaven Shiner as you open yourself deeper to elemental aether above … reaching out *through* the Watcher. Imagine in the heavens directly above you appears a crystal castle, shimmering amongst the stars. On the front of the castle is painted a violet five-pointed star upon a white background. As you focus upon the symbol and the colors, project your consciousness deeper into the presence of aether.

Feel the pentacle in your crown connecting to the symbol on the castle and imagine an enormous column of violet fire extending from your crown and up into the infinite above. Light the candle and say:

> *I conjure open the Well of Stars!*
> *To peer into the Vault of Heaven!*
> *Hail, Quakoralina! Infinite Light!*
> *From You all things emerge.*
> *Reveal your starlight in my breath!*
> *We salute thee, IAO!*

The castle melts away and reveals the great well between the worlds: an opening in the fabric of the infinite through which all things emerge. Feel Her as a presence in the central column, which now shifts into white fire. Feel Her filling the stars with Her presence. Allow Her to move into you along with the white fire on your breath. Maintain for at least a few minutes.

When you are finished, give her thanks and say:

> *Quakoralina of the Well of Stars,*
> *I thank you for your power and your presence.*
> *Hail and Farewell.*

Extinguish the candle. Return back with Heaven Shiner through the crystal castle, which shimmers, then is gone. Commune with her for a moment and then release the Watcher in the usual way. Return to normal awareness.

Aether Below: Sugma'ad, the Well of Souls

Sugma'ad is the Goddess of aether below; the Star Goddess in the underworld as the infinite darkness, the empty space of intangible nothingness from which all form emerges. She holds the earth (manifestation and form) within her formless womb. She is the Star Goddess in the underworld; the faery stars that exist within the earth, the hidden (spiritual) light within darkness (matter). It is she who looked into the mirror and saw her reflection, thus giving birth to duality and eventually multiplicity.

As an underworld figure she is associated with the fae as well as with the dead. Her title "the (Deep) Well of Souls"[43] reflects this, a reminder that the dead are part of the cycle of life and even they have a role to play in the cosmic dance. She is the chthonic aspect of aether primal consciousness.

EXERCISE: Opening the Well of Souls

As before, there is no traditional time to perform this exercise other than "right now."

Items needed:
A violet candle adorned with the following sigil:

Figure 15: Sugma'ad Sigil

---

43. Many thanks to BlueRose initiate Lynx for coining this term.

Open the Way. Invoke the celestial sphere below. Imagine the starlit expanse extending from the horizon all around you and downwards into the underworld, where you can now just begin to see the horned violet pentacle that projects into your perineum. Feel the powers of *radiance* and *awareness* flowing through you, radiating from and through the pentacle. After some time invoke the Watcher *Fire-in-the-Earth* and take some time to feel this presence as you breathe. Maintain this for at least a few breaths.

Maintain your awareness of Fire-in-the-Earth as you open yourself deeper to the elemental aether below … reaching out *through* the Watcher. As you peer into the infinite darkness between the stars, you begin to see emerge from the darkness far beneath you an upside-down castle made entirely of black onyx, upon which is painted a horned pentacle ("inverted," with two points upward) of violet on a black background. As you focus your awareness on the symbol and the colors, project your consciousness deeper into the presence of aether.

Feel the pentacle in your perineum connecting to the symbol on the castle below and imagine an enormous column of violet fire extending from your sex and down into the infinite below. Light the candle and say:

> *I conjure open the Well of Souls!*
> *To peer into the emptiness within the Earth!*
> *Hail, Sugma'ad! Infinite darkness!*
> *Unto You all things return.*
> *Reveal your darkness in my breath!*
> *We salute thee, IAO!*

The castle melts away and reveals the great well between the worlds—an opening in the fabric of the infinite through which all things return. Feel her as a presence in the central column, which now becomes made of black fire. Feel her filling the darkness with Her presence. Allow her to move into you with the black fire on your breath. Maintain this for a few minutes.

When you are finished, give her thanks and say:

> *Sugma'ad of the Well of Souls,*
> *I thank you for your power and your presence.*
> *Hail and Farewell.*

Extinguish the candle. Return back with Fire-in-the-Earth through the onyx castle, which flickers like a fleeting shadow, then is gone. Commune with her for a moment and then release the Watcher in the usual way. Return to normal awareness.

Aether in the Center: The Nameless Name, the Well of the Void

Where Quakoralina is *transcendent*, Sugma'ad is *embodied*, and together they form an embodied transcendence, which is sometimes seen as the Star Goddess in the center: "the Goddess of the Nameless Name." This is the presence of the Star Goddess that is the center that is the circumference of all. There is no particular visualization for this aspect of the Goddess. It is recommended that you simply be open to whatever arises when performing the following exercise.

EXERCISE: Opening the Well of the Void

As with the previous exercises with the Goddesses of aether you may simply choose whatever time you wish to engage this work.

Items needed:
A violet candle with no sigil

Open the Way. Invoke the celestial sphere above and Heaven Shiner. Reach through the Watcher and imagine the violet pentacle in your crown and the crystal castle in the heavens. Feel how the glyph in your crown is connected to the castle with a column of violet fire.

Focus on the symbol and the colors on the castle. Invoke Quakoralina. As she fills the overworld with her presence, the column of fire turns to white. Breathe it in. Maintain this for at least a few breaths.

Invoke the celestial sphere below and Fire-in-the-Earth. Reach through the Watcher and imagine the inverted violet pentacle in your perineum and the upside-down onyx castle in the great below. Feel how the glyph in your sex is connected to the inverted castle with a column of violet fire.

Focus on the symbol and the colors on the castle. Invoke Sugma'ad. As she fills the underworld with her presence, the column of fire turns black. Breathe it in. Maintain this for at least a few breaths.

Feel the pentacles in your crown and perineum mediating the flames deeper into your being. Light the candle and say:

> *I conjure open the Well of the Void!*
> *Holy nothingness, filled with all potential!!*
> *Hail, Goddess of the Nameless Name!*
> *I am a cell in your body*
> *You and I are One.*
> *We salute thee, IAO!*

The fires merge within you from above and from below … black and white flowing together as one. Begin to chant a wordless sound, such as the OHM. With every breath, you take these flames further into your being: Twin flames flowing effortlessly into one within you as you continue to chant, vibrating the sound through your whole being. The Well opens within you and you radiate in all the colors of the spectrum. Maintain this for a few minutes.

When you are finished, give Her thanks and say:

> *Nameless Name, Well of the Void,*
> *Sugma'ad, Well of Souls,*
> *Quakoralina, Well of the Stars,*
> *I thank you for your power and your presence.*
> *Hail and Farewell.*

Thank and release the Watchers as normal. Extinguish the candle. Return to normal awareness.

———

After you are comfortable meeting with these Goddesses individually, then you can begin to work with them toward more specific ends.

EXERCISE: Gazing the Wells

In this working, we will begin to confront our deepest fears by approaching the Goddesses and allowing their presence to reveal the origin of our fears of which we may not be consciously aware. This should be performed for each Well at least twice per week for four weeks. As always, remember to utilize your journal and record your experiences.

Items needed:
A candle of an appropriate color for the element

Open the Way and invoke whichever element, Watcher, and Well with which you will be working. In the presence of the Well, kneel before it and look inside. Allow yourself to softly gaze into its depths.

Ask the Goddess:

What is my greatest fear?

By asking the question you have formed an energetic space into which the presence of the Goddess will mediate. Just breathe in silence and allow the Goddess to guide you however she will. Notice whatever arises. Repeat the question. If you get the images of fears, ask the Goddess if this is *truly* your greatest fear, or if it is just a mask of a lesser fear. Often smaller fears will present themselves first, as they are less threatening to our psyche than the deeper, more primal fears. Just take your time. When you have spent at least several minutes in this contemplative state, end the working by giving her thanks and extinguishing the candle. Return back with the Watcher. Commune with them for a moment and then release them in the usual way. Return to normal awareness.

This work sets the stage as we continue our journey into the uncharted terrain of our inner landscape as well as our search for our lost power and the potential demons that may be guarding it.

CHAPTER 6
STALKING THE SHADOW:
DEMONS OF FRIGHT AND SHADE

If you don't deal with your demons,
they will deal with you, and it's gonna hurt.
—NIKKI SIXX, COFOUNDER OF MÖTLEY CRÜE

The Shadow is that which lurks unseen beneath the surface of our knowing. We might think of it as existing within our fetch, that part of our soul structure which is aligned to our subconscious. The Shadow, in the Jungian sense, contains all aspects of the personality which are not illuminated by the light of consciousness (talker). As a result, there are both positive and negative facets to the Shadow, but it is the negative aspects that are of primary concern to us.

The Shadow is far more likely to contain negative aspects than positive, however, just due to human nature: we are all far more likely to acknowledge our constructive traits while denying our undesirable ones. As a result, the Shadow is largely composed of those negative parts of ourselves that we deny, which allows them to fester and grow beneath the surface of our consciousness.

The Shadow isn't some horrible monster whose sadistic maliciousness is unfairly pointed in your direction. In the absence of conscious direction, it has been left to fend on its own, sometimes even becoming feral in the process. And when this happens we are far more likely to manifest a *demon*.

What exactly *is* a demon? What do you think about when you hear that word? Do you think of supernatural entities set squarely against the natural order of things and hell-bent on the destruction of the universe? Or perhaps they are spirits whose energies are unhealthy for the human being, the spiritual equivalent of a wild animal or virus or disease? Or maybe you take a more earthbound approach, equating demons with deep-seated psychological issues hidden in the Shadow, knots of power the likes of which could take years of therapy to untangle.

My use of the word "demon" encompasses all of these definitions to some degree, and I have heard initiates of our tradition use the term to describe many different types of interrelated psychic phenomena. This can easily cause confusion and so first we must be clear about exactly what we are talking about if we are to delve into the deeper work. Before we can conjure and work with our demons, we must first know exactly what a demon is to us.

While some in the Neopagan world will scoff at the belief in both demons and angels, citing them as part of the "Christian pantheon," I will remind them that both demons and angels have been around a *lot* longer than the Judeo-Christian religions, to the tune of thousands of years. One need only look to the ancient Sumerians to find evidence of both. It is our society's Christianization of both these celestial and infernal beings which has given us a skewed perspective. Once we abandon the moralistic judgments of both, only then may we begin to perceive them for what they are: part and parcel of the mechanism of the universe. In their own way, they also represent the powers of our Twins: Light and Dark, Order and Chaos, Creation and Destruction. We need *both*.

The poetic power of Witchcraft presents itself as a formidable one when we consider the nature of demons. If we approach them as mental constructs, then we run the risk of being blind to the severity of the situation. If we approach them solely as an external entity, then we have perhaps given them too much of our power.

Demonic Reality

There many different types of demons, both personal and transpersonal, with which we might deal in our Witchcraft. If I may paint with a fairly broad brush for just a moment, we might generally classify all demons as being spirits who are agents or embodiments of chaos, where angels would be the agents or embodiments of order.[44] Taking a closer look, I have taken to approaching them in the following manner: On the personal side, I refer to those issues, impurities, weaknesses, and other complexes

---

44. Devin Hunter, *The Witch's Book of Spirits* (Woodbury, MN: Llewellyn Worldwide, 2017), 235–240.

that we all possess as being "demons" with a lowercase *d*. We all have these demons. Perhaps we are inclined to drink too much or are quick to anger. Perhaps we have self-destructive behaviors that seem to rise up out of the blue, taking control over us, or we have overindulgent appetites that demand to be fed, usually to the exclusion of other, no doubt healthier, behaviors. While indulging on its own is not necessarily a bad thing, all of these behaviors can be indicative of some level of "demonic activity" when they cause a harmful disruption to the individual's life and relationships.

Humans are carnal creatures and Witchcraft is certainly not a religion that preaches abstinence. If anything, we revel in our carnality. Ours is, however, a path of power. And quite often our personal demons are siphoning away that power—little by little, day in and day out. Or, they are tugging strings here and there to manipulate us into doing things that are perhaps not in our best interests, often while lurking unseen underneath our conscious awareness.

Magical paths that do not provide a methodology for working with one's complexes can actually end up feeding the Shadow. A great deal of occult rituals and practices deal with either the overt gaining of power, or the alignment of one's consciousness with otherworldly beings, which in effect does the same. If we are not actively working to identify and break down our blocks, to heal our weaknesses, or refine our impurities, then we run the risk of empowering the very things about ourselves from which we wish to be free. Any issues, complexes, and the like that are present when we encounter greater currents of power (such as those encountered during an initiation into the Craft) are empowered along with the rest of us, so where we might become more powerful in the process, so does our shadow, as well as the power it holds over us. This is the main reason that a practice of regular purification is essential to the practitioner of Faery.

The journey of any magician is the gathering of power. As we seek to continually strengthen our magic, we gather threads of this power along the way. We learn a new technique, or we make a new spirit contact, or perhaps we are initiated or otherwise ritually "attuned" to an egregore, deity, or other spiritual collective; whatever the modality involved, an effective Witch is one who continues to learn and grow. As we grow in our power, however, we begin to move into astral realms in which we come into closer proximity with another class of Demon altogether.

This is the "capitol *D* Demon," and I see two very basic types at play. One is the aforementioned spirit or universal force which is aligned to chaos and destruction and is simply part of the necessary mechanism of the universe.[45] These "transpersonal Demons" can be petitioned and worked with, just like any other spirit, as long as the practitioner takes the necessary precautions. The other type is again on the personal side; these are when a person's complex or other deep-seated issue undergoes a type of radical transformation and has become externalized. This is often due to extreme trauma (such as torture, abuse, a horrific accident, prolonged drug abuse, etc.) which causes said complex to "hive off" from the energy body of its human "host," where it begins to draw life force on its own, forming into a personal Demon. In the lore of the Faery Tradition, these types of demons are sometimes called "Taka spirits." They can also be formed when aspects of the self are ignored, neglected, or suppressed, and over time become externalized. With its new upgraded status, this Demon begins to develop a different type of consciousness and can begin more complex manipulations as well as engage in deepened parasitic behavior with its host. These demons can negatively affect an individual's preexisting weaknesses and exploit them; this can cause mental and physical imbalances to become exaggerated, and issues such as mental illness may become more severe under their demonic influence. It is said that someone who has committed murder, for example, can potentially become possessed by their own Taka spirit, engaging in violent activities and not even necessarily being aware of doing them. To them it will have been like a dream or nightmare, while the Demon continues to break their personality.

It's easier to believe in Demons as being the poetic embodiments of our own weaknesses and desires, but perhaps even more disturbing than Demons of a personal ilk are those that are quite independent of us. These are the embodiments of chaos, destruction, and primal appetites so maligned in the mainstream religions. Their morality is not human, to be certain, but to label them as "evil" and then disregard them entirely is shortsighted and foolish. While we might wish to invoke the powers of order and creation and apply only those to our lives, it is unhealthy to limit our attention to just the powers that "feel good" in the moment. To combat a tumor, we need to kill the tumor. As an agent of death and decay, a controlled demonic presence might help with that, much more so than a goddess of fertility and life. To help remove a binding that another Witch may have placed upon us, a demon might be just the thing we need to destroy that magic and keep more from taking root. In order to create, we

---

45. Hunter.

must first destroy. To plant, we must first plow. To create art, we must first "destroy" the blank canvas.

There are a certain of these beings that the Witch may very well wish to engage in order to increase their own power, in much the way that working with a deity or angel would provide, only on a different "frequency." This isn't to say that they aren't dangerous; they are as dangerous as poisonous serpents, and only a skilled and experienced worker should engage in working with them, lest they get bitten. But for that experienced worker, the benefits of doing so outweigh the risks. It is part of the Witches work to weave and unweave, to create and destroy. "A Witch who cannot hex cannot heal."

The dangers come mainly from not knowing our own weaknesses and then giving in to them when in the presence of said Demon. Once we give them control we are their slaves, and winning back our freedom will be painful and difficult. Once we give away our power, it is *always* painful to take it back.

Of all of the demons we have talked about, it is those aligned to primal appetites that are the most concerning. These can be both personal and transpersonal, and those personal Demons of this nature are perhaps among the most frightening, as they cut so *deep*. Here we find addiction, compulsion, mindless reaction … feral beings of insatiable hunger, who numb the minds of those afflicted with their presence and compel them to do their infernal bidding. These are the Demons that attach themselves to those who suffer from addictions to drugs, sex, or *anything* so long as the relationship is an obsessive one. It is entirely possible to have such an addiction without being under the influence of a Demon (though one would argue that the addiction itself is *at least* a "little *d* demon"), but being in that compromised state leaves one more susceptible to such an entity taking advantage and moving in.

Though nowhere near as frequent as Hollywood would have you believe, Demons of this nature that are sufficiently established can and will "jump hosts" when specific energetic or psychological weaknesses in the psyche of the new host provide them the opportunity. For example, a Demon born of sadistic anger will find a more inviting home in someone with whom anger has been a problem, or with whom sadistic issues lurk in their subconscious. Compatible energies. Like attracts like. Like fleas jumping from a dead squirrel to a dog, these Demons infect their previously healthy hosts, bringing pain, misery, depression, "bad luck," and the forces of entropy.

Whether they manifest as mental complexes or as external entities bringing chaos, we feel their destructive power all the same, even as they lead us down the garden path of our desires to our ultimate destruction. We might even be able to see the end result coming, but we are often paralyzed; we can do nothing but repeat the very behavior we know could very well lead to our doom, but we are seemingly helpless to resist.

The Demon Work

In Faery Tradition, there is much work done around demons and Demons alike. In the early 1980s within the coven Korythalia, there came into being a body of material collectively called "the Demon Work," which has continued its use in those lineages that stem from Bloodrose. This work borrows ideas from those in Ceremonial Magic, and seeks to identify and transform the relationship to one's personal demons, which are treated largely as Demons in a ritual context.

This work has generally been given later in the training, after the student has had ample time to work with our various tools and inner contacts. The work itself has consisted of the teacher guiding the student into a space in which they summon their personal demons—often with very specific visualizations—which are the embodiments of imbalances, impurities, and blocks as expressed through each of the five elements. In the Hidden Temple of a particular element, the Watcher and the Well would be invoked along with the elemental tool in order to assist in the demonic confrontation as well as any subsequent work in how to actually deal with it.

Its emergence into the praxis of Faery was met with some resistance, however. Victor Anderson reportedly warned against the practice, specifically the assumption that we each already have demons in each of the five elements, and warned that a demon could be accidentally created in the process of summoning one.

This may have been what inspired my own teacher to forgo the practice in my training; focusing instead on the work with the "greatest fear" in conjunction with the Wells as given in the previous chapter. Oddly enough, however, while he did not pass the Demon Work to me in my training, he *did* do a form of this work with my husband and so through working with that additional material I have come up with my own approach to the Demon Work, which is what I offer my own students.

I'm inclined to agree with Victor's assessment; if I do not already have a "Demon of Air," for example, then performing a ritual in which I invoke said Demon might just end up creating one. Whereas before there were only complexes and issues, now that those issues and complexes have been empowered with the tools of our Craft, they begin to take on a life of their own and begin wreaking havoc in our lives.

In BlueRose we do a lot of shadow work. *Most* of this culminates around the work given with the Wells. But there are times in which this proves insufficient. We should not assume that we have *any* demons *at all*. A complex, or a weakness, or a block is not the same as a *demon* and certainly not the same as a *Demon*. Once we have decided that a complex is a demon, then we have acknowledged that it has power over us. And if we are not being accurate in our assessment, then we have just given some of our power away needlessly. Divination would be a good practice to help determine if the issue at hand is an actual demon or just a psychological pattern. Remember, sometimes a cigar is only a cigar. Not everything has a deeper spiritual or magical meaning.

On the other hand, in the event that we find we *do* have a demon, then we will need the tools necessary for dealing with it. Since our intention is to eventually learn to ritually summon a demon, we must first become proficient in *banishing* them, lest we later find ourselves in proverbial hot water.

RITE: Banishing

This teaches us how to claim our personal space physically, emotionally, mentally, and spiritually, removing unwanted influences and energies and leaving us in a state of charged balance. This exercise (or its equivalent, if you already have an effective banishing in your current personal practice) should be repeated until you feel its effects are "second nature" and can be summed up in the span of a single breath, as an informal "shorthand version." It will very likely take some time to build up to this, however, so take your time with it.

Items needed:
A Star Goddess candle
Incense burner and charcoal
Your ritual blade
Copal resin

Light your incense charcoal and allow it to get ready. Open the Way. Light your Star Goddess candle with the usual observances. Feel your connection to her through your holy daemon as crystalline-white and ebony-black flames.

Charge yourself up with this vibration of wraith force and place some of the copal resin on the charcoal, allowing it to burn and smoke. Invoke the Iron Pentacle within yourself. Feel yourself as a powerful being! The power of the iron flame within you compels all lesser spirits to flee, while the flame of the Star Goddess protects from greater spirits. Take hold of the burner so that you can begin fumigating the area. Face north[46] and imagine that your soul alignment is like a focusing lens. *Will* this wraith force to be focused like a laser, shining out from your heart center and beaming outward with a tremendous force, brilliantly blasting everything in front of you as you wave the incense smoke in that direction. With your free hand, use your blade to trace a pentacle in the air in front of you and feel your connection to the Iron Pentacle. Imagine it blazing with red iron fire in the air before you. Feel how it obliterates all obstacles, heating them up … melting them … reshaping them as if in a fiery forge. Turn to face the west and repeat this process. Then turn to face south and to the east. Finally, do the same for below and then above, ending in the center within yourself. Stay in this state for at least a few breaths, and then absorb the wraith force and use it to again align your three souls. If you feel you have too much accumulated wraith force, you may send some to your holy daemon along with a wish or prayer, as outlined in the HA Prayer (see appendix I).

JOURNALING: Your Dark History

This will be a longer journaling exercise than those given previously. You will want to spend at least ten to fifteen minutes of actual writing, but it will likely take longer to do it justice. Allow yourself to get into the flow.

Open the Way. Begin to journal about your personal history, specifically about ways in which you have made mistakes … choices you made and later regretted. Things that carry a sense of shame or embarrassment. Perhaps incidents in which you were emotionally unbalanced, reacting disproportionately to the situation. Recall especially how you may have hurt others, regardless of your original intentions. What are their names? Looking over your life thus far, what disappointments come to mind as being particularly significant?

When you are finished, you may wish to perform the Waters of Purity rite.

---

46. In the northern hemisphere–based Faery Tradition, north is usually associated with the earth element. If you are using a different elemental arrangement then begin with whatever direction you associate with earth.

You will likely wish to perform this exercise several times over the course of a few months, and even then, it will likely need to be revisited afterward. Once you have familiarized yourself with the above exercise, you can start to look for overall patterns. What types of issues have you been dealing with over a long period of time? Are you noticing that you seem to be repeating certain patterns of behavior, relationships, stresses, etc.? Now we must start to look at the overall patterns that present themselves to us as we try to boil it all down to its core.

JOURNALING: The Two Questions

When doing shadow work, we must ask ourselves what amounts to two basic questions. Open the Way and then spend at least five minutes journaling about each of the following:

1. "I am secretly afraid that I really am _____." *(Example: Bad, stupid, ugly, evil, unloveable, etc.)*
2. "All my life I have struggled against _____." *(Example: Anxiety, depression, addiction, obsession, etc.)*

Try not to edit yourself during the process. You may find that you wish to "sweeten things up" in order not to appear too "needy." Sometimes we wish to appear strong or do not wish to draw too much attention to ourselves, in which case we will not ask for help when we need it. Or, some of us might crave the attention and so will ask for help when we really *don't* need it. In between these two extremes is real life. Use this tool to help you find your balance.

When you have finished you will likely wish to follow up by invoking the Iron Pentacle to assist you in strengthening up your boundaries and a Waters of Purity rite to help you reintegrate the energies you have raised and transformed.

———

Introspective exercises such as these can provide us an opportunity to discern whatever patterns in our behavior might be present. What themes have played out over your life? Or perhaps, if we have been experiencing "bad luck" for some time, we might be able to determine patterns that can shed light on the origin of the problem and perhaps how to correct it. This is all particularly useful for discovering one's potential demons.

A Witch is a warrior: someone who is responsible.
—Oral tradition, attributed to Victor Anderson

Each of us must live life in such a way so that the good outweighs the bad. This is easier said than done, especially if our past behaviors have been less than honorable. When confronting our own shadow, one recurring theme that arises is feelings of guilt for previous negative conduct. One thing in particular should be made abundantly clear: guilt is a waste of our life force. It may feel as if we are "doing penance" for some crime or sin and that somehow our guilt is a form of justice, but in reality, it is really just directing our attention away from the problem. The life force that is going toward making us feel guilty *could* have been going toward actually correcting the problem, but instead it's just bouncing around the ego and making it (once again) all about *ourselves*. Just another self-important ego trick to keep us from actually evolving. Instead of feeling sorry for past actions, we need to do our best to *make amends* for them.

Making amends is so much more than simply offering an apology, no matter how heartfelt it may be. To make amends is to offer *justice*: restitution for a wrong. To bring balance to the scales once more. Where there has been an injury, now there must be healing. Where there has been a burn, now we must bring cooling waters. In the "Twelve Steps" of Alcoholics Anonymous, the eighth step is to make a list of those who have been harmed and then to have a willingness to make amends to each of them. Step nine is to actually make amends to them, where possible, excluding cases in which to do so would compromise someone's safety. In the event that it is not possible or safe to do so, we can again turn to magic to assist us.

RITE: The Scales of Justice

This rite is to help you make amends on a soul level to someone whom you have harmed. If you wish to share this with the injured party, that is up to you. Who you share this work with is up to you and you alone.

Items needed:
Three candles—one red, one white, and one black

A balance scale—or two paper cups, some string, and a wire coat hanger (the ones with top notches for hanging straps work best)

A pen and two pieces of paper

A pair of scissors

Two to four tablespoons of a mixture of dried herbs: hyssop and basil

A whole or part of a High John the Conqueror Root (chips will do in a pinch)

Two roses, one red the other white, with stems no longer than 6–8"

A cup of water

Gather all of your materials and set up your balance scale. Or you can make one by poking three equidistant holes near the rims of two paper cups, through which you tie three strings. Attach this to one end of the wire hanger. (If there is a top notch then this is the place to do it, as it will prevent the string from slipping.) Now do the same for the other cup on the other side. You may need to adjust the strings so that the cups hang upright and level.

Figure 16: Scales of Justice

Open the Way. Light the red candle. Invoke the Iron Pentacle. On the paper, write the name of the person whom you have wronged. Underneath their name, write out exactly what you did to this person. Explain what you were thinking at the time … and how you felt at the time. Acknowledge how they must have felt and what they went through. If they suffered hardship as a result, really look at that and take responsibility for what you did. Write this all on this page. Now, turn the page over and write out your apology. Open your heart and let it all pour out. Tell them how you *wish* you had acted and how you regret your actions to this day. Be aware of how it all weighs on you.

Fold the paper in half and place it on one side of the balance scale. With the scissors, cut the blooms off of the roses, then place the thorny stems on top of the folded paper. Watch the scale tip out of balance.

Now, light the white candle and invoke the Pearl Pentacle. On the other paper, write out everything you are going to do to make amends; to actually make it as right as you can. Will you be able to fix what you did? Do you even know how to get ahold of them? Are they even still alive? Perhaps you will donate to a relevant cause, or you will help someone else who reminds you of them, or something similar. Write it all out again, pouring your emotions into it. When you are done, fold this paper and put it on the other side of the scale.

Place the High John root and sprinkle some of the herb mixture on the side with your amends paper, and then—one by one—begin adding alternating red and white rose petals while building energy as you chant:

> *By the Pearl and by the Iron,*
> *Restore the balance and quench the fire.*

Do this until you either run out of rose petals or you have *at least* balanced the scales. If you run out of petals before the scales are balanced, you may add more of the herb mixture, continuing to chant as you do.

Once the scales are balanced, reaffirm your soul alignment and light the black candle. Feel your connection to the Star Goddess through your holy daemon. Pray for the person you wronged. Allow their image to inspire you to work toward justice from this moment forward. Perform the Waters of Purity rite. Allow the candles to burn all the way down. The thorns, stems, paper, petals, and herbs should be collected and then buried at the base of a tree or thrown into running water.

———

This rite should be repeated for every individual person that you have wronged, going back as far as you can remember. If many people were wronged by the same incident or pattern of behavior it is permissible to do a collective rite, but don't cheat yourself; you will want to make certain that every facet and relationship has been healed to the best of your ability. Any unhealed relationships that you may have "glossed over" are potential holes in your psychic armor, which can leave you vulnerable when dealing with powers and beings on the astral planes.

In the previous chapter we worked with the Wells of Creation, powerful elemental forces of creation and destruction, and through their lens we asked to be shown our greatest fear. Through each of the elemental principles, our fears were summoned and focused, and while they may have appeared in even vastly different forms in each elemental station, it is probably not surprising to hear now that *they likely are all the same fear*. Generally, there is one basic "core fear" that gets expressed in multiple ways through this process and it is this fear that our shadow uses to beat us into submission. Keep in mind, however, that without the guidance of a Faery initiate or some other person trained in this process, you will have to trust your own judgment here which can admittedly be problematic, since we are usually the very first people that we will lie to. Self-honesty is not only necessary to this process, it's also damned *hard*. This is where it would be a good idea to have a good friend or a therapist to talk to. DO NOT think that you can do this on your own because you are so strong, intelligent, experienced, initiated, powerful, lucky, blessed, or fill-in-the-blank. Your demons will lie to you, so this means you will lie to yourself. A best friend or coven member who can "keep you real" is imperative here.

This work demands that we learn to face our core fears head-on. Whatever it is that we most fear, we need to look at it square in the eye and not look away. Just like in the ballad of Tam Lin, we need to hold fast and not allow our fear to turn us away. We will face our fears and watch them transform before us.

Demons often will appear in frightening, monstrous shapes in an effort to shake our resolve. But just as often they may appear as small, impish creatures. On their own they may seem insignificant, even comical. But keep in mind that there is strength in numbers. Where one or two might even be "cute," seven or eight could be a problem, like a pack of really adorable yet feral dogs that will bite your ankles until your legs end in bloody stumps.

We most often see the results of the shadow, but not the Shadow itself; the sense of shame we may feel or the fear that we have all point in the direction of the Shadow, but it is not a direct observation. The Shadow does not reveal itself openly. Like "dark matter" it is inferred rather than directly perceived.

The Shadow employs many allies in its war against us. One of our most important jobs in this war is to deny it the resources that it uses in its waging. And in any war the most important weapon is *information*. Revisiting the journaling exercise given earlier in this chapter will help to create a sort of written record of your personal demons, which will give you greater insight into what patterns they may reveal. Every tool you have will be needed in your work to know—and potentially reclaim—the power that this demon has stolen from you.

Confrontation, Transformation, and Establishing Control

Our goal is to get to a place in which we can face down our shadow and not flinch, where we can control it and not allow it to use its tricks upon us, so that we can work toward its eventual transformation and (hopefully) reintegration. Toward this end we will employ whatever methods are necessary.

One method that is often underappreciated in regard to its effectiveness in combating fear is that of reengaging with a practice with soul alignment and the Iron Pentacle. This pentacle in particular encourages personal strength and protection, so regularly invoking it will grant the added benefit of being stronger in your power, but also more stable and secure. As a sort of informal practice, become accustomed to quickly invoking this pentacle at random times of the day. I often will run the pentacle while taking a shower, or while in between other tasks. In this way, it is always available when I need it, so if and when I may be surprised by any given situation, I can call up this strength and power at a moment's notice.

Another time-honored method is the practice of reciting a meaningful prayer. The "Litany Against Fear" is an incantation from Frank Herbert's science-fiction novel *Dune,* used there as a means to calm the mind in the face of danger. Following the poetic idea of the Hidden Kingdom, some lineages of Faery Tradition have adopted it as a means to help in their shadow work:

I must not fear.
Fear is the mind-killer.

Fear is the little-death that brings total obliteration.
I will face my fear.
I will permit it to pass over me and through me.
And when it has gone past I will turn the inner eye to see its path.
Where the fear has gone there will be nothing.
Only I will remain.

This is memorized and then chanted (either silently or out loud) when dealing with fear, either during our practice or "in the wild." Practitioners who adopt this technique will generally find that this practice helps not only in mitigating the effects that our fears have over us, but also determining their origins, which up until now may or may not have been clear to us.

A common saying in the Craft is "Where there's fear there's power." Repeating this like a mantra in the face of fear can remind us that fear is just *energy* moving through our psyche and that the most important thing in its face is to *pay attention*. It's a red flag waving in our face. When I experience fear I now sometimes think of a little man waving a literal red flag and the absurdity is often enough to get me out of my fear and into observation mode. Once there the fear no longer has the same power it once held, and I am free to examine the lesson it has for me. There is indeed power in our fears.

In many "alternative spiritualties" (especially those aligned toward a less balanced view), fear is treated like a four-letter word. Fear is seen as the enemy of enlightenment and a throwback to our base nature which keeps us separate from our "higher" nature. Even in Faery circles I have heard talk that seems to demonize the very concept of fear, equating it to something that a less evolved person deals with but not an accomplished Witch.

To this I must respectfully call *bullshit*. Everyone experiences fear. Everyone. If someone says that they do not then they are either lying or they are so disconnected from themselves that they might as well be. To fear is human, and Witchcraft is a path that revels in our humanity instead of trying to hide from it. To feel our fear is a step toward understanding it. Fear itself is not the problem; inaction in the face of it is. To have courage—to function as a warrior—we still experience our fear, but we learn to move beyond it. Courage is not the absence of fear. It is right action in the face of fear.

We will likely feel fear when we see the faces of our shadow or Demon. It will likely appear in such a way that will make us want to look away, to bury our heads back in the proverbial sand and deny that it even exists. As Witches on a path of gathering power, we can no longer afford the luxury of denial, for in the astral worlds, that which you don't know can kill you.

While we continue stalking our shadow there are other tools we can employ to help us during our encounters with it. For those who work with crystals and stones, I have found black tourmaline to be especially helpful. This stone is much prized for its powers of both grounding and protection and is actually the best protection stone I have found. Wearing or carrying a piece when you engage your shadow can provide you a greater sense of security as it acts as a barrier to energies that are infectious or harmful. Likewise, snowflake obsidian has been used for this as well.

Other protection charms can also provide a greater sense of stability while engaging this work. I would recommend the creation of a Witch Bottle to assist in this as well as the Faery practice of keeping a piece of iron on the altar. This for its protective as well as grounding properties.

DIVINATION: The Devil at the Crossroads

This is a tarot spread to help decide a more exact course of action when dealing with our shadow. First it helps us determine whether or not we are dealing with a demon, and if so, which element would be best utilized in our continued work. This spread is unique in that, for the most part, *we will only pay attention to those cards that you interpret to be "negative."* We are looking only for "hot spots"—the points of particular intensity that represent complexes or a demon (though we will also look at any positive cards that appear in the section marked "Center/Aether"). This relies on your own familiarity with and relationship to the particular deck you have chosen, as well as your own developed intuition. If you are new to tarot, then I would suggest referring to whatever instructional booklet came with your particular deck and read the cards accordingly.

Items needed:

A deck of tarot cards (any style will do as long as it retains the traditional Devil card)

Besides its capacity as "demonic detector," this spread shows us a map in which we can see through which elements our shadow presents us the greatest challenges. The challenging or negative cards show imbalances in their particular elemental areas.

We see here that each of the elements/directions is also broken into a trinity. This trinity can be viewed on multiple levels or "stations," each identified with one of the three worlds of Celtic folklore and corresponding to a component of the human soul structure and complete with an Elemental ruler.

The first station is the middleworld. Here are issues concerning the talker. These are issues with communication, with ego, and with mental clarity. This is how we move and exist in the world in terms of our interactions with others. We are consciously aware of these issues, though they may have a depth to them that we fail to fully realize. The Guardian Beasts rule this station, providing us specific keys that we may engage in order help address the particular imbalance. For example, an indication of an imbalance in this station in the element of fire tells us that the ego suffers an imbalance that the Lion can help address. To me this sounds like an inflated ego, possibly some anger issues as well. Candle work would be advised here. An imbalance in talker with water, however, indicates that the issue might be not having enough of a personal will, taking on the identity of the group, losing yourself, etc. Here the Serpent is aligned toward helping bring balance, perhaps through trance work and cleansing. Air speaks of communication issues as well as those of clear sight. The Eagle is helpful in being able to see things from a higher perspective so we can "take it all in." Earth imbalances here would be those of physical health, likely addressing health concerns that have been present for some time. The Bull can help us to garner the strength we need to push through our obstacles. Complexes expressed through aether invite us to connect to the Divine Twins of above and/or below; the Azure Dove and the Scarlet Serpent. Are we expansive or contractive? If our imbalances are above, how might we be losing the "big picture"? How are we failing to be inclusive of diversity? If below, maybe we need to pay closer attention to the little details? How are your basic needs being met? Where is your passion?

The second station is the underworld and corresponds to the fetch. This is the Shadow in the classical sense. These are issues of deep-seated emotion, shame, anger, etc. and likely ones that we are not aware that we possess. These are deep in the subconscious and provide our own personal keys into the underworld. This is ruled by the Wells of Creation, whose raw power might be particularly helpful in transforming blocks in this area. Each of the Wells/Goddesses can tell us of some quality that we may need to cultivate in order to bring balance to the situation. Arida is freshness … new beginnings. Tana brings energy, passion, and transformation. Tiamat reminds us to go deep, to look beneath the surface of what we know we feel, and face our abyss. Verr-Avna teaches us patience as well as the processes of crystallization and manifestation. Quakoralina is the light of our divine consciousness, expansion, and transcendence. Sugma'ad is about going deep into the primal, the darkness within. The Nameless Name is the wild card that brings it all together and reveals the central theme that unifies everything in the spread.

The third and final station is the overworld. This corresponds to the holy daemon. These are issues with our spirituality, our *magic*. We can become addicted to our spirituality and then disconnect from our mundane lives. Conversely, we could be disconnected from our own daemon, so wrapped up in the unimportant details and dramas of life that we fail to make genuine connections to those around us. The Watchers are aligned to this station, giving us insight as, how to address a particular imbalance by utilizing the power with which they are traditionally associated. (See appendix I.)

With this spread we are given not only the knowledge of where in our soul-structure and elemental makeup our shadow or demon is manifesting, but also a means of addressing it, for the associated elemental rulers can provide us the means of transformation.

Open the Way and shuffle the cards. "Tune in" to your shadow using whatever methods you feel are appropriate. Arrange the cards according to the following figure.

Any negative cards are revealing the presence of an imbalance. If at any point we place the Devil card, we will immediately place the next card on top of it and continue dealing the spread as given. Doing so we have marked the presence and location of our demon.

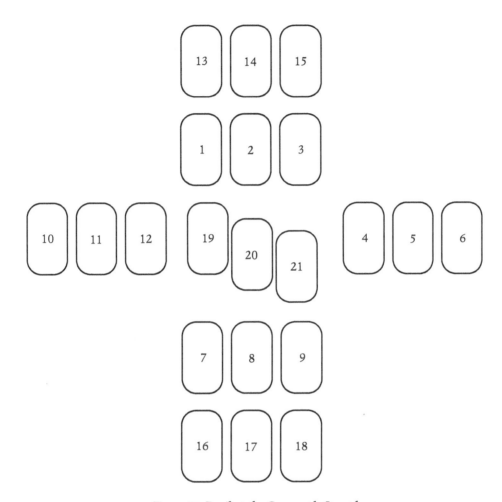

Figure 17: Devil at the Crossroads Spread

North/Earth

1) *Middleworld. Talker. Black Bull.* Structure. Money.

2) *Underworld. Fetch. Verr-Avna.* Stability. Health. Physicality. Manifestation.

3) *Overworld. Daemon. Black Mother.* Silence. Listening. Wisdom.

East / Air

4) *Middleworld. Talker. Golden Eagle.* Communication. Perception.

5) *Underworld. Fetch. Arida.* Resonance. New beginnings. Fresh start.

6) *Overworld. Daemon. Star Finder.* Mental clarity. Knowledge.

South / Fire

7) *Middleworld. Talker. Red Lion.* Ego. Potency of action.

8) *Underworld. Fetch. Tana.* Anger. Strength. Transformation.

9) *Overworld. Daemon. Shining Flame.* Will. Truth.

West / Water

10) *Middleworld. Talker. Blue Serpent.* Worldly passions. Adaptability.

11) *Underworld. Fetch. Tiamat.* Fluidity. Going deep below the surface. Astral travel.

12) *Overworld. Daemon. Water Maker.* Compassion. Love.

Above / Aether

13) *Middleworld. Talker. Azure Dove (Divine Twin).* Awareness.

14) *Underworld. Fetch. Quakoralina.* Radiance. Expansion. Light.

15) *Overworld. Daemon. Heaven Shiner.* Transcendent consciousness.

Below / Aether

16) *Middleworld. Talker. Scarlet Serpent (Divine Twin).* Awareness.

17) *Underworld. Fetch. Sugma'ad.* Radiance. Contraction. Darkness.

18) *Overworld. Daemon. Fire-in-the-Earth.* Embodied consciousness.

Center / Aether

Here we may also read whatever positive cards may arise as our strengths and allies. If the Devil card appears here in any of the three cards then the demon revealed here may be an actual *Demon*. Pay particular attention to card 20, which is the central issue. A Devil card there is particularly concerning.

19) *Middleworld. Talker.* This is the center of your talker; what you normally think of as being "you." Whatever card is here (positive or negative) is a message for you in relation to the rest of the spread. How are you embodying / holding your power?

20) *Underworld. Fetch. The Nameless Name.* This is "deep fetch" and the central issue of the reading/spread. What are you hiding? What is empowering you or holding you back?

21) *Overworld. Daemon. Guardian of the Gates.* This is you aligned, and in the center of your Witch power.

It is likely that this spread will give you much to consider. Treat a session with it as you would a meditation. Contemplate the associations and connections and record your findings in your journal.

If the Devil card does not appear in your spread then you do not have a demon, and instead will focus on your lesser complexes, which are represented by whatever negative cards do appear. If you do receive the Devil, then you may wish to repeat this spread later, both to check in on your progress in transforming it and as a means to see if there are any others present, since this reading can only pinpoint one at a time.

When you get proficient at this reading, you may wish to overlay another divination method, such as runes or bone/curio throwing. With these types of systems, you can use the card spread as a foundation, reading the bones/runes/curio as points of particular interest if they appear on top of a card or certain combinations. Experiment!

———————————

We will draw from as many sources as we need in order to get the job done. The more secure we are able to feel when engaging our shadow will increase our likelihood of being able to get it under our control. Most of this is done through *observation;* when we discover the many tricks that the Shadow uses to manipulate us they begin to lose their effectiveness against us. This alone makes your journal an invaluable tool in this particular work. Once we have deprived the Shadow or Demon of its weapons, we can begin the work of transformation.

Our shadow and all the potential demons that we possess are really just parts of ourselves, twisted and turned against us. As a result their very existence indicates that we are not running at full capacity, as a portion of our own life force is being used to maintain the demonic presence. It is for this reason that our first goal must be to transform the demon back into wraith force and then reintegrate it into our system, so that we become more powerful in the process. We have a number of tools that we may choose from for this purpose. However, as not every situation will respond to the same methods, a body of material has grown up around this work to help address different circumstances and temperaments.

CHAPTER 7
TEMPLE OF THE DEMON LOVER:
THE DEMONIC RITUALS

The process of delving into the black abyss
is to me the keenest form of fascination.
—H. P. LOVECRAFT

Many things lurk in the outer darkness. From this abyss may emerge any number of challenges, both personal and impersonal, which may adversely affect our magical workings. This is a main reason why many magical systems across the globe engage in some form of ritual cleansing, not just of the participants themselves but also of the ritual area. There are many different types of energies that may be floating around in any particular area. Perhaps the aetheric recordings of past events that have taken place there, or the natural lines of earth energy, may bring influences that can affect our minds and our moods, and therefore our magic. Simple acts such as the burning of herbs or incense or asperging with salt water can clear up a majority of insignificant (yet potentially disruptive) energies, and the Banishing exercise can do more. But there are certain times in which we may perceive that there are perhaps more than simple energies that are present.

There is a type of supposed "Demon" that many of us have already encountered. They are usually called "Shadow Beings" and appear exactly as one might think: like wisps of shadow, scurrying out of sight, just out of the corner of your eye. These are "lower spirits" and not usually a cause for concern, as they are more akin to a form of "astral wildlife," like a small rodent or a cat. They generally will hang around in the shadows, absorbing ambient energies of various types (most often "base" emotions, such as fear, anger, sexual desire, etc.) They are not "bad," per se, but they *can* be disruptive if not taken care of, especially prior to a ritual working, which may actually empower them in a negative way. While the Banishing might be effective against them, certainly, another approach has been brought into the Faery Tradition from our spiritual cousins in the Far East.

RITE: Offering the Red Bread

This ritual observance is inspired by practices of the Tibetan Bön shamanism tradition and found its way into Faery Tradition via the NightHares line. It is used sometimes as a preliminary rite to high ceremonies such as Grand Sabbats, dedications, or initiations. It is a means to give a "peace offering" to the minor "demons" or other low and obstructing spirits that might otherwise adversely affect the ritual. This gives them an offering along with a magical warning: take this offering and leave in peace, or suffer the wrath of the magician and their deities. What follows is my adaptation.

This is done in two steps. The first is to make the "red bread" and the second will be the offering itself.

EXERCISE: Making the Red Bread

This is a "simple version" using rice. Alternatively, you may wish to bake actual bread with the mustard seed and red coloring and use that instead, as bread will be less messy than the colored rice (as well as potentially more comfortable if you are performing this rite indoors and without shoes).

Items needed:
Dry white rice
Mustard seed
Red food coloring
A ceramic bowl
A baking pan or cookie sheet
Some aluminum foil (for easy clean up)

Begin by lining the baking pan or cookie sheet with the aluminum foil. Open the Way. Now, fill a bowl about half way with the rice. Now add about two tablespoons of mustard seed. Mix together. Now, add a few drops of the food coloring and MIX THOROUGHLY. You will want the color to be reddish, but it need not be "blood red." Add more as needed but GO SLOW, as it's easy to add too much color and end up with a bit of a mess. Stir until the color is fairly even.

Pour the rice onto the cookie sheet and spread thinly and evenly. Allow to dry overnight (or you can put it in the oven on a low temperature for several minutes until dry).

EXERCISE: Offering the Red Bread

This is usually done just prior to a larger working. If you are outdoors you may wish to strew the rice on the ground, but if you are indoors it might prove more useful (and less messy) to pour the offering into a bowl or on a dish.

Items needed:

The "red bread"

Some incense for an offering (and incense burner and charcoal, if needed)

An offering bowl or dish (optional)

Open the Way. From your aligned state, breathe in the essence of the Star Goddess as white and black flames and use this wraith force to bless the bread.

Imagine that you can send out a multitude of rays of light, each with a little hook at their end, that radiate out from your alignment and into each and every of the "obstructing spirits." With a breath, these rays retract and "drag" these spirits together so that they are all in one small area in front of the practitioner. They may appear to the aetheric sight as red, angry spirits, wild and feral-looking.

Hold the red bread in your left hand at waist level while you hold the incense offering in your right. Say:

> *Demons and spirits that deceive!*
> *By God Herself you must obey.*
> *Do not resist, or suffer our wrath!*
> *Receive this gift and take your leave!*
> *IO EVOHE! So must it be!*

With a snap of the fingers, offer up the red bread, throwing it down onto the ground (or alternatively, pouring it on a plate or dish and placing on the floor) while imagining a wave of intense fire and heat radiating outward from your heart center in all directions, repelling all remaining obstructing forces and spirits. The offering has been made, and now your other work may proceed. Dispose of the remains in the way of your choosing after your ritual is complete.

———

Having looked deep into the mirror of our own abyss, we have seen what frights and shades lurk there, just out of sight. We have invoked our shadow, and with the help of the Watchers and the Wells at the Ends of the World, we have gazed into different aspects of our greatest fear. But if we were to think that our work is done, we would sadly mistaken. The ego may try to convince us that we have already done our work, but most often this is a trick to dissuade us from going any deeper.

We may find that the fears that arise to our consciousness might not actually represent those deepest fears that are affecting us. Instead they may be smaller, less significant fears that the ego will throw our way in the hopes that we will take the bait and back off from our pressing insistence of getting to the core of that which ails us.

But even smaller fears can be potent ones. When we do this type of work, we may even be able to use our magic in order to combine these smaller fears and issues into a singular force with which we may more easily interact, setting the stage for confrontation, identification of the core issues, and (hopefully) transformation. And so, we again pull from our magical toolbox and engage another of the magicians most potent of tools: the Triangle of Manifestation.

The Triangle is the Holy Trinity in perfect alignment—the three worlds, the Three Souls of Humankind. It is the Divine Twins merged together, becoming a third form. That third form is our aforementioned Winged Serpent, the Blue God, who as the Dian y Glas is our own holy daemon, aka our "higher self," "deep self," or "God Soul." When we are in alignment with our holy daemon, there can be no "evil spirit" that can invade us. The holy daemon forms the triangle that will hold our complex or demon, allowing it to manifest into a form with which we may interact within the black mirror.

Though not often called upon in the Craft in this capacity, this rite will utilize the magic circle not so much as a barrier, but primarily as a means of *extraction*—to "draw out" our demons (however we are defining that term) and place them under controlled observation in the safety of our Triangle.

RITE: The Daemonic Triangle

This rite aims to safely call into form the embodiment of our shadow that we may observe it. You will wish to perform this rite several times, at least until you are comfortable with its form and effects. This may take some time, perhaps a month or more of consistent workings. My advice would be to perform it at least twice a week for four weeks and then see how you feel about it overall. There is no shame in taking more time to make certain of your own progress.

To mentally prepare for this rite, spend some time meditating on your shadow using the previous tools given. What are the themes that have arisen? What are your fears? Be aware of these as you go into this rite and be prepared to call them up in full emotional detail. You may wish to abstain from certain foods or activities for at least one to two full days prior to this rite.

Items needed:
A meditation pillow
A Star Goddess candle
A bell
A pen and some paper
A cup
A small pitcher of water
An incense burner
Charcoal
Copal resin
Dried lavender flowers
Chalk, tape, sand, or salt to mark on the floor
A black scrying mirror
A small box or jar that can be closed

Using the chalk, tape, sand, or salt, mark out a circle on the floor that is large enough for all of the tools you will be using with you sitting in the center. Outside of this circle, mark a triangle on the floor,[47] so that it is oriented pointing away from the circle.

---

47. For the invocation of hostile beings and energies, the triangle is traditionally placed outside of the circle. If you are summoning using a particular element, then the placement of the triangle would reflect that. Otherwise, you may feel free placing it anywhere outside of the circle that you feel is appropriate or practical.

In the middle of this triangle place your black scrying mirror so that its concave side faces into the circle. Light the incense charcoal.

Open the Way. Place some copal on the charcoal. Ring the bell nine times, in three groups of three. Feel your connection to the Star Goddess as crystalline-white and ebony-black flames that flow through your holy daemon, through your fetch, and through your talker. See yourself shining with these fires, this wraith force. Use this power to perform the Waters of Purity rite. Now perform the Banishing exercise as given previously.

You may do this next part sitting, facing the triangle, or standing and physically walking the circle's edge. Focus your awareness on the physical space all around you. With your breath, use wraith force to empower the circle around you and enchant it to become a whirling vortex[48] of divine intelligence. Imagine this vortex is spinning around you at such a high velocity that it appears to be *standing still* ... and you are in the calm central eye of this invisible maelstrom. Use whatever additional methods you feel are appropriate to make the circle feel solid to you, if needed. In this circle, you are "between the worlds," i.e., outside of space and time.

Invoke the Watchers and the Wells in each direction, east (Star Finder / Arida), south (Shining Flame / Tana), west (Water Maker, Tiamat), north (Black Mother / Verr-Avna), above (Heaven Shiner / Quakoralina), below (Fire-In-The-Earth / Sugma'ad), and center (Guardian of the Gates / the Nameless Name). Feel their presences: The Goddesses of the Wells as the primal, unknowable, maddening mystery that is the elemental powers of the outer darkness, and the Watchers as the focusing lenses that mediate that combined power into your circle, here and now. They each present you with a version of your greatest fear ... and the means of championing it.

If you are standing, sit down and face the triangle.

Now, with three deep and conscious breaths, empower the triangle with Blue Fire; see each line being drawn as if by an invisible hand with an exhalation, like a brush-stroke of brilliant electric blue light. Feel how this is the true holy trinity: thesis, antithesis, and synthesis. This is the true symbol and story of the Divine Twins: *1+1=3*.

Our Twins are the mystery of manifestation and so they will hold this gate open for us. Begin to call up your complexes ... your fears ... your guilt and shame. Imagine

---

48. The direction of this vortex should be that associated with "banishing" for your location, counterclockwise for the northern hemisphere, or clockwise for the southern.

that these feelings are vibrations of energy that exist within your energy body ... or frequencies of consciousness like dissonant notes in an otherwise harmonic symphony. Visually, we might see them as dark, mist-like shadows that exist deep within. Imagine how this darkness within you is drawn to the light. Like moths to flame they take flight ... rising up and out of your body like rising smoke. Imagine this smoke exuding out through the pores of your skin, like a dark vapor that is pulled by an unseen centrifugal force to the inner edges of the whirling, glowing circle all around you.

With every slow, deep breath, these energies, blocks, complexes, issues, fears, demons, etc. get caught in the wake of the swirling vortex and begin to spin around you just inside the boundary of your circle. With every breath, they spin a little faster. Faster ... faster ... FASTER ... whirling around you with tremendous speed as your breath remains slow and deep. Imagine that you can hear these dark forces whooshing around you ... humming ... spinning so fast that it all appears like a single streak of darkness all around you. Merging together as a single force. Allow the speed and the power to build. With every breath, you release more and more of whatever negative energies you have held inside you. Perhaps more than you had previously known. It merges and builds at the edges of your spinning circle ... faster ... faster ... faster!

Maintain this energetic edge for a bit. When you feel it is at its peak, recite the following incantation:

> *Whirling darkness, screaming shade*
> *Fright and demon, guilt and pain*
> *Shadow of my darkened past*
> *Within the mirror now held fast!*

On the last line and with your exhale, channel an opening in the circle / vortex before you and throw the shadow demon into the triangle. Feel this dark force being beamed into the scrying mirror within the triangle where it is securely contained.

Reaffirm your connection to the presences of the Watchers and the Wells, feeling how they are keeping you balanced and in a state of deep Enchantment. Gaze into the mirror. Feel how your demon is trapped within the triangle. Scry and see what images arise in the mirror. Do you see your demon? Look at it. What form does it take? Is it frightening? Let the fear wash over and through you. Is it pitiful? You can have compassion for it without harming yourself. Is it beautiful? What is it distracting you from? Does it refuse to be seen at all? *Command* it to appear before you. By the power of your three souls aligned, the power of the highest spirit, command it to obey with the charm:

> *Shade or Demon, come to form*
> *As calm as eye of many storm*
> *Now held to these three things I ask:*
> *Your name, your sign, your face unmasked.*

Held within the Daemonic Triangle the shadow demon must obey—at least eventually. It is underneath a sort of spiritual microscope, and now we will observe its behavior. Ask for its name…its *true* name. How does it respond? Ask again. Do you understand the name? Do you feel it is true? If so, move on to the next step; if not, continue to demand its name, drawing on the powers of the Watchers and the Wells, if necessary.

Now, command it *by name* to bare its true face. Unmasked, it reveals itself. Does it change? Unmask! Does it change again? Hold tight and fear not! Do not flinch or look away.

Next ask for its sign. This is as much its "theme" as it is a visual image. You may receive an image of a symbol or some sort of sign. Draw this as best you can. You may also treat this as you might automatic writing or drawing, allowing the pen to flow independent of your conscious thought. Or you may be particularly inspired in the creation of a sigil. Draw it on your paper to your satisfaction.

Now, with its name, sign, and form revealed you have power over it. Ask it questions. How long has it been with you? How is it fed? What strengths has it offered you? What payment does it demand? Just allow your imagination to be the medium by which this demon communicates. Try not to judge what you are receiving in the moment.

If your demon has not reveled itself to you, then you are to keep commanding it until it relents. This may take several sessions, so be patient. You may also wish to strengthen your connections to both the Watchers and the Wells outside of this exercise to help give your work here the needed impetus toward success. In this work, allies can make all the difference.

Reaffirming your connection to the Watchers and the Wells, bind it *by name* to its sigil. Burn copal and waft the smoke over the sigil.

After you have spent at least a few minutes in communion with your demon, reaffirm your soul alignment and place some copal and dried lavender on the charcoal. Offer your shadow demon the following prayer:

> *Shade or Demon, shadow form,*
> *The winds have calmed the raging storm*
> *A pleasant slumber now for thee*
> *And peace between us ever be.*

Waft some of the incense smoke in the direction of the triangle, sending it a sense of compassion and healing. Imagine a beam of divine love from your holy daemon shining into the mirror and triangle. Most likely you will experience the sensation of the demon fading from the mirror. (If not, perform the Banishing rite.) Place the sigil in the jar or box and close it tightly. Keep this out of sight and out of sunlight completely, only bringing it out after sunset, only by candle or moonlight, and only when you are communing with your demon.

Waft some of the smoke over yourself. Ring the bell three times. Perform the Banishing rite and then the Waters of Purity. Take down your circle as you would normally. Record your experiences in your journal.

———

This rite serves as the first main component of a series of workings designed to help us get to know our shadow on a more intimate level. We need to learn what its tricks are if we are going to be able to combat them. And confrontation is the only real way to learn how not to give in to our fears. Once we have confronted our shadow demon, and perhaps become more accustomed to its many forms, we can then begin the real work of transformation, for we cannot expect to enter into this relationship and remain unchanged.

As we continue to work with our shadow we must use all of the tools at our disposal in order to champion it. As we sit in its presence, we learn to allow our fear to wash over and through us, holding fast to our practices that keep us on the warrior's path. We use our magic, divination and ritual, to determine how best to proceed, and then to enact our will. If our demon manifests in one or more particular elements, then we may use the tools of that element to help bring back the balance that we seek.

In addition to using the Devil at the Crossroads spread, we can rely on our journaling practice to assist us in learning where our elemental imbalances lie.

JOURNALING: Elemental Impurities

For this exercise, each night for a week, before going to bed, take about five minutes to make a list of your weaknesses, blocks, and impurities. Mentally go back over your life since your childhood. Think about all the negative experiences you have gone through and how they affected you at the time. Have you carried any of that into your present life? Imagine that every incident you list is being packed away as if in a box.

The next night, repeat this process and see if there are any other incidents that you can think of. If not, review your previous list. If any of those items feel particularly "powerful" go ahead and list them again on today's list.

Do this for a full seven nights. On the eighth night look at your list and then distill it down. You may find that certain incidents are actually representative of a "theme" and so make a new list that shows those themes and patterns extrapolated from what you wrote the previous week. Now, beside each entry, list whatever element you feel best describes that particular issue. For example, "Quick to anger" might be labeled "Fire," "too trusting" might be "Water," and "easily confused" might be "Air."

Once this is completed, look over your list and see if there is one or more of the elements that stand out more than others. This, along with the Devil at the Crossroads spread will give you a different perspective as to where to look to find allies in dealing with your shadow.

———

Once we are aware of which elements in particular are giving us trouble, we can focus our efforts there. In the Korythalia/Bloodrose material, there is a set of specific practices and visualizations that are used in order to get in touch with an elemental shadow demon.

EXERCISE: Shadows of the Elements

This is used in order to call up the impurities or blocks that we have in relation to certain elements. Drawing from our list, choose the element that is giving you the most trouble and "plug in" the appropriate spirits and visualizations into the following formula.

Unlike the previous exercises, in this series the circle cast will be of a standard type, in that it will be used to contain the energy as well as offer protection.

Items needed:
A meditation pillow
A Star Goddess candle
A ritual tool for the chosen element
A bell
A cup
A small pitcher of water
An incense burner
Charcoal
Copal resin
Dried lavender flowers
Chalk, tape, sand, or salt to mark on the floor
A black scrying mirror

Mark the circle on the floor as you did with the Daemonic Triangle exercise. Likewise mark the triangle just outside the circle facing outward, in the direction that corresponds with the element with which you will be working.

Open the Way. Cast the circle. Empower it to be a barrier of protection. Breathe Blue Fire and empower the triangle.

Facing the triangle, invoke the Watcher of the element. Take a moment to feel their presence connecting to the associated glyph in your body. Take as much time as you'd like to get "in tune" with them.

Imagining that you are reaching *through* the Watcher, invoke the corresponding Well. Feel this goddess's presence as an overwhelming elemental power, mediated and regulated by the presence of the Watcher; an "interface"—much like how software interacts with hardware—providing a safe way to access a portion of this goddess's otherwise devastating presence.

Take hold of whatever elemental ritual tool is appropriate for this working, while tapping into the archetypal tool on the astral. Take a moment to feel how your physical tool carries this deeper spirit within it. Hold it out in front of you, between yourself and the mirror in the triangle before you, so that you focus on the tool instead of the mirror. Feel how you wield this tool with skill and with grace.

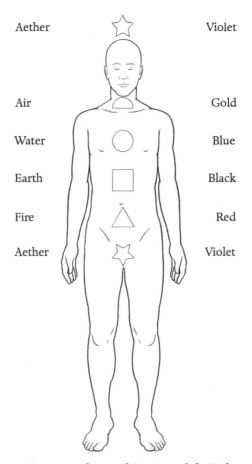

Aether — Violet
Air — Gold
Water — Blue
Earth — Black
Fire — Red
Aether — Violet

Figure 18: Elemental Stations of the Body

Reaffirm the alignment of your souls and—drawing from both the Watcher and the Well—call up your blocks…impurities…weaknesses…complexes…your *demons*. Call them to appear in the mirror before you, using the appropriate visual key:

Air: A glowing yellow eye within an eight-rayed vortex of violet fire.
Fire: A glowing red eye within an eight-rayed vortex of yellow fire.
Water: A glowing blue eye within an eight-rayed vortex of pink fire.
Earth: A glowing green eye within an eight-rayed vortex of black and dark Blue Fire.
Aether: A glowing violet eye within an eight-rayed vortex of intense white and black fire.

Visualize the appropriate key as appearing in the black mirror before you. Notice how you feel about it. This is a doorway into a deeper experience with the shadow demon. Open this door and look inside. What do you see? Command this shadow demon to appear before you in a form that you will understand. Demand its true name. Draw on the Watcher and the Well, as necessary.

Ask the shadow demon what you need to do in order to be free of it. Use your elemental tool to command it to obey. Pay attention to how it responds.

You may be able to command it to dissolve and transform. If so, receive it back through your holy daemon, which will act as a means of protection. If not, burn some copal and lavender and send it peace until next time. Thank the Well and the Watcher and open your circle. Perform the Waters of Purity rite and the Banishing exercise. Repeat this exercise once a week for four weeks for each of the five elements.

————

We have done much work to properly locate and identify what our shadow has in store for us. Now we should be intimately familiar with our complexes and our potential demons and have some idea of how we might approach dealing with them. Now comes the part in which we need to make a decision: Can we transform the demon or complex?

To do this we must ask ourselves: *Can I have compassion for this?* This is a part of ourselves that is twisted, in fear and in pain. It formed, in a sense, to *protect* us, as misguided as that was. The ideal is to transform and integrate it back into ourselves so that we once again have access to that life force. As long as this shadow demon exists, we are not whole. We seek that wholeness. We seek nothing less than our power.

RITE: The Demon Lover

Only perform this exercise after you have completed working with the elemental powers as with the previous exercise (Shadows of the Elements). This is inspired from a traditional Faery exercise which utilizes solo sex magic as the means to transform and integrate the shadow demon. You may adapt it to suit a nonsexual working if desired.

Items needed:

A meditation pillow

A Star Goddess candle

Three candles, black, red, and white
A bell
The box or jar with the paper sigil of your demon
A cup
A small pitcher of water
An incense burner
Charcoal
Copal resin
Dried lavender flowers
Chalk, tape, sand, or salt to mark on the floor
A black scrying mirror

Mark out the circle and the triangle on the floor as you did for the Daemonic Triangle rite. Place the sigil within the triangle.

Open the Way. Place some copal on the charcoal. Ring the bell nine times, in three groups of three. Feel your connection to the Star Goddess as the crystalline-white and ebony-black flames that flow through you. Use this power to perform the Waters of Purity rite. Now perform the Banishing exercise as given previously.

Empower the circle and the triangle as you did in the Shadows of the Elements exercise, and invoke the Watchers and the Wells.

Call up your demon as was done in that exercise, and allow it to be pulled from your energy body as before. Feel the swirling vortex around you. Focusing on the sigil, command it by name into the triangle/mirror with the incantation previously given, or another of your choosing. Light the black candle. Make a declaration that the demon is now bound and subject to your will. Command it to appear before you in the mirror. Ring the bell three times.

Now, with the image of your demon before you, we will work the transformation.

Reaffirm your soul alignment. Identify with your holy daemon. Allow this part of you to draw from the powers of the Watchers and the Wells. Feel your place in the center of the universe … you are the child of the Mother. You are her lover, sibling, and other half. You are the Twins, combined as One. You are the Blue God, Dian y Glas … and through him: Melek Ta'us. Feel the presence of the Peacock Angel … his body surrounding you, his peacock feather wings your own.

See your demon. See the face it wears before you, and the Peacock Angel's heart swells with love and compassion. Feel compassion for your demon. Feel for it as you might a wounded child or animal that lashes out. Feel how it is a part of you, though disconnected and distorted. Feel genuine compassion. *Fierce* compassion. By the light of your *daemon*, send that love to your *demon*, shining like a light from the heart of your alignment and into the heart of your demon. Light the white candle and say:

> *I am the child of the Mother,*
> *I of she, and you of me,*
> *Child, sibling, mirrored-other,*
> *Transform I pray, my demon lover!*

Allow the image of the demon to change before you. Continue to send it love and compassion like a light beaming from the alignment in your heart. Like Janet from the ballad, hold fast and worry not … do not allow fear to confuse you. You are here for a purpose. Lovingly *but firmly* command the demon to assume its authentic form. Command it by its name and by its sign. Draw on the powers of the Watchers and the Wells, as needed.

Be open to whatever actually happens in your experience. Here we must rely on our own psychic skills of observation and discernment. If we are at all proficient in trance work then we will know the difference between an authentic astral/trance experience and a mere flight of the imagination, the meditative equivalent of watching television. The goal is to send love and healing to the demon and provoke it to transform. We may also (again, lovingly but firmly) command it to transform. No matter what disturbing and/or alluring images and emotions may arise during this process, we must not be distracted by them. Look at your demon *directly in the eyes* and command it into loving submission. It may transform into a beautiful image. Be open to how it feels. Here, in the light of your daemon, it reveals its true intent. If you feel that it is sincerely transforming and submitting, then move on to the next section below. If not, you will want to continue trying. If it still will not effectively submit, then you will want to end the rite as the end of the Daemonic Triangle exercise, by blessing your demon with peace and slumber while wafting the smoke of copal and lavender over its sigil and yourself. Close the circle as normal and try again another day.

If your demon, however, *does* submit and transform, then call up a sense of erotic passion for your demon, light the red candle and say:

Into our eyes, the light of love
Into our hearts, sweet passion's flame
Into our kiss, a fevered moment
*In our embrace, Her Holy Name!*49

Holding the image of your demon before you, and feeling a genuine sense of love and compassion for it in your heart, open yourself sexually to this being.[50] Imagine the wings of the Peacock Angel—your wings—stretching out and upward. Facing your demon, looking at it directly in the eyes and feeling that love and passion, use your arms and gesture as if you were hugging your demon, imagining pulling it close and you kiss. Imagine your wings wrapping around your demon lover, pulling it closer. Pull it close…closer…open your heart and pull it inside of you. Feel yourself joining together as a singular being. The lover and the beloved. Two halves of the same love.

Burn the sigil in the flame of the red candle. Take a bit of the resultant ash and put it in your cup and then fill with water. Perform the Waters of Purity rite.

Take down your circle-space as you would normally. Extinguish all but the red candle, which you allow to burn all the way down.

———

You may need (or simply wish) to perform this rite more than once with a particular demon. In some cases, the results of this type of working can be both gradual and cumulative. After performing this rite once a week for three weeks, you should have an idea of whether or not it is working for you. If you feel you are achieving results, then continue to work with it until you are able to successfully transform and reclaim the demonic presence. If after six weeks you have still not been able to successfully transform the presence then you will want to shelve it and move on to the next exercise.

---

49. Adapted from my poem "The Love of Kings," from my book *The Stars Within the Earth*.

50. It would be traditional to engage in masturbation for this working, building energy with your pleasure and finally merging with your demon during your orgasm. There may, however, be times in which you will wish to forgo the overt sexual aspect of this working (perhaps in cases where the demon in question is aligned to some aspect of sexuality, for example). In these cases, you should substitute another type of visionary/energetic modality, such as bringing two candle flames together to light a third candle, or pouring two vessels of water into a third. Use your imagination!

Since at this point we have been engaging in a semi-regular practice with our shadow and gotten familiar with several different techniques in dealing with it, we are ready to take our shadow work to the next level.

The Temple of the Demon Lover is—as all hidden temples are—a specific place on the astral that focuses energies and layers of consciousness in a certain way, in this case one that assists in the transformation of one's demons. The original form of this temple was discovered by BlueRose initiate Puck DeCoyote, who gifted it to our line. While that exact temple is a private space and not suited for those who have yet to undergo certain initiatory experiences, I used this as a point of inspiration and went on a series of journeys to find the keys to a similar type of space that would be better suited to work with the public. Enter the Temple of the Demon Lover.

TRANCE JOURNEY: The Temple of the Demon Lover

This exercise / trance journey should be used after you have familiarized yourself with and effectively performed the Demon Lover exercise at least a few times and journaled your results. This exercise can assist in bringing up deeper complexes from our shadow and moving them into our conscious awareness that might otherwise have gone previously unnoticed.

You may wish to record yourself reading this script so that you can use it as a meditative tool.

Open the Way. Breathe deep. Set your intention to travel into the underworld to seek the Temple of the Demon Lover. Imagine an opening in the ground before you in whatever form you generally use for such workings. Enter this opening and move down into a cavernous space. Feel the air grow cool and damp. Imagine you can hear the echoing drops of water in the distance. You feel yourself moving down and to your right, as if you are spiraling as you move. There is a faint silvery light that has no visible source that just barely illumines the winding path downward.

You come to a large room in the cavern and in the center is a large silver pool. You walk over to look into it. The surface is perfectly still and reflective like a mirror. You see your own reflection, but also something else … what appears to be a dark castle set against a night sky. Breathe deep … and when you are ready, dive into the pool.

Travel through the mirror of the silver pool
in the land below,
to the world above.

The water is cold at first, but then … there is no cold. Then there is no *wet*. Here is no … sensation … you are floating amongst the stars. The castle before you, made entirely of clear crystal. It sits atop a dark Olympian spire of a mountain; miles and miles of stone steps form a staircase that leads from the abyss below and into the very heart of the castle.

You are drawn to the steps and find yourself now standing upon them. You climb … all the way up until you reach the castle gates.

As you reach the gates, you are greeted by a guardian. Notice how they appear to you. You will be asked a question. Answer correctly and you will be given entrance. If not, you will be turned away and you will need to return later when you are ready.

When you are given the "green light," the gate will open for you, and you may step inside. The inside of the castle is just as strange as its outside; made entirely of clear crystal, and set against the starry expanse, it appears to be black, with a plethora of stars and galaxies. You follow the hallway which curves to the right, and you are led in a spiral inward, to the heart of the castle when you find an empty room with a single chair in the center. On the floor around the chair is the markings of a circle, a small distance outside of which is marked a triangle pointing outward.

You walk over to the chair and sit down. As you get comfortable, you notice that straight ahead of you, inset into the far wall, are two seated figures, silently watching you. The Faery Queen and King reach out their hand to one another and rise as one. In her free hand, she holds a silver branch. In his, a golden sword. Together they walk from their thrones to stand just outside the circle before you. One of them asks you why you are here … what demon are you here to transform? Provide the answers to what is asked of you.

The Queen releases her brother's hand and begins to shake her silver branch. The sound is like little silver bells or chimes … a pleasant tinkling sound that purifies the space and awakens the fetch. She then drags the end of the silver branch on the ground behind her as she walks clockwise around your circle. Little silver sparks erupt where her branch drags on the ground. And little sparks ignite into silver flames, as she casts a circle around you with silver fire.

It is the King who steps closer now, pointing his sword directly at your heart. His blade seems to glow with a golden fire, and this flame leaps forward and into your body where it roots out the shadow demon(s) and forces them to the surface. Like a black smoke or vapor they flow from you ... little issues and complexes ... negative feelings ... that bad memory from school ... that trauma ... that embarrassment ... from when you were little ... from that early morning last week ... they *all* flow up and out of you and into the space of your circle, streaking around you like dark wraiths.

Take a breath of power. The King swings his golden flaming sword upward, and the shadow demons are caught in its wake, flowing out from the silver circle and into the triangle, which now glows with golden fire.

The Queen knocks her silver branch on the ground three times: THUD! THUD! THUD! And as it is trapped in the triangle before you, you see the shadow demon for what it truly is. The Queen and King begin to walk counterclockwise around the triangle, the King pointing his golden flaming sword into the triangle, and the Queen dragging the silver branch on the ground behind them.

This seems to weaken the shadow demon's resistance, making it susceptible to suggestion and magical command. Consider that it is a part of you, broken apart and wounded. Open your heart to it even as you command it *by name* to transform back into the life force from which it came. See if you can make the shadow demon dissolve back into energy. Toward this end, the Queen and King may offer you the use of their magical weapons. What does it feel like to hold the silver branch? Use the silver fire to cleanse, entice, and compel the shadow demon. How about the golden sword? The golden flame transforms, illuminates, and defends. What magic do these tools offer you here? How are they different? How can you use them here? Can you transform your shadow demon? Holding love and compassion in your heart, use either golden sword to slay your shadow demon, or the silver branch to compel it to make love to you ... either way, striking at its heart and causing it to burst into an explosion of silver and golden fire.

If you do not feel this occur, just maintain the space and keep trying. It may be that you will need to return at a later date to try again. But once the shadow demon has been transformed into fire, that fire begins to swirl like a cyclone, still trapped within the triangle. The Queen and King gesture toward the triangle and it *moves*, rotating on the floor so that it points *into* the circle. Reaffirm your soul alignment and then call this power into your circle ... feel this metallic fire swirl around you as you take seven deep breaths, breathing in this flame, reclaiming your power, now freed from its demonic form. Take this power back inside yourself, feeling recharged and complete.

The Queen and King stand before you, each holding their weapon once more. He draws the remaining golden fire from the triangle back into his blade. She walks around the circle counterclockwise, drawing up the silver fire into her branch. They stand before you, again holding hands. They cross their weapons over their bodies so that the two weapons cross each other.

> *The silver branch and golden sword*
> *Shall lead the way,*
> *Shall mark the word.*

Open your heart in gratitude to the Queen and King and they walk *backward* toward their thrones, still holding each other's hand. In unison, they sit. And in the blink of an eye, they are gone.

You make your way out from this central space and back to the castle gates. You exit the castle and begin to climb down the stone steps that lead down into the blackness of space. As the darkness swallows even the steps, you find yourself floating in the darkness amongst the stars. You see—off in the distance—a silver mirror and you are drawn toward it. With a breath, you move *through* the mirror and find yourself emerging in a cavernous room, filled with the smell of damp earth. You follow the path up and to your left, spiraling up … higher … higher … higher … until you emerge here in the middleworld … into your room and into your meditating body. Open your eyes to gaze at the light of the Star Goddess candle. Take seven slow breaths, allowing all of your experiences to come back with you. Take three more breaths and call your power back from the candle. End as you would normally. Record your experiences in your journal.

———

There are some demons that will not easily cast aside their identity. Perhaps they have been with us for a very long while, becoming even a trusted friend of sorts. Demons acquired in childhood can often be the most difficult to challenge, as they have become so ingrained in our lives it may be difficult to see where one ends and the other begins. And if we discover that their intent is not so much malicious as it is *protective,* we can perhaps begin to see the benefits of keeping them around. Maybe now with a few rules in place.

___

From Demon to Familiar Spirit

If we feel transforming and reintegrating the demon is not a possibility (or we have tried multiple times and failed), then we may "repurpose" the demon by giving it a new task to perform. If we are to have demons, then we must turn them into our allies, our Witches' familiars. As my good friend and fellow Faery initiate Veedub often said of hers, "Hey! You work for *me* now!"

We must decide what we would like our demon ally to do for us.

JOURNALING RITE: The Demonic Gift

If you have been working with the previous material in earnest and for the suggested numbers of repetitions, then by now you should not need to physically mark out the circle or triangle unless you wish it. Spend at least five to ten minutes for the journaling portion of this rite. Repeat this entire rite once per week for three weeks.

Items needed:
A Star Goddess candle
Copal resin
An incense burner
Charcoal
Your journal and a pen
A black scrying mirror
Sigil for your shadow demon

Open the Way. As you have done before, cast a circle and empower the triangle, which is placed outside the circle in the direction of your elemental shadow demon, or in the west if no element has been assigned. Place the sigil inside the triangle before the mirror.

Call up your shadow demon by name. Imagine it appearing in the mirror before you. Take some time to connect to it. When you feel ready, begin to ask it questions, writing down the answers much in the style of automatic writing, in which you will simply allow your pen to move on the paper. Ask it how its power might be best put to use to serve you. Remember your alignment and your allies in the Watchers and the Wells.

When you are finished, thank your shadow demon and burn some more copal. End the ritual and you would normally. Perform the Waters of Purity and the Banishing rites.

———

This exercise can inspire us toward a practice specifically tailored to redirecting our shadow demon toward behaviors that are in alignment with our own benefit. Toward this end we can employ our divinatory tools to assist us at more clearly mapping out how we should proceed.

DIVINATION: The Devil's Tree

Here we will use our skills at divination to assist us in seeing what feeds and sustains our Demon, as well as how we might best engage it toward the reclamation of our power.

Items needed:
A deck of tarot cards with only the major arcana

Open the Way. Remove the Devil card and place it in the center. Shuffle the remaining cards and lay them out according to the diagram.

The Devil is, of course, your Demon. What lies beneath your Demon is its *root*; it is its origin, but also that which feeds and sustains it. This can give us insight as to how to avoid giving it more of that nourishment and perhaps even learn what might prove to be an effective and more suitable substitute. What lies above the Devil is its *branches and fruit*; the skills and powers it possesses that can potentially be brought into service, both for left-hand and right-hand workings. The fruit, branches, and the roots can all be an integral part of any pact that you may devise and into which you may enter with your potential demon familiar.

Though the cards are laid out in the order given in the diagram, they are read in the following order:

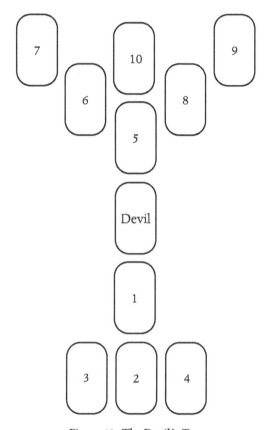

Figure 19: The Devil's Tree

3, 2, 4) The roots. Read from left to right, these cards tell a story about how this demon came into existence.

1) The base. What nourishes your demon. This is what your demon needs in order to feed.

5) The trunk. The raw energy that this demon brings into the world.

6, 7) The left-hand branch. Read together, these represent the powers of cursing that this demon can bring.

8, 9) The right-hand branch. These together are the demon's potentially beneficial powers.

10) The fruit. The culmination. The unification. The advice. The fate. The legacy.

———

Once we have an idea as to how to repurpose our shadow demon(s), then we can use our tools to create our own ritual tailor-made toward this end. At this point in your magical practice, you should be more than proficient in the creation of an effective ritual, drawing from the concepts and exercises presented here. Use the basics of the Demonic Triangle rite and, instead of blessing or banishing your shadow demons, *compel* them to serve you in the specific way that you have discerned to be appropriate. You may wish to devise and use a sigil that aims to do this, perhaps drawn overlaid upon that of your shadow demon, which you can keep in its special box or jar. You will want to develop a relationship with your shadow demon as you would any other type of spirit ally. This will take some time, likely the better part of a year or more as you work in conjunction with the Watchers, the Wells, and your personal ancestors and spirits. Once trust has been established, then you may find that what was once your demon has now become your familiar.

PART FOUR

THE FORBIDDEN RITES

You the Wine and I the Cup

When does align the sun and moon
with the holy star of blue
then that star, like silver cup;
an empty vessel opens up.

O spirit!
You are the star-filled wine
Pour into me, both bold and sweet
Then let me taste my fill of you
And you may then dance with my feet.

O spirit!
Grant your power and your presence
The world you will see with my eyes
And I with yours, to gaze quintessence
That I may see beyond all lies.

O spirit!
Come in love and healthy purpose
And if our wills align as one
You and I to each will be in service.
And so, our pact is made and done.

Together let our flames burn brighter
Together let us speak as one
Together we shall rise much higher
And gently part when we are done.

CHAPTER 8
TWO FLAMES INTO ONE:
THE ART OF DIVINE POSSESSION

The possession of anything begins in the mind.
—BRUCE LEE

Possession. In the popular mind, it conjures images of demonic activity ... tortured vessels and violent exorcisms ... hooded figures and conspiratorial Satanic rituals. We think of movies like *The Exorcist* or TV shows like *Supernatural* in which dark forces hell-bent on causing pain and suffering violate the sovereignty of otherwise good people, causing them to commit horrendous, transgressive, and often violent acts, leaving them broken and in despair. Or perhaps one pictures frenzied dancing around a bonfire to the sound of drums, participants having ferocious seizures, speaking in tongues, and consorting with dark spirits for forbidden Voodoo rites. While these seem miles apart to the religiously diverse and the magically inclined, both scenarios are equally shocking to the larger culture—the Protestant Christian mindset that influences much of the religious thought and social interactions in the Western world. They are shocking because they touch a deep and primal fear, one that organized religions have tried to conquer for millennia but have ultimately failed: the fear of losing control.

No matter the imagery, there's one thing that most people agree on: the person who is possessed is *no longer themselves*. They are not in control of their actions, and might not even be aware of them. I spoke previously about the teaching of a person being possessed by their Taka spirit and potentially committing acts that are contrary to their own nature without that person's conscious knowledge. This is what most people think of when they think of possession: a malicious invasion from an outside spiritual force; a parasitic condition rendering the host tortured and helpless.

While this type of possession does exist (often mistaken for more common mental illnesses), it is certainly not the only form or the most common. In Haitian Vodou, Cuban Santeria, Brazilian Umbanda, and other forms of African Traditional Diasporic religions, practitioners are known to become possessed by the Lwa or Orisha. These are powerful spirits that are venerated and prayed to, and who may inhabit the bodies of their practitioners and engage in any number of activities, such as talking, singing, dancing, or drinking, all potentially without the knowledge of the "horse," the human practitioner who has become a willing vessel through which the divine power of the spirit may incarnate and interact with the earthly plane.

But African religion is not the only one to have a history of such intimate encounters with spiritual entities. Altered consciousness and contact with deities is a hallmark of the Norse *seiðr*. Shinto and Buddhism each have a belief in spirit possession, as do Christianity, Islam, and Judaism, each with varying degrees of acceptance and/or fear. The ancient Egyptians and Greeks likewise believed in such phenomena.

These likely all draw from the older, foundational practices and worldview of what we might call transcultural shamanism, in which animism and trafficking with spirits was (and remains) a frequent and foundational occurrence. It is a common function for a priest or holy person to commune with the spirits in some form or another in order to obtain information otherwise unavailable and then bring it back for the betterment of the community.

When done correctly, divine possession is a beautiful and sensual experience. It is a loving embrace with a spirit in which we have made a conscious decision to allow ourselves to act as a vessel for a higher consciousness. It is akin to making love, and so it is understood that in this intimate state we are more vulnerable and permeable. Our own consciousness opens up like a flower, and we are naked before the spirit, a tender offering of presence and sensuality.

Divine possession is a symbiotic relationship. There are many benefits for both the spirit and the practitioner in the arrangement. For the spirit, it is the opportunity to become embodied and to further interact with this world, as well as to be *fed*— nourished by the wraith force raised and offered by the practitioner. For the practitioner, chief among these benefits is the embodied knowledge that comes from this connection. When a spirit or a deity inhabits our consciousness, we are privy to certain things: inspiration, wisdom, knowledge, power, healing. There is often a type of blessing that occurs—an outpouring of wraith force in some form, from the spirit to the practitioner, that benefits the practitioner.

There are also benefits for the community. Often possessory rituals involve some type of oracular divination in which members of the congregation are given advice or even personal readings. The spirit or deity is able to speak directly to the congregation, who are able to ask questions, receive insight, and participate in ritual acts together. This can be a very powerful form of magic that can touch many lives at once.

There are many stories of the practitioner who would engage in strange and even seemingly miraculous behavior while in the possessed state. Tales abound of individuals safely jumping off of roofs or walking through fire unharmed or drinking entire bottles of rum and not getting intoxicated. Often these practitioners will retain no memory of what transpired during the possessory state but are left with a sense of being blessed at having had the experience.

We have explored one aspect of the Witches' intimate relationship with spirits when we did the work of enlisting the aid of our Demon to make them our ally. Witchcraft has a long and varied history when it comes to spirits, as well as with spirit possession, but front and center must be the idea of the Witches' familiar. During the era of the English and Scottish Witch trials of the sixteenth and seventeenth centuries, many details regarding the Witches' familiar were recorded. Often, they were said to suckle from the "devil's mark," a mole or blemish that not only marked the person as a Witch, but also provided a physical (and even sexual) link to their familiar. One example comes from the Salem Witch Trials of 1692 in which Sarah Good was accused of having a familiar spirit in the form of a little yellow bird that would suckle from in between her fingers.

When seen through the lens of the poetic, we can see this as an example of the Witch offering wraith force to the familiar spirit. This is an act of communion that strengthens both parties and brings them closer into alignment with each other. Some practices involve this spirit temporarily inhabiting the body of the Witch in order to be nourished or otherwise empowered.

In Wicca, the rite of Drawing Down the Moon is specifically a possessory rite in which the High Priestess acts as a channel for the Goddess to speak to the participants in the circle. She becomes the Goddess incarnate. Recognizing that there are different degrees to possession, this event might take any number of forms, from the priestess merely reciting a piece of inspiring poetry (perhaps lightly feeling the presence of the Goddess with her), feeling inspired and allowing the deity presence to guide her actions in the circle, to full-on possession in which she is transported beyond herself and *might* (or might not) be a conscious witness to what transpires in the circle. In some modern Witchcraft traditions, there is a practice known as "aspecting," which is aligned to our topic here. It has been suggested that it is the same practice as possession, just one that uses a different terminology, one that does not have the potential negative baggage that "possession" often brings with it. This is laudable, certainly, but in a religion in which poetry matters, the words we choose each carry different vibrational tones, and those tones subtly influence the flow of wraith force, which affects the magical working. To my ear and spirit, "aspecting" seems lighter, more mental…less embodied. While *possession* seems…full…rich…deep…and visceral. To me, they exist on the same spectrum, but are not identical. Both of these experiences (and all their variants, alongside and in between) are potential tools in our bag of Witches' tricks, regardless of the terms we choose.

It may be helpful to our study if we map out this spectrum, starting from the lightest and moving gradually into the heaviest forms. Teachers from the Reclaiming Tradition (which finds its roots in Faery/Feri) have done a lot of work around aspecting and trance work and have offered up the following list of four stages or "levels" of this work. I present it here in a slightly edited form.[51]

1) Enhancement. This is the lightest stage and is when the priest/ess experiences a heightened awareness of their surroundings and sensations become more intensified. The priest/ess may experience a sense of the spirit's presence but retain full control of their actions and thoughts.

2) Inspiration. This stage involves the priest/ess feeling the spirit presence but still retaining full control. At this stage language may become more poetic and the priest/ess may speak on topics which they previously had no knowledge of.

3) Integration. This is the level that most people think of as "aspecting." This involves the spirit speaking through the priest/ess, and/or engaging in actions

---

51. This is based on the work of Robin LaSirena, "Aspecting in the Service of Deity," *Reclaiming Quarterly* 86 (2002): 22–23, 56–58, accessed July 26, 2017, http://reclaimingquarterly.org/86/RQ86-18-Theme-Aspecting.pdf. Here slightly edited by me, I place the poetic speech element in the second category instead of the first.

through the physical vessel. Often people report feeling as if they are somewhat "displaced," or "pushed to the side" during the process, though they are still able to retain control of their actions, if need be. The priest/ess may retain their memories intact, or they may find them to be fuzzy afterward.

4) Possession. This is the level in which people are able to do things that they otherwise could not, such as displaying great feats of strength or endurance or offering healing to the vessel or other participants. Often people will report having little or no memory of the experience, though those more skilled in this work will retain their consciousness and memories nearly intact.

When people speak of "full possession," they are often referring to level four and will assume that this means that the priest/ess will not be conscious of whatever events transpire during the experience. This is likely because at this stage it is far more difficult for the average experiencer to remain present during the experience, giving the false impression that this level of intensity *must* be accompanied by the loss of the individual's consciousness during the event. Even among some Faery initiates, this myth plays out where participants will be trained to *expect* a full loss of consciousness, and this is seen as a mark of intensity for the rite. To this I must offer a differing opinion.

Several initiates who worked closely with the Andersons have reported to me that Victor taught the importance of being "double-headed" in this work. This refers to a type of "dual-consciousness" in which the deity or spirit is fully present while the consciousness of the priest/ess is *also* fully present. This is the true "full possession," as anything short of this is not fulfilling the fullest potential. (For how can a possession be "full" if one of the parts is missing?) This is the goal of all possessory work in the BlueRose line. We strive to retain our individual consciousness while in full concert with the spirit. In this we are able to get the full benefits of the experience.

One such difficulty with possession work is that if practiced in such a way so that one's consciousness "exits the building," so to speak, then we run the risk of engaging in behavior that is unsafe or unsavory while in the possessed state. I have seen trained priests and priestesses engage in some pretty shady behavior, only to blame it on the spirit they were supposedly carrying. Brandishing of knives, being careless with fire, and making unwanted sexual advances toward other participants are just the tip of the iceberg when it comes to what some people will claim is the fault of the spirit. This is, needless to say, sloppy Witchcraft at best, and outright fraud at worst. And in a tradition that likes to think of itself as a sort of "Witchcraft elite," it does nothing but undermine that assertion.

Even practiced and knowledgeable practitioners may, from time to time, experience possessions in which they do not retain their full memories. This can be for any number of reasons: the practitioner might be tired or in need of food; or they might be emotionally unsettled for a reason unconnected to the working; or the "astrological weather" might be such that it makes the working more difficult; or the information discussed during the event was private and not for the ears of the priest/ess, etc.

At this point I feel compelled to share a personal story. Years ago, I was invited to take part in a ritual that was being led by another line, adjacent to my own lineage. The material we each worked with was fairly close in style (as is the majority of Faery in its "home" of the San Francisco Bay Area), and so it was relatively easy for me to simply join into their ritual structure, following their lead, as it were. I was asked to carry Dian y Glas, while the person who invited me was to carry Nimuë.

I consider myself a priest of the Blue God and had done possessory work with him and other deities prior, so I was no stranger to this type of work. I had struck what I believed to be a nice balance in my practice. It had been quite a while since I had experienced any difficulty while doing this type of work and so I felt pretty confident about it. Before the rite began, one of the attendants asked me if I needed a "tender"—someone to tend to my needs, such as helping me get back into my body and grounded after the rite, as well as helping with whatever physical things I may need as a result of being in the deep trance state (food, water, etc.). I replied politely in the negative and probably said something to the effect of "No need; in our line, we were trained to be self-sufficient." And with that, she left me to my ritual preparations.

The rite began and all was well. When the time came for the Blue God to be invoked, I felt him come through me with the usual sensations; a light, buzzy feeling and a sense of sensual confidence. While the ritual was taking place, the Blue God was blessing the participants, by using my peacock feather wand, lightly caressing their faces and speaking to each person in the circle. This was where things started to go sideways. It was around this point that I remember that my consciousness was not in the circle. My experience was that I was thirty to fifty feet above the rite, bathing in the fog that was rolling in across the tops of the redwood trees. It was quite pleasant, and I slowly started to realize that I had been in this state for at least several minutes. At about the moment that I fully realized that I was no longer paying attention to the ritual, my consciousness abruptly snapped back into my physical body where I was shocked to find that the wand I was holding had become entangled in one of the participant's hair and was quite stuck. I suddenly was standing in a group of people with everyone looking at me. I was embarrassed and started to gently untangle the wand from their hair. As soon as it was free, the Blue God was back running the show, and I was off to the side (my usual "position" when doing possession) and the rite continued as intended. At the climax of the rite there was a pole that we had wrapped with ribbons to represent different energies of which we were letting go. Nimuë and Dian y Glas picked up the pole and threw it out of the circle as the final act of magic. I remember that as soon as the pole left our hands I collapsed. I fell down on the ground with a thud, like a sack of potatoes—and just as graceful. (I will say that it was the most relaxing experience of falling down I have ever had.) At seeing me fall, the woman who had offered to be my assistant came over to me to make sure that I was fully back in my body. She asked me to repeat my name, which I did, as proof that it was really me whom she was talking to and not the deity. I was fine, thankfully. Just a bruised ego. But I left that circle a little wiser than I had entered.

What I was able to surmise is that there is an effect present in group ritual in which we can get "caught in the wake" of certain practices and energies. It was the custom of that lineage to do possession in the manner in which the priest/ess is not consciously aware of their surroundings, believing this to be "proof" of the intensity of the experience. And me with my Piscean nature just "went with the flow" of things and I ended up in the treetops instead. Next time I would make sure to have an assistant, if I were to practice possession with others who do it differently, and I would work harder to stay grounded and present.

Possession can be a powerful experience for the coven as well as the priest/ess who is carrying the spirit or deity. In terms of group involvement, it can provide an opportunity for an oracular experience, the spirit or deity offering advice or giving members information that is relevant to their lives. Or it can be the focus of a spell or rite, with the spirit offering power and direction for our magic. If the priest/ess is grounded and double-headed for the experience, then they will be privy to what transpires during the rite, which means that they will have benefitted from whatever wisdom was shared, as opposed to the single-headed priest/ess having to be "filled in" afterward by another participant.

Another benefit for the priest/ess who is being possessed is the possibility of receiving a deep healing or blessing from the spirit in question. Again, I share a personal story. This is actually a story of one of the most powerful possessory experiences I have ever had. This was many years ago at one of the "Feri Camps" that a few other initiate-teachers and myself offered. These were private retreats in which we experienced Faery magic and ritual in a shared, communal space with teachers from different lines who represented different perspectives and practices. For this camp, which was themed around Samhain, we were working with the concepts of death and destruction. I was tasked with carrying the Arddu while my friend Karina was to carry Ana. We were outside the ritual area, mentally preparing for the rite, but I was concerned because the day before I had badly twisted my ankle. It was quite swollen and I could hardly put any weight on it without severe pain. I even needed assistance just to walk from one place to another. But the show must go on, as they say, and so I figured I would just do my best and see what came of it. I hobbled over to the preparation area where Karina and I began our invocations.

From the get-go, I knew that this was going to be a powerful experience. Karina and I both began to speak in poetry, each of us speaking a line, only to be answered with a rhyming line from the other. I remember part of my mind being quite amazed at what was transpiring, as I had never had that happen to that degree before. It was uncanny. By the time the ritual participants invoked Ana and the Arddu (thus giving us our cue to enter the space and let the deities do their thing), we were so entranced that it felt like we were floating. I also was no longer experiencing the physical pain from my injury. I was still present, but I was off to the side, so to speak. A normal state for this type of work.

Entering into the ritual area, Ana was seated atop a large chair, raised and in front of a large fireplace, giving an ominous appearance. Arddu, by contrast, was among the participants and was tasked with speaking with them and potentially bringing some of them up to have an audience with Ana, based on the wishes of the deity.

I remember speaking with several of the participants (but for the most part do not remember what was said to them, as that was *private*, between the deity and the individual). I also remember that in one case it was I and not the deity who chose *not* to bring a certain person up to have an audience with Ana, proving to myself that—even though this experience felt very *deep*, I was still in control … when I wanted to be. Another thing I remember is that the Arddu wanted to *dance*.

Now I enjoy dancing as much as the next club queen, but I have never been one for causing a spectacle on the dance floor. I remember beginning to dance…and dance *hard*. Arddu was *stomping* his feet…like a bull…and becoming quite exaggerated in his movements…*my* movements. After a minute or two it stuck me that I still wasn't feeling any physical pain.

I continued to watch my body dance around the room and figured that I would probably pay for it the next day, but for then it was an exhilarating delight. The Arddu continued his work for the group, bringing people up to see Ana and also prompting the group to release their fears, which the Arddu transformed. When the ritual ended, and the deity had left my body, I was both exhausted and exhilarated. Food and drink were given to us (for possession is hungry work), along with a small amount of chocolate.

There were two major revelations that I had about possession from that experience. One is that I learned that possession can be *addictive*; as soon as I was out of the state, I had the feeling that I wanted to *do it all again*—to have that power inside me once more. The experience was extremely pleasurable, and I felt elated and relaxed, the same state of afterglow that is most often associated with sex. Really *good* sex, at that.

The other revelation was that I had been completely and miraculously healed. There was no swelling, no bruising, and no pain at all. I could put my full weight on it, when only a couple of hours prior it was painful and difficult to put any at all. I was stunned. After I ate I figured that it was probably the endorphins from the possession state that were acting as a sort of natural pain killer and, again, that I would likely pay the price the next day. But the next day the results were the same. And so it remained. I had been healed by the Arddu, and not in some abstract or even emotional sense. This was tangible. Physical. It was the real deal.

As we prepare ourselves for the practical work of learning possession in the Faery Tradition, it should be understood that we must speak first and foremost about *self-possession*. Before we can even entertain the notion of inviting another consciousness into our being, we must first be clean and clear within ourselves and aligned in our three souls. We must have a strong and healthy relationship with all three souls, be able to feel and move energy, have a fairly good handle on our shadow demons, and be able to receive clear guidance from our own holy daemon.

Speaking on the subject of full possession, Victor Anderson said, "if your godself (or in Vodou we call *maître tête*) gives permission for a spirit to work with you and through you, then you go into a kind of sleep and you take part in it, but you never give up your individuality. You are never conquered, you are never screwed over by something. You remain yourself. In Hawaiian, we call it *noho*, which means "to sit." But it cannot happen if your personal god forbids it."[52]

But lest we relax our attention and begin to think that we can let our guard down, we should remember that there *are* real dangers to doing this work, and not just the "mundane" ones that I described earlier. Victor warned of spirits that could break the personality of the practitioner, or could otherwise infect them with cruel and terrible ideas.

The trick to avoiding this is a series of no-nonsense rules and practices, chief among them the ability to remain aligned with our holy daemon. This alone will go far toward guiding the process and offering us protection. Another is knowing with whom you are working. We do not do possession with just any spirit. We must build a relationship over time…build trust. Otherwise, these "alien beings" could touch deep, unconscious aspects of our psyches to use against us, quite possibly without our conscious knowledge.

Preparing the Vessel

Before we jump right in to invoking a spirit into our body/psyche/soul-structure, we must make sure that our vessel is a sound one. If we have been maintaining a robust and regular spiritual and magical practice, then we will have encountered our shadow demons and have (hopefully) worked to champion them. This is the number one concern with doing this type of work, as inviting a spirit inside ourselves empowers those parts of ourselves that are hidden, deep, and unconscious. In the presence of a spirit or a deity, those hidden parts can become endowed with greater intensity, potentially causing us (and those around us) some level of difficulty and perhaps even harm.

Assuming that we have done our shadow work and are ready to take this next step, we should ask ourselves: Why? Why do we want to do possession? Is it to impress our covenmates or teachers? Is it to receive some hidden knowledge from the spirit? Is it so that we can experience the spirit or deity in a more intimate, embodied way? Or perhaps we want to prove to ourselves that magic is real and losing oneself in an act of

---

52. Transcribed from a recording of a talk given by Victor at PantheaCon, 1996, in San Jose, CA. Spelling and punctuation are my own.

ecstatic Witchcraft would fit the bill? Once our intentions are clear, then we can begin the real work toward preparing ourselves to carry a higher consciousness in this way.

If we have been doing our regular work then we have already come a long way toward this preparation. If you are able to go into trance and remain lucid and focused for the duration, then this is a good indicator that you might be ready to take things to the next level, so to speak.

EXERCISE: The Mother's Body

This simple exercise is usually taught to Faery students early in their training as a sort of relaxation exercise but is later revisited as a means to prepare them for the eventual work of possession. This should be repeated until you are able to achieve the desired shift in consciousness in the span of a couple breaths. You may continue to move forward with the other work as you work toward this.

Open the Way. Feel your body and allow yourself to fully relax. Imagine that you are floating in peaceful darkness. With every breath, you rise and fall as if on the ocean waves. With every breath, you are lulled deeper into trance. Breathe deep.

Imagine that your whole body is becoming empty and hollow as you continue to float effortlessly on the waves of your breath.

With your eyes closed, remember the flame of the Star Goddess candle before you. Imagine it is like a star in an otherwise dark and empty expanse. Breathe deep, and imagine this light is coming closer to you. Imagine breathing it in … and this light flows into your hands. Imagine that your hands become full of this light … they are bright, and warm, and relaxed. With your next exhale, imagine that your hands and this light melt away, and you say:

My hands are the Mother's hands.

Breathe deep. And breathe this light down into your feet. Feel them becoming full, and warm, and relaxed. With your exhale, they melt away and you say:

My feet are the Mother's feet.

Breathe deep, and continue this practice, filling and melting your arms, legs, belly, chest, back, buttocks, sex, shoulders, neck, throat, and head, each time affirming the particular area of the body as being identified with the Mother.

When you have done every area of your body that you can think of, breathe this light into your whole body all at once and allow the entirety of your body to melt away as you say:

My body is the Mother's body.

Continue to repeat this as you breathe, slow and deep. Feel how your body is an extension of the Great Mother, who nourishes and sustains us all. Notice whatever insights may arise for you. When you are ready, open your eyes and imagine coming back into your own body. Wiggle your fingers and your toes. Stretch. End your session as you would normally. If you are having trouble coming back, make sure to look at your reflection in a mirror and say your full name three times. Touch a piece of iron or hematite. Get something to eat. Take a shower. Record your experiences in your journal.

Contracts, Boundaries, and Responsibility

Once we feel we are ready to embark on possession, we need to establish some ground rules. First, it is a good idea to only do this work with spirits with whom you are intimately familiar. Think of possession as a type of sex. Are you going to have unprotected sex with someone you just met? Without trust? Considering that there is no such thing as a "possessory condom," this makes our preliminary work with a spirit or deity essential to our safety. Some spirits just don't "smell" right. Trust your intuition. If anything feels off, then that might be a good indicator that their energy is not right for you. Or at least not right for this particular moment.

In the Faery Tradition, individual covens or lineages tend to form their practices around varied deity forms, making these the most common spirits worked with in terms of possessory training. In this, Faery is wide open: "All gods are Faery gods," which is to say, whichever gods or goddesses with whom you already work are just as valid as any other. If you have a preexisting working relationship with a deity, and you have a desire to work with that deity in a more intimate way than your current practice offers, then your choice is clear. But for those who may not have a particular deity or spirit with whom they work, this requires us to make some choices.

The first choice to make is whether or not you actually wish to engage in this work. Reading about it is one thing. But practicing it is quite another. And due to the intimate and sexual nature of this work, it would be inappropriate to simply jump into it with your eyes closed. Choosing just any spirit or deity for this work because possession sounds cool and you need a partner is really no different than a virgin hooking up with a stranger at a party because they wanted to "get it over with." Possession should be a beautiful experience, and with the proper care and preparation it can be just that. But if undertaken lightly and with no foresight, it can be a traumatic experience akin to any physical-world encounter that we may feel fits the sexual analogy.

Another thing to keep in mind is that this work is not for everyone. Even some Faery initiates do not work with possession. If you are not personally called to this work, then I would suggest simply reading about it and leaving it alone until such time as you may be inspired to use these techniques with a particular spirit of whom you are fond.

When this work is being taught in a coven, class, or one-on-one setting, there are experienced people present for real-time reactions. Even in long distance sessions over the phone or webcam, there is the opportunity to interject should something drift and miss the mark. Alas, here in book form we do not have that luxury, which is to say that *you* do not have that luxury. What is that luxury, you might ask? That of a tether, a life vest, a safety net. You will have to be all of these things for yourself, which means you have to be smart. You have to know your own mind. If you suffer from severe mental illness or have serious trouble distinguishing between fantasy and reality, then this probably is not the work for you. If you are depressed or suffering from anxiety, then this may not be the work for you.

You also have to take precautions. Make sure that your area is safe. My advice would be to pay extra caution to clothing or jewelry items that may get caught on candleholders or robe sleeves that get burned in candle flames. If you are in an altered state of awareness, then you may not realize right away if your robe sleeve has caught fire, so better to nix the robe and go sleeveless. (I just might be making an argument for going skyclad for safety purposes!) You may also wish to have a fire extinguisher at the ready and make sure that there are no objects that can be easily disturbed should you begin moving or dancing.

And finally, if you feel you have trouble coming back, or are experiencing any other sort of mental, spiritual, or psychic disturbance during one of your sessions, perform the Banishing rite and then focus on self-care, such as grounding work. Eat some food (whole grains and proteins are good—avoid alcohol and a lot of sugar). Stretch your muscles. Go outside and feel your feet on the soil. Take a shower. Have a cup of tea. Turn on your favorite song. Watch a favorite sitcom on TV. Do something *mundane*.

JOURNALING: A Pact with a Spirit

When engaging our chosen spirit, we must first decide on the details of our contract. This journaling exercise will give us a magical space in which to explore the boundaries that are necessary toward establishing and maintaining a healthy relationship with the spirit with whom we have chosen to become more intimate. If done properly, it need only be done once per spirit, unless you later decide you wish to change the details of your agreement, in which case you will need to engage in a new negotiation.

Items needed:

A pen

Your journal

A candle of your choosing to represent the spirit with whom you will be working

Open the Way and then journal for five to ten minutes on the following questions: How long will you wish to be in the possessory state? Fifteen minutes? Half an hour? An hour or more? What is it that you wish to accomplish by having the spirit move through you? (Provide healing? Help writing an invocation? Something else?) What are some things that you DO NOT wish to do while in the possessory state? (Like engage in unsafe activities, violence, unwanted sexual behavior, etc.) State your boundaries. Be specific.

Once finished, rewrite this into a simple list of rules that will be a contract with the spirit. We will use this contract in our later work. You may wish to embellish it with the sigil of your spirit and any other symbols that you feel are pertinent. "Sign" it by making a mark on it with some of your body fluid. Empower it in the way in which you would normally charge a sigil, making sure to include the presence of the spirit and feeling their blessing and consent. (Honestly, if the spirit does not want to consent then nothing will happen and you will have wasted your time.)

Alternatively, you may create a sigil *of the contract itself* (perhaps along with your spirit's sigil) and use that instead of the "longhand" version for use in later ritual workings. It makes for an easier (and far more Witchy-feeling) tool during the ritual. End as normal.

EXERCISE: Opening to Divinity

In keeping with the tradition of the Hidden Kingdom, this exercise is inspired by one given in the fantasy novels of the late Robert Jordan in his series *The Wheel of Time*. I highly recommended this series to my Faery students, as it gives some incredibly lucid descriptions of the use of magic through an elemental lens.

Open the Way. Imagine yourself in the form of a new rosebud. With petals tightly bound, held together by the outer green sepals. Imagine that the rosebud is growing…and now blooming…silken petals in vibrant color unfolding. Imagine the distinctive scent of the rose as you expand into full bloom. Feel your energy body unfolding with the petals. Feel the ecstatic joy of being this flower…your delicate petals extended outward in exuberant celebration. Feel this for a moment.

Now, imagine that there is a divine light emanating from the heavens. Warm…like golden sun. Feel this sunlight warming your petals. Imagine this light shining *through* your petals. Notice what it feels like. Now, imagine that you can *hear* this light. What does it sound like? What does it smell like? Taste like? Does it inspire any thoughts or emotions?

After you have done this for a few minutes, call your power back from your Star Goddess candle and end as normal. Write down your experiences in your journal.

———

Once you have familiarized yourself with the basics of this exercise, you can feel free to use imagery that is specific to whatever spirit or deity with whom you wish to work. For example, if working with the goddess Hecate, we might imagine ourselves as a garlic flower, instead, to keep with her symbolic associations.

EXERCISE: The Candle of Possession

This is a simple exercise used in order to strengthen both your ability to invoke a spirit into your body and also to establish a strong boundary. It should be repeated periodically over the course of your magical career, but especially in the days prior to engaging a formal ritual possession with a spirit or deity.

Items needed:
A candle representing the chosen spirit or deity
Your spirit contract or empowered sigil for the contract

Open the Way. In your aligned state, open yourself up to the presence of your spirit or deity. Perform an invocation to them and light their candle. As you focus on the candle flame, imagine that the presence of your spirit is slowly growing within you. You may wish to chant, sing, or hum in order to help build this presence. Or, you may wish to simply chant their name over and over in a rhythm. You may imagine their presence like a light that fills you from your feet all the way up to your crown. When you feel that this presence is reaching a peak, take a deep breath and imagine collecting all of this power and consolidating it into a single breath. With your exhale, send this power into the flame of the spirit candle. Feel it move out from you and how this presence is no longer inside you. Say a prayer of thanks and extinguish the candle. Take three breaths of silence and then repeat the whole process from start to finish. Do this at least three to five times. End as normal. Record your experiences in your journal.

EXERCISE: Pulling the Thread

Once we have been able to touch the presence of our desired spirit, we can begin to gradually take them into our body/mind/soul structure. This exercise can be used to help build our skill in pulling them inside as well as give us an easy means of letting them go afterward. Like the previous exercise, this should be repeated periodically so as to keep us skilled in its use, but especially prior to any ritual working in which possession is a part.

Open the Way. Perform the Candle of Possession for your chosen spirit. Focus on your spirit and imagine that there is a silver thread that connects you to them. This thread flows into your holy daemon, down into your fetch, and up into your talker. Take a few moments to really feel this thread. When you are ready, imagine slowly pulling this thread so that your chosen spirit is drawn closer and closer to you with every slow, deep breath. When you are finally able to pull the spirit in through your daemon/crown, pay attention to what this feels like. Feel this spirit being pulled into your daemon, fetch, and finally your talker. Feel how your souls have created a space to hold this spirt within yourself, guided and protected by your holy daemon.

When you are ready to draw things to a close, take a breath and imagine letting go of the thread, which has the effect akin to letting go of a helium balloon. On your exhale release your connection … relax your body. End your session as you would normally and—as always—record your experiences in your journal.

EXERCISE: Automatic Writing

Now we will take this to the next level. This exercise is about allowing our talker to be more active during the process while still focusing on the spirit/deity.

Items needed:

A pen

Your journal

Open the Way. Perform the Candle of Possession and then Pulling the Thread. When you feel the spirit/deity's presence within you, take hold of your pen and just allow it to flow over the page. Don't worry at first about forming words or complete sentences; just allow whatever to come through. You may find that you are drawing or doodling. That's fine; just allow the presence to guide your hand. You may find that you want to draw certain shapes … or that certain words are coming through. Try not to think about them in the moment. Do this for at least five minutes. Then read over what you wrote; what the *spirit* wrote. Does it make sense? If not, do you notice any patterns, such as repeated words or letters or even shapes or symbols? End as you would normally.

———

This begins the work of engaging the talker in this process. I would recommend that you repeat this exercise several times over the course of a month to really get things going before you attempt the next one.

Dealing with the Censor

For a majority of people doing this work, the main obstacle will be self-doubt. Like so much in life, this demon, more than most, causes good people to fail, sometimes before they even begin. Confidence is a powerful antidote, but like courage not being the absence of fear, confidence is not the absence of doubt. It is a *belief*. And that belief is deeply rooted in *trust*.

It might sound like a pretty tall order to ask you to simply have faith in yourself, but that's exactly what I'm going to do. And either you will or you won't. And it's really pretty much that simple. Either you will make the *decision* to have confidence in your capacity to learn to do this work … to talk to spirits … to enlist their aid … or you won't. You must simply decide that you are more powerful than you know or have known. You will choose to believe in your higher self, your holy daemon, that it is guiding you, and wants to protect you. And that will be that. You don't need to place your faith in anything else … not in me, not in the Faery Tradition, not in Witch-craft … just in *yourself*. You do not need to be a perfect being to make this happen. You are flawed, as we are *all* flawed. But the Blue God is your *holy daemon*, and he is the child of the Mother, just as you are the child of the Mother. The spark of divinity is within you. You only need learn to kindle it into a fire.

We are charged with building our inner flame, our holy fire. And when our very human doubts will undoubtedly arise, we will greet them head-on. We will look at them square in the eye and allow them to wash over and through us, like our fears. And then we will tell it where to go and what to do. And it will assist us in building our fire. When it arises and we *notice*, we will take our power back from it and we will use that power to redouble our efforts to strengthen our practice.

Litany Against Doubt

The demon doubt that rises here
Shall fuel the building of my fire
Until my fire is burning bright
And then my demon tends the fire.

Let your doubt point you in the right direction. Feel your doubt. And then … do it any-way. Let go … say what wants to be said…

EXERCISE: Speaking with Their Voice

Similar to Automatic Writing, this exercise is about engaging talker in this work and strengthening that connection.

Items needed:
A recording device or app

Open the Way. If you will be recording your session, begin recording now. Perform the Candle of Possession and then Pulling the Thread. When you feel the spirit/de-ity's presence within you, take a moment to really identify what their presence feels like. Check in with your body and your emotions. Making these sensations a focal-point, begin to hum softly, imagining this sound strengthening your connection to the spirit and helping them to move through you and into your voice. You may be inspired to sing or to form words, but don't force it…just allow whatever comes through to come through. Spend at least five to ten minutes with this and then end as normal.

As an alternative, you may wish to have a poem or invocation prepared. In this case, recite this instead of humming. You may find that you are inspired to go off script but even if not, just focus on the sensation of the spirit while you vocalize. Even if you just default back into humming, singing, chanting, etc. you will have engaged and potentially honed your skill a bit. As always, repetition is necessary for a skillful practice. So practice, practice, practice! This should be repeated at least until you have achieved some moderate successes with it. If after several weeks of concerted effort you have still not had success, then you may move on, resolving to make another series of attempts at a later time.

———

If you have a good session then your recording can be useful in helping you learn to retain more and more of the experience intact, as well as allow us to have the information of whatever transpired immediately at our fingertips. Often, we will forget certain parts of a session, only to have it all come back when we hear the recording in our own (sometimes somewhat altered) voice. I find this especially useful when the spirit is offering poetry or song but even sometimes when just offering observations or other commentary.

Returning the Center

The skills that we are seeking in this work do not come easily to many. For a few, this will all already be second nature, or these exercises may awaken something or help you connect the dots, and you will be able to do this work easily on your own. For the rest of us, we will need to put in many hours of practice, training our minds and our spirits exactly how we wish them to work together, in concert with our holy daemon. This is all an experiment, of sorts, in human consciousness—an experiment that has been going on for at least 100,000 years. And in all experiments, there is the chance that something may go awry. Since we are working with opening up our consciousness, it is a good idea to remember our foundational skills of grounding and alignment. If you feel at any time that you are having trouble coming back or that you are having thoughts that are disturbing or you feel are not your own, stop this work immediately and revisit your basic grounding practices. Remember all the usual tricks: touching a piece of iron, tasting salt, drinking water, eating protein, eating a small amount of chocolate, taking a shower, etc. If all else fails, call a friend, turn on the TV, and watch something light.

Summoning the Bones

Since one of the specific benefits of the possessory experience is that of oracular divination, we are going to combine possession with one of the most primal forms of traditional divination short of reading entrails. That is, throwing the bones.

There is something so very Witchy about throwing the bones. Beyond just the act of throwing a tangible object and seeing where and how it falls, to know that this object you now hold was once part of a living creature that had its own consciousness, not all that unlike our own, reminds us of the fragility of life and acts as a point of connection between these two worlds.

Some specialty shops carry animal bones for purchase and you can make quite a collection from teeth, vertebrae, and the odd baculum or rib. Each of them can carry a different meaning for you, based on the type of animal and the specific type of bone, and over time you will have created a divination set unique to you.

Because they are bone, they are associated with the dead. It is quite easy to draw in the spirits of the dead when using actual bone, making their use hard to argue against.

Almost immediately I can hear my vegan friends in protest, but hear me out! In the Craft we honor the forces of life and death. The bones of an animal carry the spiritual essence of that animal whether we like it or not. I am not advocating the killing of animals (though I personally have no problem with it if done quickly and for food, as I am a definite omnivore), and I can see no greater way to honor the spirit of the animal than to use its remains to help re-sacralize the spiritual relationship between humankind and the rest of the animal kingdom. But if that is not enough to convince you, then you will be happy to know that I have thought of you and present a vegan alternative: crystals, stones, and wood. These can all be seen as the "bones" of the mineral and plant kingdoms, and you can even add to this list certain manufactured items, such as jewelry, or other charms, chosen for their symbolic nature.

In fact, even if you *are* going to be using actual animal bones as part of your divination set, it would be wise to add items from these other categories as well. You will want a system that is well rounded, with pieces that represent both positive and negative qualities, as well as certain archetypal energies. For more on how to create a divinatory throwing system using bones and other curios (and how to effectively use it), see Michele Jackson's excellent book, *Bones, Shell, and Curios.*

DIVINATION: Throwing the Bones

This is a simple method for performing an oracular divination while in the possessed state.

Items needed:

A personal collection of bones, shells, crystals, pieces of wood, jewelry, and other
   curios that you will use to form your personal set

A cloth on which to throw the items

A pouch or bowl in which to hold the items before throwing

A recording device or app

Prepare the items in the pouch or bowl. Lay out the throwing cloth.

Open the Way. Start your recording. Perform whatever additional exercises or techniques you feel are necessary to effectively call your chosen spirit or deity into the possessory state. While in this state, toss the items onto the cloth and observe how they land. Some may fall near each other or even touch. Others might be far away. Allow the spirit to speak about this. What do you feel? Allow the voice to come through. Allow the spirit-sight to draw different associations, new conclusions. Allow the spirit to give the reading; you are just providing the vessel.

After a few to several minutes, thank the spirit as you would normally and end your session. You may journal your experiences now, and again after listening to your recording at a later date. Make sure you are fully grounded before driving or performing other dangerous tasks.

————

If you take the time to work with these (or similar) exercises, then you will find that it is much easier than you may think in order to have these types of ecstatic experiences. If you are performing these alone, remember to take extra precautions for your physical safety, and if you start to feel like you are experiencing depression, anxiety, or bouts of "missing time," discontinue the practice, perform the Waters of Purity rite, and practice grounding techniques instead.

CHAPTER 9

OCCULTUS MALEFICUM: THE HIDDEN ART OF OFFENSIVE WITCHCRAFT

Black magic operates most effectively in preconscious, marginal areas.
Casual curses are the most effective.
—WILLIAM S. BURROUGHS

This is usually how it starts. Something happened that crossed a line. Perhaps it had been building up for a while…a series of disrespects or even worse…just now finally reaching a limit. Or it could have been sudden, perhaps a violent or cruel act that caused harm to you or someone you love. Or even on a larger scale, a political act that harms the people, the land, the innocent…while billionaires and bureaucrats reap the rewards of a skewed system. You are *angry*, and rightly so. So what are you going to do about it?

You're a Witch. Witches have a long historical record of cursing their enemies. From blighting crops to drying up cows to tormenting their victims with their demon familiars, the stories of—and belief in—the efficacy of the Witches' curse have endured from the earliest stretches of history and into the present day. At least this is true where *non*-Witches are concerned. For actual Witches, however, the path forward isn't quite as clear.

In 1954, a public relations campaign began that changed how much of the world saw the practice (and religion) of Witchcraft. That year Gerald Gardner's book *Witchcraft Today* was released. This was the first book written by an actual Witch, and he intended to set the record straight when it came to misconceptions of this often-mis-understood religion.

As Wicca took its place in the public eye, it found itself in a position to shape popular opinion, and so it took to the task of presenting to the world the truth about Witchcraft. This truth included certain religious guidelines, most notably "The Wiccan Rede," which set forth a fundamental guiding principle of the religion that intimated that practitioners should do no harm, and "The Threefold Law," a magical tenet suggesting that energies raised and sent by the practitioner will be returned upon the practitioner three times over. I have it on good authority that this is not exactly what this means to those actually initiated into the Gardnerian tradition of Wicca (where all of Wicca originates), but whether or not the Threefold Law is actually what it sounds like is beyond the point. What matters is that most people *think* that is what it means, and because of this it has served what I believe to have been its main and original purpose: to soothe the fears of a largely Christian society so that those who identified as Witches might be able to creep up out of the shadows and stretch, just a bit more. While it very well may have deep esoteric meaning for the initiates of Gardnerian Craft, for the vast majority of those practicing some other form of Wicca outside of the traditional framework of initiatory lineage (as well as those who are just casually informed about the Craft), the Threefold Law is just that: a *law*. And anything outside of that law is out of bounds, and not "authentic." This has sometimes proven to be a bit of a wedge when it comes to other traditions of Witchcraft that do not adhere to the publicly accessible version of Wiccan praxis.

This public relations campaign has been largely effective. Especially where Neopagans and their supporters are concerned. I would venture to say that the vast majority of those who identify as Pagan today are at least aware of the Threefold Law and Wiccan Rede, even if not by name. Word on the street is that a *real Witch* would never violate someone's free will, and so a practitioner who turned to the darker magic of *maleficum* would be demonstrating their opposition to an authentic Craft. Some modern Witches might even be *afraid* of throwing a curse, thinking that to do so would rebound on them "times three." (Apparently scientific thinking is a rarity in Witchcraft circles today. I'm thinking that Newton would roll over in his grave.)

Modern Witchcraft had set to distance itself from its historical predecessor, which *delighted* in the very acts the contemporary incarnation would publically condemn. But even still, certain elements have remained, hinting at an older worldview that was in opposition to the now near-official position of the growing movement. Even a central liturgical device used in almost every Wiccan tradition—the Charge of the Goddess—was based on older folklore which explicitly described the Witch as a poisoner who was to torment and kill her oppressors. Those parts were concealed and rewritten, giving us the beautiful poem from Doreen Valiente that we all know and love today. But as beautiful and inspiring as that is, it also quite clearly shows a move (even if perhaps well-intentioned) toward the "Disneyfication" of the Craft, in which a vital part of our heritage and history is whitewashed and those who possess ethics or morality that is different from the established norm are rejected and reviled.

In Leland's *Aradia*, we see the original text upon which Valiente's is based, and we see quite a different picture of the Craft. We are presented a Craft that is a religion of thieves, murderers, wanderers, vagrants, and the poor. Witchcraft is their redemption, their defense against a system that would oppress and disempower them, a system that very probably was the reason for their loathsome state to begin with. Witchcraft gave these people a means to fight back, and often the stakes would be life and death.

Today, we find ourselves in a position that it not entirely different. Certain segments of our own populations are increasingly vulnerable to oppression and violence, even from our own government. As a white cisgendered male, I am privileged in that I do not personally fear when I am pulled over for speeding, for example, where my friends with darker skin do not share in my sense of personal security. They routinely prepare for the worst in a way I had never even imagined, because for them it *is* a matter of life and death. As a gay person, I have been on the receiving end of discrimination, threats, and even violence, and so I do know something about how the ruling class subjugates its people. And as a warlock, I know the importance of putting my magic where my mouth is.

The Faery Tradition of Witchcraft is decidedly at odds with its more publicly recognized cousin in that we have no stated ethic that would ostensibly prevent us from throwing a curse. No Wiccan Rede or Law of Three exists within our lore and so many have taken that to mean that in Faery it's free rein when it comes to darker magic. The fact that Victor Anderson reportedly threw hexes at his enemies probably did very little to quell this belief, and soon it became a sort of badge of honor amongst our clan that we had no prohibition against such work. This, of course, was a double-edged sword, but in Witchcraft is there any other kind?

Faery is a warrior tradition. When practiced correctly, Faery is a martial art in that it can provide a means toward self-development as well as self-defense. When we are attacked we do not turn the other cheek, but neither will we mindlessly react with violence, magical or otherwise. A warrior will mindfully respond by assessing the situation and then deciding on an effective course of action. There are times in which that action may need to be aggressive in nature. To illustrate this, I will share my version of a story that was shared with me from Anaar, and which was shared with her from Victor Anderson.

MYTH: The Warrior's Choice

Once, a long time ago, there was a man who lived a simple life on a farm with his family. He had not always been a simple man, for he used to be a samurai, and a very skilled one at that. He had spent many years in military service but times had changed and the samurai were no longer needed by this new world. He chose the simple life of a farmer, and had come to regret the act of killing; and so, hiding away his armor and his sword, he swore never to take another human life again.

Many years passed and he lived a hard but happy life. He loved his wife and his child, and their farm provided all they needed to live. One day word came that there was another ex-samurai who was terrorizing the countryside. He would travel from village to village, challenging the strongest men to fight. If they refused, he would burn and destroy their village, forcing them to do battle. If they agreed, he would best them and then burn the village anyway. He had done this to many villages, and none could oppose him. It seemed that the evil samurai would destroy the entire country.

On this day, the farmer was out in the field when he saw smoke rising over the horizon and he knew that the next village had fallen to the evil man. Just then a man in dark armor rode up to the edge of the farmer's field.

"I know who you are," the evil samurai said. "You were once among the best of the samurai, but you have disgraced your training. You hide away like a coward. Come out and fight me!"

"I will not," the farmer said. "I have sworn never again to take a human life. If you wish to do battle, just slay me and let it be done."

"No!" the evil samurai said. "If you do not fight me, then I will burn your farm, I will rape and kill your wife and murder your child. If you do not fight me then I will kill everyone in the village and their deaths will be upon your head."

Daunted, the farmer agreed. "Because you force me," he said, "I will do as you ask. Return tomorrow at sunrise and we will do battle."

As the night grew long, the farmer went to his old hiding place and retrieved his armor and sword. All night he cleaned and polished his armor and weapon, his training as immediate as the back of his own hand. When the sun rose, he stood in his field, the morning sun gleaming off his meticulously polished armor, and the evil samurai approached.

"Now we do battle," the evil samurai said. "I have waited for this day a long time."

The farmer bowed in reverence and respect and then drew his sword and they commenced their fight. Swords clashed and armor was struck. Each drew from their considerable training as they lunged and struck and blocked each other's blows. "I do not wish to hurt you," the farmer said. "Lay down your arms and let us resolve this peacefully."

"I will not!" the evil samurai said. "I would rather die than surrender. I look forward to your death and the death of your family!"

"Very well, then." Knowing that there was no other way, the farmer moved as quick as lightning and struck the killing blow, and the evil samurai was no more. His lifeless body fed the land with his villainous blood and the farmer was filled with a great sadness. He had gone against his solemn vow and had again taken a human life. He was heartbroken—not just for his broken promise, but also for this man, evil though he was. Now that he was dead there could be no change, no healing, no reconciliation. A heaviness sat in the farmer's heart like a stone, and it weighed on him heavily for many days.

Soon the nearby villages caught word of the death of the evil samurai at the farmer's hands and they began to rejoice. The many who had been living in fear now could live freely. But the farmer was not happy.

A monk came to visit the farmer to speak of what happened, and the farmer told him of his vow and how it had been broken.

"It is indeed a dishonor to break your vow," the monk said. "But do you regret what you did?"

And the farmer replied, "No! I would do it again."

Some choices are like no choice. We may think we know how we should act but life will demand we make difficult choices for the greater good. Was it "bad" to take a human life? Yes. But was it "wrong"? Sometimes there are no good choices. And we are asked to make them anyway.

———

When we strip away the layers of religion that have been woven over the magical system that is the heart of all Witchcraft, we find that the magical system does not impose an ethical code upon its adherents. We are each asked to do what we believe to be "right," based on the situation we find ourselves in. "A healthy priest makes all things sound."[53]

While many a Neopagan practitioner will cite "karma" as a reason not to engage in martial magic, the Faery Witch sees the fallacy of such an argument. The world is not a place in which all things are fair and balanced and good. If we or our loved ones are attacked, there is no shame in defending them. This, of course, is not an attempt to convince the pacifist otherwise, but to remind the Witch of their heritage and history, as well as the reality of the world in which we live. Like it or not, the universe is a violent place. Those in the Craft who will do what is necessary in times of need should not be vilified for doing so. To assert that those who would engage in cursing are "not real Witches" would be hurtful, if it weren't *laughable*. The assertion is demonstrably false, as our very history proves. But even still, to each their own. Some Witches might be fine with giving away their teeth in some misguided attempt at "enlightenment," but most often what they really find is an artificial sweetness the likes of which causes cancer on a spiritual level.

This idea that we must *never* cause harm is ludicrous; to eat, we cause harm to the animal or the plant that feeds us. To breathe, we kill microorganisms, and even to clean our house is to harm and kill the bacteria that would invade our bathroom surfaces. Even in our dealings with other human beings, there are times in which we may need to perform actions against another that are, in some form, violent. One would certainly hope that these cases would be exceedingly rare, but for self-defense I for one am in favor of the hex or curse.

If not for self-defense, then what about the defense of one's family or the innocent? In a warrior tradition, we are asked to mindfully respond to every situation and do what is needed in order to make it *right*. If a rapist or a murderer were threatening

———

53. Faery oral tradition, credited to Faery initiate, teacher, and author Francesca DeGrandis.

our community, would we sit around and raise a cone of rose-pink love-light in the hopes of converting them to a greater understanding? Over the course of over thirty years practicing the Craft at the time of this writing, I have known several people who have gone exactly this route and I have yet to see this succeed on any level. At best, it leaves the practitioners with the smug sense of having "done what they could" (they didn't) and at worst it simply enables the evil to continue unabated.

If Witchcraft is a nature religion then we must be prepared to take our teachings from nature and not from some fantasy of how we wished the world to be. If I am struck, it is natural for me to defend, but I will not act in anger or for revenge. I will be calculated, using only as much force as necessary in order to subdue my attacker, and preferably using their own energy against them. Like a form of magical *aikido*, if they push, we *fall*, bringing them down with their own force.

My observation is that cursing, like all of magic, is on a spectrum. On the smaller end, we have jinxes—little annoyances that we might place in someone's path, perhaps to distract them or slow them down. Though there is no traditional distinction in Faery Tradition between a hex and a curse, I personally feel that hexes would come next in our spectrum, being those types of workings that are more than just an annoyance, perhaps encouraging someone to fail at some endeavor or to cause them to suffer in some way. Curses definitely are the "big deal." These are workings intended to cause harm, more than just suffering. They are not something in which I would engage for a trivial reason. I have rarely found it necessary to cast a hex (though I certainly have done so). If I have come to the point in which I feel I am justified in placing a *curse*, then things have gotten serious. Both for them and for myself.

Even if we are not intending to engage in the act of throwing curses ourselves, it would do us well to familiarize ourselves with the subject if for no other reason than it would prove useful in learning how to defend against them or remove them from others. Where we are fond of telling ourselves that those who would have enough power to do such a thing should have "evolved" to the point in which they would never engage in maleficum, again we find ourselves living out a saccharine fantasy that bears no resemblance to actual reality. *A lot* of people throw curses, and a good number of them are at least moderately skilled at doing so. It doesn't take much, actually. Just some intense emotions and a moment of clear focus. And for some people, magic is a natural talent. And especially if they are untrained (or unaware), then we can find ourselves in the middle of a very messy problem.

Usually the person throwing the curse is a family member or loved one (for only someone who is bound to you in love can hate you enough to throw an effective curse). I have seen this in my clients over the years, and have talked about this at length with my peers who likewise work magically with the public. It happens. And it's very real.

I have been on the receiving end of a curse on more than one occasion. The first time was when I was just nineteen. I had a quick and intense love affair with another magical practitioner, who proved to be just a little bit unstable. When I declined their offer to leave my life and family behind me to join them hundreds of miles away, they decided on revenge. Several days after he had returned to his home city I received a letter that was a dark love poem, the sort that implied "if I can't have you, no one can." It was striking, but I didn't think much of it other than it seemed a bit overly dramatic at the time.

That night, while at work, I started to have a strange experience. Out of the blue, I started to get fuzzy-headed, and my vision became impaired, my sight appearing as if viewed through rippling water and a dark, creeping cloud slowly rolling in from my periphery. I also noticed that I was becoming verbally confused, and the formation of complete sentences was becoming increasingly difficult. I had to leave my shift early and make my way home. This proved to be a difficult task, as by this point my sight had almost completely left me, with only a small area of the field of my vision unaffected. By the time I got home I had the mother of all splitting headaches and I immediately lay down. Not ever having had a migraine before, I had no idea what to expect, and the pain became so intense that I was convinced I must have had a tumor. But no matter what it was, there was nothing I could do but bury my face in my pillow in a dark room with quiet music playing in the background.

I passed out and dreamt of this person standing at the foot of my bed. They crawled up on top of me and the experience was non-consensual to say the least. The next day I was still experiencing pain and difficulties, though not quite as intense as the night before. Later that evening, I attended the weekly healing night at the local metaphysical shop. I didn't talk about my magical experience, as I didn't want to feed into the fear, and truth be told I was still a bit in disbelief. (Surely I was just being dramatic, no?) What the reader told me gave me chills. They told me immediately that I was under psychic attack, that the attacker was male, and that I knew who they were. They even were able to tell me the direction that this person was from our position, which I knew to accurately reflect the location of their home. They worked their mojo on me, the headache lessened, and I walked away a believer. I went home and proceeded to perform a reversing spell, burning the dark love letter in my cauldron with some reversing herbs and setting up a mirror to reflect the fire light in the direction of their home. I chanted and raised energy and felt it all *push* outward as I sent it all back to its source. After it was all done, I felt *much* better and the symptoms did not return.

A few days later I got a call from a mutual friend. She told me that his life had abruptly fallen apart: he lost his job for gross negligence…he was picked up by the police because he matched the description of a criminal…and he ended up having to move, all in the span of just a few days. All of this I took as "proof" that my spell had worked.

Years later I would run into this person once again and I decided to confront him directly about the incident. He confessed and apologized to me for having done it, adding that he had definitely "learned his lesson" when all hell broke loose for him immediately afterward. I decided not to tell him that I had reversed his spell, leaving him to believe that it was the "karmic consequences" of his negative actions. But then, I suppose it really *was* the result of karma, only karma doesn't work on its own. It requires agents to act in the world.

Witches, I believe, are among those agents. We are called to look at the world and to act within it, upon it, to make this world a better place. This doesn't mean that we need to address each and every ill in the world (and certainly not if it means that we would harm ourselves in the process), but we do need to take responsibility for our actions, as well as our *inactions*. When we see evil and we do nothing, then we are in part responsible for it.

If one suspects that the dark arts are at play, the first step would be to do the Waters of Purity rite or some other personal purification exercise. Then we need to ask ourselves *why* we think a hex or curse is at play. It is all too easy to jump to the far more interesting conclusion that one has been hexed rather than face the fact that things just kind of suck because of a lot of really boring mundane reasons, not the least of which is that we are depressed, or unmotivated, or experiencing the denial of any number of our own shadow demons. We shouldn't suspect a curse just because we are having a bad day—or a bad week. If we are having a bad month or a bad year then we might want to do some divination to check things out, but even then, usually there would be other mitigating factors to point in the direction of a curse. Have you been having accidents? Near misses? More than three in a week? What about conflicts with family members or coworkers? Or perhaps it is the area of money. Have you experienced three or more financial losses in a single month that were out of the ordinary? These are not hard and fast rules, but guidelines to get us thinking about how we are viewing the situation. Remember that a large part of magic is *perception*. If we believe that we are cursed then we might as well be.

DIVINATION: To Diagnose a Hex or Curse

Items needed:

A deck of regular playing cards

This technique relies on reading either red or black cards, and nothing else. It can actually be used for any yes/no questions and has been shared in many places and in many variations. This is my favorite.

Open the Way. Shuffle the deck and ask, "Have I been hexed or cursed?" while you are shuffling. Focus on how you feel: on that which would bring you to even ask the question. When you are ready, stop shuffling and deal out five cards in a row facedown. Then one by one, left to right, turn them over. Black cards indicate a no response while red indicates yes. In this you can see the degree of the curse by the presence of red cards. If all five cards are black then the answer is a clear no. If all are red then that is a clear yes. The degree of red to black will determine the severity of the curse, if it is determined there is one.

The spread can be read as follows:

5 black—0 red = No curse or negative magical energies are present.

4 black—1 red = A blip of dark energy exists in your energy field, but likely your natural defenses will ward it off.

3 black—2 red = There are dark energies present. You may have been jinxed.

2 black—3 red = Sufficient dark energies are hanging around you. You may have been hexed. Do a cleansing immediately.

1 black—4 red = There is significant harmful magic in your situation. You have probably been hexed or cursed. Rituals of purification and protection are in order.

0 black—5 red = There is a hex or curse present. It's time to bring out the big guns and get a handle on things again.

If it is revealed that there is dark energy, jinxes, hexes, or curses afoot, then you may shuffle the cards again and ask more specific questions. You will want to determine if it is a jinx, a hex, or a curse. You will want to know if you personally know the caster. (If not, were they hired by someone that you *do* know?) Ask questions that help you determine the who, what, when, where, why, and how. These are *all* important pieces of information that we may need in order to effectively break the curse.

Other divination methods can be employed, as per your personal taste and practice. Many Witches form a special bond with the tarot and seek certain cards for determining the presence of a curse. Cards like the Tower and the Devil carry a particular charge when viewed through the lens of the curse and may indicate the presence of one if they show up in a reading on the subject. A pendulum is a quick and easy tool for determining yes/no questions, and can be used to redirect the flow of energies. Some who develop a practice of throwing bones may have special bones, stones, or other curios that represent a curse to them, making it a particularly useful tool for dealing with this subject. The White Plate method is a favorite among some conjure doctors.[54] In it, they would anoint a candle with oil and then take a white plate, passing it all over the subject and then through the smoke of the candle. If the subject had been cursed, then an image of the tormenting spirit would appear in the smudges on the plate. Many a magical practitioner who deals in this sort of work will have their own preferred methods of diagnosing maleficum.

Should your divinations point toward a curse, it can be quite alarming. But if you or someone you know is plagued by maleficum, you should immediately perform acts to purify and energize your energy body as well as your immediate environment.

Breaking a Curse

As practicing Witches, we have some natural protections against allowing most hexes or curses taking hold. Just like having a healthy physical body helps fight off disease-causing bacteria, so too a healthy energy body can ward off much if not most of the negative energies we encounter on a daily basis. For a Witch of practice and power this protection is increased, another benefit of psychic tools such as the Iron and Pearl Pentacles; they increase our power and our grace. Severity and beauty—two qualities

---

54. See Chas Bogan *The Secret Keys of Conjure*, Llewellyn.

necessary for the work we do between the worlds. As a rule, we Faery dance with spirits, not harass them. But if necessary, we must be prepared to assert our authority.

This authority is that of our own *divine* authority; the holy light of the Star Goddess with us all that is the Blue God, the Dian y Glas, the holy daemon. Our own higher self is the consort and other half of the Star Goddess. We literally see ourselves as being part of the living body of God Herself. "I am a cell in the body of the Goddess!" Victor Anderson once said. "And I demand my rights!"

The basic Faery exercises of Soul Alignment, the Waters of Purity, and working with the Iron and Pearl Pentacles form the basis for a series of practices which are aimed at strengthening the practitioners' magical power as well as their ability to be open to receiving (and sharing) that power. Along with an additional practice of running energy in some form (such as those found in Qi Gong, Tai Chi, Yoga, Reiki, etc.), a powerful method for maintaining psychic and magical health and strength is formed. But even healthy individuals can use an immune boost, from time to time.

EXERCISE: The Violet Shockwave

This is given here as a formal exercise, but it is intended to be a psychic device that can be invoked in an instant, manifesting like a sudden explosion, to cleanse yourself and your immediate environment by scrambling whatever aetheric patterns are present.

As a practice, it should be done sparingly, as prolonged exposure to the particular energy invoked in this exercise can be overtaxing and potentially burn out the practitioner, leaving them unable to sense or move energy, at least for some time afterward. Use with caution and respect.

Open the Way. Orient yourself to the directions. Open yourself to the land and your environment. Even if you are in a building, that building is on the land. Feel the horizon all around you. You stand in the very center of a circle made from the horizon. Feel how you are centered between above and below. Perfectly centered. Our souls aligned, like three lenses, through which you now invoke…

> *Aetheric bolt to earth from heaven*
> *The violet lightning flame,*
> *Which strikes with serpentine precision*
> *And now the slate is clean!*

On the last word of the incantation, a bolt of violet lightning strikes *through* the aligned lenses of your souls, and this violet lighting strikes a violet *flame*…an explosion like a liquid bubble of violet fire erupts from within the alignment in our center and moves outward like a shockwave, burning, transforming, scrambling, scrubbing, breaking, tearing, healing, shaping, *cleansing* everything within you, and as you throw out your arms in a sweeping gesture, now out around you…extending into the whole of the room you are in. Feel your own *divine authority*; your holy fire ignited by the flame of God Herself. This was the lightning bolt from heaven…the current of heavenly fire afforded you by the Star Goddess, a sign of your royal power as a Witch, consort to the Queen of Witches Herself. Bask in this glory, *your* glory. The glory of a cell in the body of the Goddess Herself.

End as normal.

———

If our defenses get low, we might become susceptible to negative energies. When we are sick for a prolonged period, or suffering from depression or anxiety, our natural psychic shields may be insufficient to ward off an actual attack. An effective curse will target a natural weakness and so those who suffer from certain mental conditions may be more susceptible in those areas. But before those without an official diagnosis rejoice their good fortune, anyone and everyone has weaknesses, and so anyone could potentially be infected by maleficum. Everyone has an Achilles' heel. Bottom line: don't get smug. Be impeccable.

The first step toward removing any unwanted or harmful energies or spirits should *always* be the Waters of Purity rite. This should be followed by ritual bathing. Since this is something that most traditions teach early on in magical training I will not spend much time with it here, save to say that in my experience a repetitive practice of it is best. I would usually prescribe thirteen successive nights of said bathing when dealing with a curse, which may or may not be part of a larger series of rites, depending on the severity of the situation. You may wish to incorporate additional energy exercises as a means to keep your energy flowing, lest it stagnate or become "clotted," neither of which are healthy scenarios.

There is no singular rite to undo a hex or a curse in Faery Witchcraft. Each curse is as unique as its caster, and so it is helpful to know where and how the curse originated. Who cast it? Why? What kind of magic was used in its sending? These are helpful questions because the more information we have about the type of spell used against us the better chances we have to more easily deflect it or render it harmless. Again, we may turn to our divination tools for better insights as how best to proceed. Tools like the Lenormand may provide us insights as to what type of magic may work best. Cards like the Whip speak of the necessity of purification, while the Flowers speak of using herbal magic. The Ship that travels over the sea is magical baths, while the Sun is candle work. The Birds may be chanting or singing. The Ring: a pact with a spirit. The Coffin: ancestor work.

We can also use the suits of the tarot to help determine a magical approach. When doing a reading on your situation look for the four suits. Each represents an elemental power and therefore a type of magic which is making itself known through your reading. Pentacles are crystals, herbs, money, and healing magic. Swords are written word spells, sigils, fumigation, and mental magic. Wands are candle spells and fire magic. Cups are potions, waters, teas, and baths, as well as emotional, astral, and trance magic. A predominance of major arcana cards represents the element of aether and speaks of ecstatic workings, divine possession, and the like. A predominance of inverted or reversed cards may indicate that a Reversing is the best course of action.

A Reversing Spell is one that reverses the direction of the cycle of some energy or otherwise sends back said energy to its source. It can be used to turn around a situation against the predicted pattern, or to cause a spell to rebound upon its caster. Since this is the type of spell that uses the attacker's energy against themselves, this is my preferred method of ritual defense against magical attacks, should said attacks be able to penetrate my passive defenses. In my experience, this is a great method to use when dealing with prolonged attacks as this will usually stop (at least temporarily) the attacks, giving us some breathing room to set up protections and whatever additional steps we feel are necessary.

SPELL: Reversing

To reflect a hex or curse back to its source, this spell is based on that which I learned from Hoodoo teacher and shop owner catherine yronwode.[55] It calls for a traditional double-action candle in both red and black. These are usually jumbo sized, and will

---

55. catherine yronwode. "Reversing Spiritual Supplies in Hoodoo Rootwork," accessed August 3, 2017, http://www.luckymojo.com/reversing.html.

be black on the bottom half and red on the top half. These candles are traditionally butted before use, a process achieved by cutting off the tip and then carving a new tip on the bottom, making the black end the new top, thus reversing the physicality of the candle. If you do not have access to a red/black double-action candle you may substitute a black candle, also prepared by butting.

Items needed:
A butted black and red "double-action" candle (alternatively, a black candle will do)
Reversing oil (a traditional blend might contain powdered crabshell and camphor)
A nail or other sharp, pointed instrument to carve on candle wax
A small mirror (alternatively, a small sheet of aluminum foil)
A photo or other "personal concerns" of the target (optional)

Open the Way. Breathe and charge yourself up with wraith force. With the nail or instrument, carve the name of the person who has sent the curse your way onto the black end of the candle, but do so in "mirror writing," that is to say that if held to a mirror the reflection would appear as normal writing. Concentrate on them all the while.

Next, dress the candle with the oil using exaggerated outward motions as if you are throwing or pushing the negative energy outward with each stroke. If you have personal concerns you may add them to the now-oiled candle. If you have their picture, dress it with the oil as well and then place facedown on your altar and place the mirror over it, faceup. If not, just place the mirror on your altar. Now place the candle on top of the mirror or foil. You may wish to melt the end of the candle first to give it added stability. Light the candle and say, with absolute conviction:

> *Candle turned against itself*
> *I conjure you to now repel*
> *The darkness and invading force*
> *By light reflected to its source.*

Spend a few moments in that state of Enchantment, feeling the wraith force of your spell reversing the flow of energies away from you and back to their point of origin, the mirror assisting in their reflection. When you are ready you may end as normal and allow the candle to burn all the way down.

The remains are traditionally buried at a crossroads, but the mirror may be reclaimed as long as it is intact and you do not look at your reflection within it. Wash it in salted water to which you have added hyssop and a bit of rosemary, then wrap and keep for any future reversing spells you may perform.

———

The beauty about this type of spell is that in the event that you are incorrect about the origin of the curse there will be no ill effect upon the one mistaken for the culprit. In this case the spell would likely do nothing, though it *may* actually find the one truly responsible in spite of your mistake, *if* your spirits are powerful and clever enough, that is.

RITE: The Left-Hand Wheel

This is my version of a traditional Faery spell to reverse the direction of a tenacious situation, or when working against a recognized impetus.

Items needed:
A candle (your Star Goddess candle will do)
Your ritual blade

Open the Way. Light your candle and cast a circle. Invoke the Iron Pentacle into your body and then from that space invoke the Pearl: Love, Law, Knowledge, Power, and Wisdom. Allow the Pearl to move you into a space of open acceptance.

Feeling this state, call up the situation you wish to change. Feel it here with you in the circle. Feel the flow of its energy moving clockwise in the circle. It is natural for it to move this way.

Now, take hold of your blade in your left hand. Hold the knife in the flame of the lit candle, feeling it charge up as it heats. Say:

> *By heat of fire and cold of steel,*
> *A march toward destiny, although:*
> *Widdershins reverse the flow!*
> *I now turn the left-hand wheel!*

Silently, move to the north and stab your blade into the energetic band of the circle. Feeling the blade enmeshed with the energy of the circle, drag the circle counterclockwise a full 360 degrees, feeling the entirety of the circle beginning to spin like a top. Building energy with your breath, send this spinning power flying off to disrupt the natural direction of the energy. End your circle as normal.

Occultus Maleficum

Despite the negative press the art of cursing has received, the ways of maleficum in traditional Craft have boldly continued, if often quietly under the surface. A common saying in the Craft is "A Witch who cannot hex cannot heal." This is a reminder that magic in itself is *amoral*; it does not possess some inherent ethical or moral quality. It is simply a force of nature. It can be no more "good" or "evil" than a river, or a forest fire, or an earthquake. Certainly, we might drown in the river, or be burned in the fire, or we might lose our home in the earthquake, but these things are not moral or immoral … they simply *are*. We would not waste our time blaming the river or the fire for what it had taken from us. We would work to rebuild, to heal. Magic simply *is*. What is positive or negative is the intention behind the working. Just like the electrical current that is used to power your home or to execute a murderer, the magic behind both is the same.

Our intention is a type of current that we can tap into, as are our emotions. In fact, we need to bring the two together as one in order to effectively petition our daemon for the power to do effective magic. This is another facet of the soul alignment which we have been working with thus far. Once talker and fetch are in harmony then petitioning the daemon for a magical working becomes increasingly easier.

All magic requires some level of skill. But magic for, let's say, prosperity, doesn't carry the same level of danger that a curse would. Certainly, there is risk in all magic, for we are engaging the intricate web of universal possibilities and it is nearly impossible to see all the potential outcomes of the spell we may wish to cast. This is why it is generally taught that the first step to any spell is divination. When we use our divinatory tools we are given a deeper perspective, which (hopefully) we will then use to better steer the direction of our magic.

In Faery Tradition, it is often taught that one must first be "clean" in order to throw a curse and remain unaffected. This is only a half-truth, as in reality there is *no way* to be unaffected by *any* spell that we cast. The energies of every spell we cast move through us *first*, and so what we mean by "being clean" is having no energetic blocks that could potentially and adversely affect the flow of magic, thus impairing the spell. When dealing with energies of a more negative nature, the stakes are raised to the next level. Those blocks are potential weaknesses, and if we have weaknesses within ourselves that can give that negative energy a then we may suffer accordingly. Imagine a biologist handling a deadly poison. If they are trained and take the proper precautions then they can do so unharmed. But if they are careless, perhaps forgetting to wear protection clothing or working while they are fatigued, they might make a careless mistake and may end up killing themselves. Cursing is dangerous work.

There is one emotion more than others that makes one vulnerable to the dark powers of a curse, and that is guilt. If we are harboring feelings of guilt then this is like a hole in our natural psychic armor. This is what often gets exploited in a hex or a curse. If we wish to be safe from being cursed we must be free of guilt, making purification work essential to our magical survival. We work to minimize the negative effects that the curse we cast will have upon us. But rest assured there is always a price to pay.

One famous story concerning this price is from early Wicca concerning World War II, in which the then-secret coven performed a rite in order to prevent Hitler from invading Britain. They gathered at night to dance skyclad around a fire to raise a Cone of Power, implanting the telepathic message in the minds of Hitler and his army: "You cannot cross the sea, you cannot cross the sea, you cannot come, you cannot come." The magic apparently worked, and Hitler never invaded. The price was paid, according to Gardner, when some of the more elderly coven members died shortly after the working.

This is obviously an extreme example dealing with a large target, but it serves as a clear warning. To effect change requires energy. The larger the change the greater the need for energy to achieve it. With this in mind it should come as little surprise that one of the secrets to effective cursing is to use as little of one's own energy as possible. With workings such as the Reversing, this is relatively easy. But for heavier workings we need to find ourselves an external source of power.

One of the influences (or resonances, depending on how you look at it) of early Faery Tradition is the practice known as Huna. Originally sold as the rediscovered survival of the nearly lost spiritual and magical practices of the precolonial Hawaiian people, it is now quite evident that it is a creation based on the personal research and subsequent practice of the late Max Freedom Long (1890–1971), a white man who appropriated pieces of Hawaiian language and culture to inspire and inform a new spiritual system of magic. Victor Anderson had long claimed to have been one of the last Kahuna,[56] and so his use of Hawaiian terms was no more surprising than when he mentioned practices and myths from the Celtic, or South American, or Basque cultures. He claimed to be racially connected to many cultures in this life, while also drawing from his remembered past life experiences.

While there is a body of lore that is passed in the oral tradition that uses Hawaiian terms and supposed practices, I, as a non-Hawaiian, will refrain from appropriating their culture further and so direct the reader to the invented system of magic, stripped now of its cultural window dressing, which forms the basis for some strains of magical thought in Faery Witchcraft tradition.

Early works regarding the system of Huna described the "Death Prayer," in which the magician enlists the aid of "evil spirits" in order to magically kill their victim. This is necessary for this type of work because the higher self of the magician is the usual source (or at least conduit) of power for their workings, but it is not interested in actions that are not in line with the evolution of the magician's soul development. Without the assistance of one's higher soul, the magician must turn to an alternative power source.

This is not unlike other magical practices, such as Palo or Ceremonial Magic, that harness spirits for their magical power. These spirits are often housed and fed, or sometimes even trapped against their will, depending on the need and the temperament of the individual magician. Indeed, we have even opened the door for that ourselves by working with our Demons as the Witches' familiar. A cautionary word, however, for those who may feel emboldened at the possibility of being able to inflict such a heinous attack on another without fear of retribution or reprisal: a magician's spirits, like the proverbial chickens, always come home to roost. Or feed. Should you ascertain how exactly to enlist the aid of the kind of spirits that both have the power and the inclination to engage in such work, consider that even engaging those types of spirits has a tendency to slowly corrupt the magician over time. How quickly depends on how often and how powerful these types of workings are. But like all magic, we become aligned to what we invoke. While I am a defender of hexing and cursing

---

56. This is the traditional Hawaiian name for a wise-person or shaman. Since we have determined that Huna isn't actually Hawaiian, and with respect for Victor's use of that term to describe himself, I will now use the culturally neutral term "magician" instead.

in principle, in practice one must be aware that doing this work will change the magician. I have seen those who engage in *maleficum* somewhat frequently and they become twisted, anxious, and paranoid, seeing magical attacks and heretical infractions around every corner. It's a downward spiral. The more they curse, the more they feel they *need* to curse … or they feel the need to fend off non-existent curses coming their way. In their way lies madness. Sometimes literally.

This is yet another reason why it is often stressed that one must do purification rites immediately after engaging in "the dark arts." We don't want to get stuck in a negative mindset, for that will only manifest more stress and negativity in our lives. We need to switch gears, so to speak. In Hoodoo, it is sometimes taught that one should wash their hands with Florida Water after doing this work. This is both to spiritually cleanse the magician from any lingering negative energies and effects, but also serves to physically wash away any residual (and potentially inflammatory) oils that may still be present, even after washing with soap and water. Either way, it's a good idea to wash your hands after Witchcraft.

The Righteous Hex

Before exploring some of the techniques to cast hexes and curses I wish to take a moment to speak on the subject of righteousness. This is often the state of mind in which the Witch or magician will find themselves when considering throwing magic offensively. These emotional fires often rise quickly and can be a considerable fuel for darker workings and are sometimes sufficient for bypassing the aid of the daemon altogether. This is primal magic, the magic of raw rage and the clarity that this emotional fire can sometimes bring.

But there is cause for caution; righteousness can be a twisted lens through which to assess our situations. When in that seemingly elevated state we may believe that we are the only ones who are seeing things clearly and that it is our "duty" to punish those who would draw our condemnation. Here tread carefully, for these are deceptive flames and through them we may believe that we are seeing the face of evil, when perhaps the truth is not quite as luminous.

So how do we determine if our perceptions are true? Again, we should turn to our divinatory tools. And our journal.

DIVINATION/JOURNALING: Cursing and Clarity

This is an exercise consisting of both divination and journaling, allowing us to gain a greater clarity on the subject of cursing and our motivations one way or another.

Items needed:
Your tarot cards or other divination system
Your journal
A pen or pencil

Open the Way. Focus your attention on the one you wish to jinx, hex, or curse. Ask yourself what it is that you really want to accomplish with this working. Are you looking to hurt someone? Why? Justice? Is this *really* justice or is it just to make your ego feel good? Is this really about revenge? How will this action bring a greater harmony to the situation? If you are feeling justified in a working then this means that you have a sense of moral balance. How does this action align with that balance? Do a reading (or series of smaller readings) with these questions in mind. As you do, journal your findings. When you are done, continue to journal for about five to ten minutes on any related feelings or thoughts you have on the subject.

———

When I am considering throwing a hex or a curse I have certain personal rules that I follow. These keep me focused on what is important and also help prevent me from potentially going off the deep end of things.

1. Do it for justice but never revenge.

Justice is an important thing to fight for. The oppressed are starving for it and our heritage as Witches is intimately entwined with its seeking. But if we cannot see the difference between it and revenge, then we are victims of our own anger and denial and have no business throwing a curse.

Revenge is the lashing out at and hurting of someone in order to make us feel better in the short term. We may feel that our revenge is really justice, but if we look closer we will see that only true justice will right any wrongs that have been committed while revenge will bring about more imbalance. Revenge initiates a never-ending cycle of retaliation, whereas justice will provide closure. Justice is about bringing balance to a situation;

it will provide closure and healing, restoring balance and righting (as well as it can) the original wrong. Revenge is nothing more than just lashing out, plain and simple. In a warrior tradition, the difference is that our actions are used to bring balance and healing. Justice is stopping further hurt from being done and doing what we can to heal that hurt that exists. Nothing more. Revenge is personal. Justice is impartial.

2. Wait at least three days between deciding to throw a curse and actually performing it.

This prevents us from committing a "curse of passion" and potentially doing something that we would regret later. If they are truly deserving of a curse, then they will still be so three days from now, when cooler heads have prevailed. Fiery anger is a dangerous and deceptive power. It distorts our perception just as a real flame distorts our vision around a campfire. If you are so mad you are seeing red (outside of the cursing rite), then this is not the time to be casting a curse. While you very well may have the emotional power necessary to pull it off, you more than likely do not possess the necessary mental focus to do it effectively and safely. Wait until your anger has grown cold. Hot anger is messy and unpredictable. Cold anger is a focused anger, and is excellent for strategic workings.

3. Be free of the quality on which you are focusing in your target.

In other words, don't be a hypocrite. We must remember that the magic we are directing to our subject must first be channeled through ourselves. If our intent is to "punish" our subject for, let's say, gossiping, then we might find ourselves feeling some of the negative effects of the curse if we are likewise engaging in gossip. This is similarly true of any inherent weakness in the subject that we may wish to exploit, such as a specific fear or physical ailment. If we also possess those same weaknesses, we may find ourselves negatively impacted by the magic used to exploit them. This too is a good reason to perform purification work immediately after engaging in cursing.

4. Make sure the punishment fits the crime.

Sending someone a death curse because they slandered your name isn't exactly bringing balance to a situation. In a religion of poetry, I think we can do better, both morally as well as artistically. If they are speaking falsehoods, then the curse might include the truth taking center stage, perhaps a truth about the slanderer, or exposing them as a liar. Or perhaps a taste of their own medicine? In the case of a rapist or domestic abuser perhaps the curse is for them to be sloppy and get caught—and convicted—of their crimes. May justice guide your hand and wand.

5. Give them an "out."

If I am doing this work for justice and not revenge, then this means that this curse is a *means to a greater end*. And that end must be the correction of the overall problem or some level of restitution. It is a way of making amends. If I am cursing someone to experience some torment, I will want that torment to end should they accept responsibility for their actions and make their own restitution. In fact, sometimes I even tack on a blessing at the end in the hopes that this will help solidify the work toward restorative justice. As long as justice is served it does not matter who serves it.

————

Once you have cleared the way for your work, you will want to decide what level of maleficum you wish to impart: jinx, hex, or outright curse. A jinx you could do on your own; a sufficiently charged fetch can accomplish as much. Possibly your fetch may even be able to pull off a hex, though that is more difficult. But a curse will likely need to have outside spiritual assistance, since your holy daemon may not participate. I say "may" not participate because while some of the old lore stipulates that the daemon/God Soul will not contribute to the throwing of curses, in my experience this is not always true. Sometimes a righteous curse can even be a divine one. And to this I offer another personal story.

It was many years ago and I had been an initiate of Faery for not quite two years. An Elder in our Craft, now deceased, who carried a long history of venomous attacks and sexual predation, publicly stated that he was going to curse me. Referencing "black candles and pins" on an internet forum, he described just how he was going to throw such a curse, for the crime of sharing a personal story of how he had attempted to manipulate my husband and myself into an unwanted sexual relationship, using his eldership in the tradition as a stick and the promise of "nearly lost queer lore" as the carrot. After watching this person verbally abuse many in the community to the degree of attempting to get entire lines of our shared tradition "invalidated" in the eyes of others, and hearing so many other stories of how this person had sexually abused his own students, I decided to speak out. This obviously upset him and inspired the accusation that I was now an "oathbreaker" because I was not "protecting" this person who was a brother of the Craft. Upon first hearing that he was planning this curse (a friend in the tradition gave me a "heads-up"), I honestly didn't think anything of it. I figured they were blowing off steam as I believed (naively) that actual initiates of our shared tradition would not behave in such a foul way (I have since been relieved of that particular blissful fiction). So, I did nothing.

A couple days later, I was visited by a strange energy and sensation. I was at home, walking upstairs, and I suddenly felt both light-headed and a bit dizzy, as if I were standing on the deck of a moving boat. My aetheric sight showed me what I can only describe as an energy form that was like seaweed, slowly undulating in a trance-inducing rhythm, all yellow-green and feeling somewhat sickly. I was surprised! I had expected my passive defenses to have taken care of it, but this was, after all, an initiate *and* an Elder in our tradition. They had many years to grow in the Power and I was feeling the effects of that in the most eerie and off-putting way. I knew what I had to do. I gathered my materials, a candle, some salt, Uncrossing oil, some hyssop, some dragon's blood resin, and my incense burner, and I set to draw myself a bath. I smoked myself with the dragon's blood, and then added the salt, hyssop, and oil to the bath with a prayer of empowerment and purification. As I bathed I felt the "seaweed effect" lessening, until it was no more. I got out of the bath and had a most striking experience.

I can only describe it as my daemon descending upon me and I was completely self-possessed. I was filled with a sense of complete calm, focus, and power. I also was experiencing a very clear vision of an ornate and beautiful harp, the kind that this Elder was known to have played with considerable talent. I was filled with the knowledge—as if it were a certainty in my bones—that if I wanted to send this curse back to its source, then all it would take would be for me to reach out and pluck—and break—one of those visionary harp strings, but to do so would have meant the death of that person.

I will admit that I considered it. This person had gone very far to fabricate stories about myself as well as others in an effort to discredit us and had caused a lot of people a lot of pain over the course of thirty years. But I decided against it. I would not be brought down to that level. That punishment did not fit the crime as far as I could see, and so I would not be part of it. I sat down on my couch and aligned my souls and calmly waited for the vision and sensations to leave me.

Even later I would feel the presence of that visionary harp in my mind and knew that I could use it, if I wanted to. I never did.

————

There are very few hexes or curses that are passed down in Faery Tradition outside of individual covens or lineages. Perhaps one of the better-known curses (amongst Faery initiates) is the "Medusa Mirror," which details the creation of a magical device that is aligned to a particular Olympic spirit, as well as to various Dark Goddess forms, and used to repel magical attacks or even to kill your enemy by getting them to look into it. Created during the total eclipse of the sun or moon, certain sigils are placed on a mirror's back, and an herbal mixture is used to "smoke" the mirror before placing it in the magical triangle and focusing all of one's hate, anger, and terrifying mental images into it. Much care is given in the text to ensure that the practitioner never looks into the mirror themselves, before, during, or after its ensorcellment, even specifying that a special bag should be used that indicates which side is the back of the mirror (and therefore safe to behold), as the mirror will need to be recharged every month during the full or dark moon.

For those who have read this chapter in the hopes that I would spell out exactly what to do, step by step, in order to cast a hex or a curse, you will be happy to know that I have already done so. Assuming that you are already experienced in magic, if you have read this book from the beginning, and practiced the forms that I have given, then you will have the tools necessary to devise a hex or a curse on your own, which would be far more effective for you and your situation than any "stock curse" I would provide. If you are not yet magically experienced, then me telling you step by step wouldn't really help you much anyway, unless your goal was to curse yourself—in which case have at it. Sometimes the most potent magical lessons are those learned when everything blows up in our faces. I can personally attest to this. It is largely because of my magical *failures* that I am an experienced warlock. Nothing will grant you power and skill without having first done the work. There is no substitute for experience.

Should you decide to attempt throwing a hex or a curse, I hope that you consider employing my methods and guidelines. We have enough sloppy magical practitioners running around throwing hexes like so many monkeys flinging feces from the tree-tops. While the hex and the curse have a definite role to play in a Witchcraft that seeks justice for the oppressed, we should refrain from using it in a knee-jerk reaction to perceived or even actual attacks. Faery is a warrior tradition. We hold ourselves to a higher standard. If you seek Faery you need to be aware of that.

Afterword

Change is the law of life.
And those who look only to the past or present are certain to miss the future.
—JOHN F. KENNEDY

It is a poetic truth passed as sacred lore: to be initiated into the Faery Tradition of Witchcraft is to become a racial descendant of the faery race. As such we have "eaten of the fruit" offered us in their realm and are forever changed by the experience. Where this newfound identity leads some to retreat from this world altogether into one of tribalism and secrecy (much as in the old folktales of the little people receding away beneath the hills and mounds), for others (as is also depicted in the old tales) it is a call to action, to stand one foot in each realm and exist fully between the two, working toward reestablishing the sacred relationship between humanity and the living planet. In this we are charged with shifting the collective consciousness of humanity toward the magical once more.

Regardless of specific tradition, the spread of magical paths such as the Craft is an indicator that this shift is happening and has been for some time. More and more people are turning toward spiritual worldviews that affirm, rather than deny, the living divinity in all things. But this shift has come quite late in the game. The powers of industry and greed have overwhelmed the fragile ecosystem and we are all beginning to see the terrible price for such avarice. The first thing sacrificed on our altars must therefore be the bliss of our own ignorance. We must look into the mirror, individually as well as collectively.

The shadow work presented here begins with the hunt for our personal complexes and demons. But it can go so much further. Once we have a handle on our personal demons, it becomes time to start trying to tackle the collective ones. One need only turn on the news to see how these transpersonal demons of racism, misogyny, homophobia, and the like are rising up and threatening human rights. We see how once-trusted governments are turning to the techniques of fascism to suppress opposition to the state. These are troubling times. And troubling times call for Witchcraft.

But in all of this what can we as individual Witches do? It might be tempting, especially for the Witch who is also a political activist, to take up magical arms, cursing and jinxing all who would oppose freedom and environmental sustainability, and indeed it may be necessary for some of us to do just that. But for others, their magical calling will be in the areas of healing—to mend the bodies, minds, and hearts of those who have been injured by the machine of the oppressor. Still others will be called to make music and art, to help sustain the movement in its myriad of possible forms. And throughout all of it, we are each reminded that we need to do everything in our power toward our own self-possession and self-care.

As someone who has engaged in political actions and who has many friends who are activists, I can say with certainty that what is really necessary in maintaining our ability to bring justice to the world is remembering to practice self-care. We simply need to take time off from our big W (Work) and give ourselves time to relax, regroup, and integrate. As we move into an uncertain future (for is there really any other kind?), we must take steps to ensure that we are getting what we need. *"All work and no play makes Storm a dull Warlock."* We need to find what nourishes us. What gives back to our souls? What makes us laugh? Makes us feel powerful? What helps us heal? What does our fetch want? We must make a real effort to ensure that we are able to provide these things, for ourselves and for others, so that we do not burn out.

But neither can we get stuck here, trapped in a comfortable prison of bliss. It is still a prison—and one of our own choosing, because it feels so much better than when we look at the real work outside. Denial often starts because we can't deal with everything all at once, and so we break down … we retreat into ourselves, blocking out the rest of the world. It's almost always meant to be temporary, but sometimes we just conveniently never seem to make it back around to dealing with our (anxiety- and depression-inducing) *issues.*

We need to live more fully in the present, but also we need to make real plans for the future we want to create. Each of us is being called to make a contribution to the future. These need not be grand gestures. The future is built with the smallest and most insignificant-seeming choices that we each make every day. Most of those choices are unconscious or unknown.

Witches, Warlocks, and other magical practitioners have a series of tools that we can use in order to help guide our culture in a direction that is more open, more inclusive, more intelligent, more compassionate, and yes, even more prosperous and safe than what we have had thus far. Magicians are architects of reality, shifting perception and drawing down inspiration and power from higher (and also lower) planes, impregnating the fertile mind of our collective being with new possibilities. While our traditions offer us the foundations necessary to engage the mysterious otherworlds (and interact with their inhabitants) we must be willing to explore beyond those foundations, expanding our knowledge of magic and the Craft as we do. We cannot expect to engage this new world with the dogmas of the old one. Traditions offer us much in the way of outer forms. These forms may lead us to the threshold, but it is we—stripped bare of all convention—that must take that final leap into the unknown.

As we deal with our own shadow, learning more about our own power as we do, we find ourselves in new territory; no longer chained by our fears, we have faced them down and watched them change before our eyes in an attempt to dissuade us from our mission. But we have held fast, prompting the transformation of our fears into power. We have championed our demons and we have set them toward the realization of our own will, deepening our magic and then, hopefully, using that magic in a way that helps strengthen the spiritual alliance between humankind and the rest of the earth's inhabitants.

We are the ones who stand between. We are being called to fearlessly bridge two worlds together, merging them within ourselves as one: the magical *and* the mundane. Light *and* dark. The spiritual *and* the physical. The beauty *and* the horror. Not opposing worldviews, but two sides of the same coin, our beloved Twins at play once more, guiding us toward this "radical holism," within and without. Magic isn't something that only happens when we stand at our altars brandishing a blade, or chanting spells, or miming arcane sigils by candlelight. It is a consistent practice of attention, breath, and spiritual awareness that we carry inside of us wherever we go. In this our whole world is transformed, ignited into holy flame by the fires of magical consciousness and inhabited by beings and powers beyond the realm of the ordinary.

Once inaugurated into this expanded universe, we must learn to work with the powers that present themselves to us, each in our own little corners of the world, so that we can do our part to participate in the sacred marriage of the land and the spirits. Wherever you are, *go outside*. Get to know the land, the major natural features of your area. Talk to *those* spirits. What do *they* have to say? Journey into the underworld and build your relationships there. Know that to do all of this we must look deep into the black mirror of our souls, the dark abyss which houses our deepest terrors but also offers us the prize of the true initiation—not into any human lineage or priesthood, but one of union with the soul of the universe, *if* we are able to conquer our demons and claim our power back from deep inside them. Only then does the true journey even begin.

Appendix 1
Basic Concepts and Practices

These are foundational concepts and exercises of the Faery Witchcraft tradition that are referenced in this text, here given in simplified forms adequate for working with the material in this book. For a more in-depth look at these exercises and more, please see my book *Betwixt and Between: Exploring the Faery Tradition of Witchcraft*.

Our tradition can be thought of as "a monotheistic religion with many gods."[57] This is to say that we recognize a primary deity, but that deity is seen in a multitude of ways. Poetically this being is referred to as "the Star Goddess" or "God Herself," and she is the womb of all creation from which all things proceed and to which all things eventually return. She is traditionally represented on a Faery altar by a large, black pillar candle. The lighting of this candle represents the first ritual act of any Faery ceremony and the rite is ended when it is eventually extinguished.

EXERCISE: Opening the Way (Three Souls & HA Prayer)

This is a foundational grounding and centering exercise used in BlueRose as a beginning to all other work that we may do. It is actually a few exercises merged together into one, and includes Soul Alignment and the Holy Fire rites. Given here in a simplified, formal format, you will wish to learn how to incorporate this into any informal work you may do, i.e., internally with a couple breaths and without tools, etc. Whenever "Open the Way" appears as a component to an exercise given in this book, it will be assumed that you will use your Star Goddess candle and follow this basic formula.

Items needed:
Your Star Goddess candle
Some matches or a lighter

---

57. Faery Grandmaster Anaar.

Take a deep breath and relax. Take another. Imagine points of stillness and silence at the ends of your breaths. Breathe into them and imagine they grow larger with every breath until they meet in the center.

Imagine your talker, your ego-self, as a miniature golden sun shining in your head. Tune into your thoughts and let them go. When you feel clear, breathe deep and imagine a bloodred full moon in your lower belly … in your guts … in your sex. Your fetch is primal and you tune in to your body sensations and your emotions.

Breathe deep and imagine a star of Blue Fire shining above your head. Your holy daemon … your personal god … your God Soul … imagine it guiding you from above.

Breathe deep and return to the sun of talker … imagine a symbol that represents your three souls aligned. See it shining in your talker. Breathe deep and send this down into the moon of fetch. With every breath, imagine you are drawing in wraith force from the world around you and into your fetch … into that symbol.

Take four deep breaths of power and on the fourth and final exhale, cock your head backward and send the power and the symbol up into your holy daemon and exclaim, "HA!" Imagine your symbol exploding in the daemon and now raining down around and through you with a liquid pearlescent light. Imagine your fetch moving upward, while your talker moves downward toward your heart … the movement of talker drags the daemon downward where all three align in your heart center and appear like an eclipse. Say:

> *Shining star and moon and sun*
> *Aligned within this vessel of the earth,*
> *Together now, the Three made One*
> *Our single voice, in union, given birth.*
> *We are the three who speak as one,*
> *We are the three who speak as one,*
> *We are the three who speak as one.*
> *So must it be.*

Imagine yourself shining with the light of your own divinity like a flame … your holy fire. Take a moment to orient yourself to the directions (north, south, east, and west, above, below, and center). Feeling yourself in the perfect center, light the Star Goddess candle and say:

Holy Mother,
In You we live, move, and have our being.
From You all things emerge.
And unto You all things return.

Feel how the light of the candle flame and the light within yourself are one and the same. Your fire and Her fire are one. All flames are one flame.

To End Your Sessions

Having finished your other work, return your attention to the flame of the Star Goddess candle. Feel the unity of your fire with Her own. Draw your power back from the flame and breathe it down into your fetch to nourish and empower you. Recite the "Holy Mother" prayer. Extinguish the candle. Breathe three breaths of silence.

RITE: Waters of Purity

Most often referred to by the Hawaiian name *Kala*, which means to loosen, unbind, or forgive, this is a simple purification exercise that is a staple in Faery work.

Items needed:
A cup or glass of fresh water

Open the Way.

Step 1: Think of something that is troubling you. Notice how it makes you feel…emotionally and physically. Imagine this feeling is like a dark smoke or vapor that flows out of your body and is drawn into the water with every breath, leaving the cup full of a toxic "sludge." If you have nothing specific you need to cleanse, you can skip ahead to step 2.

Step 2: Drawing from the light of the Star Goddess, feel her flame flowing into you, through your daemon, down into your fetch, up through your talker, and out through your mouth, and you breathe this light onto the surface of the water, transforming the dark sludge into a crystalline-rainbow light. You may wish to chant or hum to help facilitate this transformation. This may take the span of several breaths.

Step 3: Feeling this light at its peak, reverently drink the water, imagining this light shining within you, breaking down blocks, and bringing you a calm balance.

End as normal.

The lore stipulates that our first urination after performing this rite is to "finish" it. I see this as releasing all energies that do not belong to us, and being returned to the cycle of water.

EXERCISE: The Iron Pentacle

This is a psychic diagnostic tool that explores five fundamental concepts with which we often have blocks or imbalances and which are essential to forming a strong magical will. In Faery training, much time is spent contemplating and doing rituals for each point of the pentacle. For now, just meditate on them and feel how they can inform you when you are out of balance.

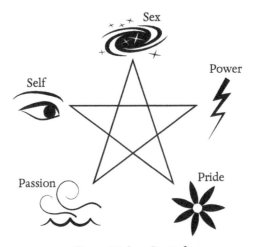

Figure 20: Iron Pentacle

Open the Way. Imagine the points in the following locations of your body and with the following symbols:

Sex: Center of forehead / Spiral galaxy

Pride: Right foot / A flower blooming in the sun

Self: Left hand / An open eye

Power: Right hand / An oak tree, a lightning bolt, or a lightning-struck oak

Passion: Left foot / An ocean wave

Imagine these points and their symbols in each of the stations in your body. Contemplate each point and ask yourself, "What is Sex (Pride, Self, Power, Passion)?" Notice how you feel about each. Imagine wraith force flowing between each point, forming the star in your body. Build up a charge with your breath and allow the energy to move faster and faster between each point, revving up the energetic pentacle within you. When it feels like it is at its peak, feel yourself strong and open like a red, five-petaled rose. Say:

In the name of the Iron Pentacle I claim my being!

EXERCISE: The Pearl Pentacle

This is the counterpart to the Iron Pentacle. In fact, it is really the same pentacle, just seen from a different perspective. Where the Iron was *personal*, the Pearl is *transpersonal*. Each point on the Pearl is the same as the Iron, only extended outward like an open hand.

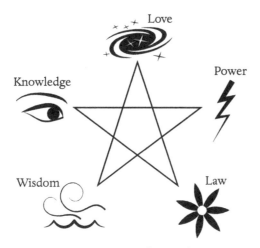

Figure 21: Pearl Pentacle

Open the Way. Invoke the Iron Pentacle. Breathing into Sex, see it transform with your breath into Love. Do this for each of the points using the following formula:

Sex: Love

Pride: Law

Self: Knowledge

Power: Power

Passion: Wisdom

Imagine the hot, red, iron energy transforming into the cool, watery light of the Pearl. Feel yourself calm and open. Sing or hum as you move the energy calmly between the "new" points. Feel yourself open like a white, five-petaled rose. Say:

In the name of the Pearl Pentacle, I claim my world!

RITE: The Western Gate

A rite for accessing and honoring the Beloved ancestors and the Mighty Dead.

Items needed:
A white (or red) candle
Your ritual blade
An image of a skull (optional)
A mirror

Opening the Gate

Set up the skull in the west along with your candle. Position the mirror in the west so that it is either hanging on the wall or propped up facing you. Open the Way. Sitting or standing before the skull and candle, light the candle and imagine how it is calling the realm of the dead closer to you.

Stand before the altar with your blade in your hands and recite the following incantation:

I stand between the worlds of fate
And summon forth the Western Gate
By my blade I part the veil
Across the sea we set our sail.

Use your tool to "slice" open the space before you and the mirror with a vertical slash. See it separating the veil. Breathe into it and then reach into the edges of this "crack in the worlds" and then with a quick sweeping motion of your arms, open the gate, ending with your arms open, imagining the veil-gate open wide before you. Recite:

By moon that hangs low in the sky,
By ancient sea, the earth's own womb,
I call the Gate to open wide,
That leads to life beyond the tomb.

Take a moment to feel this power shine upon you from the gate and know that YOU are the gate—the opening and the mirror are but extensions of your spiritual power.

You may light any special candles representing the specific Mighty Dead that you wish to work with (Victor, Cora, Gwydion, etc.) and call out their names, along with any titles, or descriptions of accomplishments that are relevant to their mythology. Take some time to honor their presence.

Closing the Gate

Holding the blade in one hand, extend your arms out to your sides so that your chest and stance are wide open as you face the gate.

Breathing into the very edges of the energetic gate, grasp ahold of them and pull them in toward each other in one quick motion as you exhale quickly. Imagine the vertical slash of light before you and seal it closed with Blue Fire from the tip of your blade slowly moving from the bottom upward until done. Trace a pentacle over the area, feeling this repair, and bless the fabric of reality. Affirm:

The gate is closed.

Extinguish the candle. Perform the Waters of Purity rite. End as normal. Record all of your experiences in your journal.

CONCEPTS: Hidden Temples/Beasts/The Watchers

The Hidden Temples are the astral constructs that represent a reverential intersection between the practitioner and the elemental power. The Beasts are a class of Guardian spirits that are rooted in the middleworld. The Watchers are Guardian spirits that are rooted in the overworld. And finally, the Wells are Goddesses that are rooted in the underworld. There are various concepts and symbols attached to each. What follows is a table mapping out these symbols and concepts for you to use in your work with them.

The Five Elements of Faery Tradition					
	Air	**Fire**	**Water**	**Earth**	**Aether**
Hidden Temple	East, Spring Meadow at Dawn	South, Summer Desert at Noon	West, Autumn Beach at Dusk	North, Winter Forest at Midnight	Above, Below, and Center, All times, No times
Glyph	Golden yellow half-circle (flat side down) in the throat	Upward-pointing red triangle beneath the navel	Blue circle in the heart center	Black (green-glowing) square in the solar plexus	Above: Violet pentacle in the crown. Below: Inverted violet pentacle in the perineum Center: Rainbow light of the Blue God
Beast (Middleworld)	Golden Eagle	Red Lion	Blue Serpent	Black Bull	★
Watcher / Power (Overworld)	Star Finder / Knowledge	Shining Flame / Truth	Water Maker / Love	Black Mother / Wisdom	Above: Heaven Shiner Below: Fire-in-the-Earth (Pure consciousness)
Well	Arida, Well of Sunrise	Tana, Well of Liquid Flame	Tiamat, Well of Watery Abyss	Verr-Avna, Well of Deep Space	Above: Qua-koralina (Stars) Below: Sugma'ad (Souls) Center: The Nameless Name (Void)
Tool	Wand	Blade	Cup	Cube	Above: Black mirror Below: Cauldron Center: Cord

APPENDIX II

POETRY AND INVOCATIONS

Faery is said to be a bardic tradition, meaning that practitioners are called upon to be poets, storytellers, artists, musicians, and the like, tapping into the creative powers of the universe and expressing them for the betterment of the self, coven, community, tradition, or even the world.

An essential component of Faery is the magical and ritual use of poetry. When we read or listen to poetry, we enter into a type of light trance in which we are able to move beyond our normal, waking consciousness and into a state of magical awareness and connection that I refer to as *Enchantment*. When we are in this state we are better able to work our magical wills, as well as to gather knowledge from non-conventional sources. We have moved beyond the confines of the *rational* and in doing so are able to reach out and touch powers that to us would otherwise be invisible and unreachable.

What follows are poems which are meant to be fully engaged. The two Scottish ballads are my rewriting of various traditional versions. They are intended to remain true to the originals while still offering something new. Read them aloud. Imagine them as trance journeys unto themselves. Allow them to inspire you.

Also included are the BlueRose invocations for the Faery Watchers, the ancient otherworldly beings which guard and guide our tradition.

A Ballad of Thomas the Rhymer

True Thomas slept upon a hill
And there a vision did he see:
A lady wondrous and bright
Riding near the old oak tree.

Her dress was all grass green and silk
Her velvet mantle just as fine
And on each strand of her horse's mane
Were silver bells of fifty-nine.

True Thomas, he took off his hat
Kneeled low and with bended knee
"A Blessed Day, O, Queen of heaven!
Your like on earth I've never seen."

"O Thomas, no," the lady said
"That name does not belong to me;
For I am the Queen of all Elfland,
And I have come to visit thee.

"Harp and play, Thomas," she said,
"Harp and play along with me;
But should you dare to kiss my lips,
Your body's sovereign Queen I'll be."

"I may be rich or I may be poor,
But never daunted shall I be."
With that he kissed her rose-soft lips
While underneath the old oak tree.

"By contract you are bound," she said,
"And so you now must go with me;
And you must serve me seven years,
Through whatever fate by chance we'll see."

Majestic on her milk-white steed,
And he behind took up the end;
And whenever those bells did ring
That steed flew faster than the wind.

On they rode, and further still
They flew faster than the mind

Until they reached a desert land
And all of life was left behind.

On they rode, and further still
And came they to a garden green.
"O Lady we can eat our fill,
These fruits I shall here pluck for thee."

"O no, Thomas," the Elf Queen said,
"This fruit may not be touched by thee.
For every curse that's born in hell
Is upon the fruit of this country."

"But here lie down, O Thomas True,
To rest your head upon my knee;
And dine on bread and claret wine,
And I will show you wonders three.

"O see you there that narrow road,
So tightly fraught with thorn and stone
Behold the road of righteousness
Though nearly all leave it alone.

"And see you there, that widespread road
With fruit and flower, figs and dates,
There lies the road of wickedness,
By some confused for heavens' Gates.

"And do you see that good fine road,
That winds around the grassy hill?
That is the road to my own Elfland,
Where you and I must journey still.

"O Thomas you must hold your tongue,
No matter what you hear or see;
For if you speak while in Elfland,
You'll not return to your own country."

On they rode, and further still
To wade through rivers above the knee;
And saw they neither sun nor moon,
But heard the ancient roaring sea.

So in the darkest of the night
They moved through blood up to the knee;
For all the blood that's shed on earth,
Runs through this land that lies between.

Next, they stopped at an orchard's edge
And she plucked a fruit from a branch so high
"This for your wages, True Thomas,
To grant the tongue that can never lie."

"My tongue is mine and mine alone,"
To her he said so carefully.
"Keep thy peace," the Elf Queen said
"For as I say, so must it be."

So Thomas then became the True,
But from the Queen one more decree:
"You may choose another gift:
Master the harp, or prophecy."

True Thomas, prophet of old Scotland
Who spoke the truth of what would be,
True Thomas, who moved between the lands
Awoke beneath the old oak tree.

Gifted a coat of elven cloth,
And the finest shoes of velvet green;
But seven years had come and gone
While Thomas on earth was never seen.

A Ballad of Tam Lin

Forbidden are the maidens all
With eyes and skin so fair
To grace the woods of Carterhaugh
For the elf Tam Lin is there.

By Carterhaugh who comes and goes
Must leave within those woods
Their rings of gold or grass-green cloaks
Or else their maidenhoods.

But Janet dreams of Carterhaugh
And sews hem above her knee
And slips away to Carterhaugh
As fast as she could flee.

When she arrived at Carterhaugh
At the well, a milk-white steed
But no Tam Lin there to be found
And so she took no heed.

She'd only plucked a double rose
Like two, but only one
When then appeared, the young Tam Lin
Who said, "What have you done?"

"Why do you pluck the double rose?
Why do you break its wand?
Why have you come to Carterhaugh
Without my clear command?"

She said, "These woods of Carterhaugh
By right belong to me,
I'll come and go by Carterhaugh
I'll ask no leave of thee."

He took sweet Janet by the hand
And then her heart did swell
And there upon the wooded land
They knew each other well.

Then at the breaking of the day
the rising of the sun
Fair Janet homeward made her way
As fast as she could run.

Four and twenty ladies fair
Were dancing in the hall
And Janet, pale with golden hair
Was fairer than them all.

Four and twenty gentlemen
Were playing games of chess
And Janet walked among them all
As green as ocean glass

Then she did hear her father dear
He spoke both calm and mild
He said, "Sweet daughter do I fear
That you may be with child."

She said, "Dear father, if now I go
With child, I'm to blame,
But no lord here about your hall
Shall give the babe his name."

"If my love were an earthly knight
and not an elfin grey,
I'd love the babe each cold long night
And every blessed day."

So she returned to Carterhaugh
With heart so dark with loss

Among the weeds and jagged thorns
Among the Stag's Horn moss.

"Why do you pluck the poison herb?"
Spoke Tam Lin beneath a tree.
"Why must you harm the little babe
That I have sired with thee?"

She said, "If you were a human knight,
Then would my heart be gay.
I'd love you both each cold long night,
And love you every day."

"If my love you'd have," Tam Lin did say,
"Then this much to you I'll tell:
That I was once a human child
And from my horse I fell.

"I was caught by Faery's Queen
And then was made her slave
And forced to serve for seven years
But now I fear my grave.

"For each and every seven years
She pays a tithe to hell
And I'm so young and full of flesh
I fear it be myself.

"If you would but accept my love
And do just as I said
I may then return to earthly land
And there we may be wed.

"On Hallowe'en at midnight hour
At Miles Cross do hide
And as the fairy folk there gather
From the dark upon them spy.

"First let pass the night-black steed
And then let pass the brown
But to the milk-white run with speed
And pull the rider down.

"Hold me tightly in your arms
And hold me in your heart
And ne'er let go, though fright and shade
Will try these plans to thwart.

"First within your arms I'll change
Into a hissing snake
But hold me close and fear me not
I am your child's namesake.

"And then within your arms I'll change
Into a feral bear,
But hold me close and fear me not,
I am your love so dear.

"And then within your arms I'll change
Into a lion wild.
But hold me close and fear me not,
And you shall love your child.

"And then within your arms I'll change
Into an iron hot
But hold me close and fear me not
And injured you'll be not.

"At last within your arms I'll change
Into a glowing coal
Then quickly into waters cast
Me down into the well.

"And then I'll be your own true love
I'll be a naked knight,

Then cover me with mantle green
And keep me far from sight."

Dark and gloomy was the night
And eerie was the day.
As Janet hid with green mantle
Just as Tam Lin did say.

Then at the stroke of midnight's hour
She heard the bridles ring
First passed the black, then passed the brown,
To the white she did then spring.

She pulled Tam Lin, the rider down
The Faery Queen did scream
And then by magic not of earth
All became a twisted dream.

Tam Lin within her arms he changed
Into a hissing snake
She held him close and feared him not
He was her child's namesake.

And then within her arms he changed
Into a feral bear,
She held him close and feared him not,
He was her love so dear.

And then within her arms he changed
Into a lion wild.
She held him close and feared him not,
The father of her child.

And then within her arms he changed
Into an iron hot
She held him close and feared him not
And injured she was not.

At last within her arms he changed
Into a glowing coal
She quickly into waters cast
Him down into the well.

And then she saw own her true love
He was a naked knight,
She covered him with mantle green
And kept him far from sight.

The Faery Queen did rage and roar
About the broken spell
For stung the loss of her favored knight
And now no tithe for hell.

"Oh had I known," said Faery Queen,
"This day he'd go from me
I'd have plucked his eyes out then put in
Two eyes carved from a tree."

And so it was that brave Janet
And young Tam Lin then fled
Unto her home, her own true love
And in that love, were wed.

Invocations of the Watchers

"Star Finder, Star Finder, Star Finder!
In darkness deep between the stars,
You glide and soar on wings of light
Watcher of the rising sun
We call your knowledge and your sight!"

"Shining Flame! Shining Flame! Shining Flame!
Within the candle and the star
Burning vortex, spark and flash
Watcher of the liquid flame
Reduce illusions all to ash!"

"Water Maker! Water Maker! Water Maker!
In darkness deep, you dream and sleep
In love and madness reawaken
Watcher of the Watery Abyss
Arise in passion, thou ancient kraken!"

"Black Mother! Black Mother! Black Mother!
From forest dark, you now emerge
With pungent scent of goat and earth
Watcher of the Well of Space
To a thousand young you've given birth!"

APPENDIX III
THE DIVINE TWINS IN FAERY LORE

The Divine Twins are mysterious beings who are at the very heart of the Faery Tradition. They appear in a multitude of different ways in many different cultures and so we can look to many sources to see their dance playing out on a mythic scale. In traditions such as Wicca, they might be expressed as polar opposites (such as the Oak King and the Holly King), and while they can certainly be as such in Faery, we recognize that they are part of the same being, and so they are not truly opposing each other.

A full account of the numerous groupings and permutations of the Divine Twins as worked with in the Faery Tradition would probably be an impossible task, given the fierce diversity of our practices. What follows are but some examples of how the Twins manifest for practitioners of our tradition. Some of these pairings will make perfect sense while others may raise an eyebrow or two. Contemplate them. Go into a trance, align your souls and then *meditate* on them.

Female	Male
The Star Goddess	Melek Ta'us
Nimuë	The Arddu
Ana	Dian y Glas
Mari	Krom
Ana	The Arddu
Nimuë	Dian y Glas
Dove	Wolf

Female	*Female*
The Star Goddess	Nimuë
Nimuë	Ana
Mari	Lilith
Male	*Male*
Melek Ta'us (or Dian y Glas)	Lemba
Red Man	Green Man
Dian y Glas	The Arddu
Christ	Lucifer
Stag	Wolf
Oak King	Holly King
Ungendered or Changeable	
Serpent	Dove
The Ibeji of Yoruba	
The Marassa of Vodou	

GLOSSARY

Aligned (**Alignment, Soul Alignment**): The desired result of the practitioner's three souls working in perfect harmony.

Ana, or Anna: Most common name for the Hag or Crone goddess in Faery. She is the spirit of Witchcraft.

Anderson, Victor and Cora: Seminal teachers of the Faery Witchcraft tradition.

Ankou: Breton name for the Dark God of Death. See *Arddu*.

Arddu, the: Common name for the Dark God of Sex and Death. He often appears as the *Baphomet*.

Arida: Goddess of the air element. See *Goddesses of the Elements*.

Baphomet: Androgynous god of radical holism.

Beasts (**of the Quarters**, or **Guardian Beasts**): The name given to a class of four Guardian spirits who appear as the animals: eagle (air), lion (fire), serpent (water), and bull (earth), and who were introduced into the Faery Tradition by the lineage of Vanthe. In BlueRose they are seen as the Guardians of the Crossroads in the middleworld. See *Guardians*.

Black Heart of Innocence: A Faery symbol of the nature and sexual state of the human soul, akin to that of children and wild animals. Also (though rarely) the Black Rose of Innocence or the Black Fish.

Bloodrose: The coven (and later lineage) of Bloodrose was among the largest and most active of the teaching covens in the 1980s. It was unique for the time, in that it offered classes to the public and sought to develop a cohesive body of material from the poetic liminality that was a hallmark of the teachings of Victor Anderson.

Blue Coven: A traditional name for a coven whose members are not sexually active with each other for their rites. See *Red Coven*.

Blue Fire: A particular vibration and visual tool for magical energy, usually described as the electric blue color of a natural-gas flame. See *Wraith force*.

Blue God: A major deity in the Faery Tradition, the Blue God is the firstborn of the Star Goddess, is her "son, lover, and other half" and is the divine spirit of humankind. He possesses dual iconography that incorporates both avian and serpentine imagery, wedding them both together as the "winged serpent." As the youthful *Dian y Glas* he embodies our individual "holy daemon" while as *Melek Ta'us* he is the collective *daemon* of humankind.

BlueRose: This is the name of the lineage I founded within the Faery Tradition. Since blue roses do not exist in nature, they have become a symbol of the mysterious and are used in that capacity in many places for that reason. Also used as a visual key for connecting to the *holy daemon*.

Daemon, Holy: See *Holy Daemon*.

Demon: A class of spirit aligned to chaos or destruction or that of a feral appetite. These can begin as personal issues or complexes within the *shadow* or may be independent of the practitioner altogether. Not to be confused with *daemon*. (Oh, the difference an "a" makes!)

Dian y Glas: The son and firstborn of the Star Goddess. He is the spirit of youth, beauty, potency, and individuation. He is also an individual's *holy daemon*. See *Blue God*.

Divine Twins: Dual offspring and consorts of the *Star Goddess* often thought of as separate in other traditions (such as the Oak King and Holly King of Wicca) but understood in Faery to be aspects of the same being.

Enchantment, State of: A spiritual state of being in which the practitioner is aligned and standing in the center of their power. A state of balance, power, and connection. The ecstatic union with the divine in which we recognize that magic is real and all things are possible. The preferred state of being when engaging in magical work.

Feri: This spelling of the name of our tradition was coined by Victor Anderson in the 1990s in an effort to help distinguish our tradition from the many others that also bear the name "Faery/Faery/Fairy." While I have used this spelling (and many others) in the past, I tend to prefer that of "Faery" as I feel it better evokes the folkloric current in which BlueRose works, and was the common spelling used at the time of my initial exposure to the tradition.

Fetch: The animal, child, or "lower" soul in our personal trinity. Fetch is concerned with keeping the body alive and in gathering wraith force. It speaks not in words but in images, feelings, and symbols. It is in direct communication with the holy daemon.

Goddesses of the Elements: A poetic grouping of deity powers that are the primal architecture of the five magical elements: air (Arida), fire (Tana), water (Tiamat), earth (Verr-Avna), and aether (Sugma'ad/Quakoralina).

Gray Dove Coven: A traditional name for a coven consisting entirely of gay men.

Gray Wolf (or **Gray Hound**) **Coven**: A traditional name for a coven consisting entirely of lesbian women.

Green Man: Aspect of *Krom* as the spirit of plant life. Lover of the *Red Man*.

Guardians: The Guardians are ancient spirits that are part of the architecture of the universe. Generally associated with the directions and the elements, they appear in the larger Faery Tradition in two sets: the *Beasts*, who are associated mainly with the middleworld, and the angelic *Watchers*, who are associated mainly with the overworld. They serve to protect us when in need, but also to protect the universe itself.

Harpy: Name of the coven into which a young Victor Anderson was initiated and which operated in southern Oregon in the 1930s and '40s.

Hidden Kingdom: A core concept in Faery Tradition that is expressed in certain lines stating that authors, artists, poets, and others can tap into the creative powers of the universe and express certain mysterious spiritual truths, even if they are not consciously aligned to a spiritual/magical tradition or even aware of the truths they are expressing. This justifies the inclusion of literary materials into liturgical practice.

Holy Daemon: The name that BlueRose uses to describe the "God Self" or "God Soul" in our personal trinity. This is also known as the *Dian y Glas*, or *"Blue God."* From the Greek "daimon," meaning a tutelary spirit or one's genius, i.e., "higher self."

Infinitum, the: Poetic term originating in BlueRose for the sevenfold grouping of deity forms popularized by Bloodrose, consisting of the Star Goddess giving birth to a gender binary, each expressed in triple form: *Nimuë, Mari,* and *Ana,* and *Dian y Glas, Krom,* and *the Arddu.* Sometimes called "the lemniscate deities." These goddess names were obviously taken from Robert Graves' 1949 novel *Seven Days in New Crete.* See *Hidden Kingdom.*

Iron Pentacle: A core psychic diagnostic tool and teaching device of Faery Witchcraft that encourages the practitioner to cleanse and balance their personal relationship to each of its five points: Sex, Pride, Self, Power, and Passion. It is often used as a visual mandala to ritually invoke said presences, or as a divinatory tool to analyze issues that may be affecting their magic. It is said that in Faery there is only one pentacle, and so the Iron's counterpart, the *Pearl Pentacle,* is seen as this same pentacle, only viewed from a different perspective.

Korythalia: A Faery coven which operated in the San Francisco Bay Area sometime in the 1980s and which was a precursor to Bloodrose.

Krom: Sometimes spelled "Crom." Common name given to the Horned God in Faery Tradition. He is often depicted with golden skin, the head of a stag, summer flowers around his neck, and an erect phallus. He is the spirit of light and heat and is sometimes called "the Summer King" or "Harvest Lord." See *Twr.*

Maleficum: Latin term for harmful Witchcraft and magic.

Mari: Most common name for the mother goddess in Faery Witchcraft. She is the living body of the planet, the moon, and the sea; the life force of all of creation, both terrestrial and celestial. Related to the Basque goddess of the same name, she also has resonances with the Christian Virgin Mary.

Melek Ta'us: A Yazidi angel who is the first emanation of the light of god, and the lord of earth. In the Faery Tradition, he is an aspect of the *Blue God* and the collective god soul of humanity.

Nimuë: The maiden goddess of Faery. She appears as if a young girl, but is also the sexual innocence of a wild animal.

Oath Mother: Non–gender-specific traditional term used for the person who administers the Oath during initiation. Since not all lineages of Faery Tradition engage in the practice of swearing oaths, this is only used in some lines.

Pearl Pentacle: A core teaching device in Faery Witchcraft that offers the practitioner an opportunity to cleanse and balance their relationships to its five transpersonal concepts: Love, Law, Knowledge, Power (or Liberty), and Wisdom. See *Iron Pentacle*.

Personal Trinity: The Doctrine of the Personal Trinity or the Three Souls is a core teaching of Faery Witchcraft that states that humans have three souls (or three parts to the soul) which each have their own modes of operation and must be brought into alignment.

Quakoralina: A major aspect of the *Star Goddess* as well as the goddess of the aether element when expressed in the above. See *Goddesses of the Elements*.

Red Coven: A coven in which the members are sexually active with each other in their rites. See *Blue Coven*.

Red Man: Aspect of *Krom* as the spirit of animal life. Lover of the *Green Man*.

Scry, Scrying: The art of gazing into a reflective object, such as a crystal ball, a mirror, or a bowl of water, so as to allow the psychic vision to reveal images.

Shadow: This is the collection of all aspects of the self of which the self is not consciously aware. The shadow will contain both positive and negative qualities, but due to our nature it is more likely to be predominately negative. This is the abyss into which the Witch must gaze in order to gather their power.

Souls, Three: See *Personal Trinity*.

Star Goddess: Also, "God Herself." Poetic term given to the ultimate deity of the multiverse, the origin of all creation. She is pre-gendered, but depicted as "she" because of her primal role of giving birth to the universe. Her "son, lover, and other half" is the *Blue God*.

Star Goddess candle: In most lines of the Faery Tradition it is custom to have a large, black pillar candle placed centrally on the altar to represent the *Star Goddess*. The lighting and extinguishing of this candle are the formal opening and closing of any Faery Tradition ceremony, often in accompaniment with the "Holy Mother Prayer." Some lineages practice the carving of certain signs and sigils upon this candle to further align it with our primary deity.

Sugma'ad: A major aspect of the *Star Goddess* as well as the goddess of the aether element when expressed in the below. See *Goddesses of the Elements*.

Taka Spirits: Aspects of the personal shadow that break off and become a type of Demon.

Talker: In our personal trinity, the talker is roughly equivalent to the ego, though as a layer of spiritual consciousness is encompasses more than just that psychological designation. It is the focal lens through which we direct our will into the world, fed by *fetch* and guided by the *daemon*.

Tana: Goddess of the fire element. See *Goddesses of the Elements*.

Tiamat (Heva Leviathan Tiamat): Goddess of the water element. See *Goddesses of the Elements*.

Twins, Divine: See *Divine Twins*.

Twr: Welsh for "tower." Common name given to the Horned God in Faery Tradition. He appears to me as a sharp, angular, white spire standing directly in front of the blazing sun and casting a long shadow. See *Krom*.

Verr-Avna: Goddess of the earth element. See *Goddesses of the Elements*.

Watchers, the: Collective term for certain (fallen) angelic presences that are aligned to the elemental principles. See *Guardians*.

Wraith force: "Life force," "magic," "mana," "prana," "chi," "ki," "numen," "the force." This is the force that empowers our magic. It can be worked with in many different ways, the most common in Faery Tradition being the *"Blue Fire,"* but traditionally also seen as red, white, green, gold, violet, and black. According to tradition, this force may be worked with safely in any of the natural colors of the rainbow, though an alternative form of "Blue Fire" (which Victor equated to limited, personal life force) carried a stern warning from the founder.

Wraith threads: These are energetic threads that connect us to other people, places, and situations. Sometimes referred to as simply "cords" or "aka threads."

BIBLIOGRAPHY

Adler, Margot. *Drawing Down the Moon: Witches, Druids, Goddess-Worshippers, and Other Pagans in America (Revised and Updated)*. New York: Penguin Group, 1986. Originally published 1979.

Anderson, Cora. *Childhood Memories*. Portland, OR: Acorn Guild Press, 2007.

———*Fifty Years in the Feri Tradition*. San Leandro, CA: privately published, 1994.

Bord, Janet. *Fairies: Real Encounters with Little People*. New York: Carroll & Graf, 1997.

Briggs, Katherine. *An Encyclopedia of Fairies: Hobgoblins, Brownies, Bogies, and Other Supernatural Creatures*. New York: Pantheon Books, 1976.

DeGrandis, Francesca. *Be a Goddess! A Guide to Celtic Spells and Wisdom for Self-Healing, Prosperity, and Great Sex*. San Francisco: Harper San Francisco, 1998.

Evans-Wentz, W. Y. *The Fairy-Faith in Celtic Countries*. Mineola, NY: Dover Publications, 2002.

Faerywolf, Storm. *Betwixt and Between: Exploring the Faery Tradition of Witchcraft*. Woodbury, MN: Llewellyn Worldwide, 2017.

Gaiman, Neil. *Preludes and Nocturnes (The Sandman, book 1)*. Vertigo Comics, 1988. Reprinted in 2010.

Gardner, Gerald. *Witchcraft Today*. Citadel, 2004. Originally published 1954.

Graves, Robert. *The White Goddess: A Historical Grammar of Poetic Myth*. New York: Noonday Press, 1975. Originally published 1948.

Grimassi, Raven. *Hereditary Witchcraft*. St. Paul, MN: Llewellyn Worldwide, 1999.

Herbert, Frank. *Dune*. Ace, 1990. Originally published 1965.

Hunter, Devin. *The Witch's Book of Spirits.* Woodbury, MN: Llewellyn Worldwide, 2017.

Jackson, Michele. *Bones, Shell, and Curios: A Contemporary Method of Casting the Bones.* Forestville, CA: Lucky Mojo Curio Co, 2015.

Leland, Charles Godfrey. *Aradia, or the Gospel of the Witches.* Custer, WA: Phoenix Publishing, 1990. Originally published 1890.

Starhawk. *The Spiral Dance: A Rebirth of the Ancient Religion of the Great Goddess.* New York: HarperCollins, 1979.

Steiger, Brad. *Secrets of Kahuna Magic.* New York: Award Books, 1971.

Stewart, R. J. *Earth Light: The Ancient Path to Transformation Rediscovering the Wisdom of Celtic & Faery Lore.* Rockport, MA: Element, Inc., 1992.

———*The Living World of Faery.* Somerset, UK: Gothic Image Publications, 1995.

———*Robert Kirk, Walker Between Worlds: A New Edition of The Secret Commonwealth of Elves, Fauns & Fairies.* Roanoke, VA: RJ Stewart Books, 2007.

———*The Underworld Initiation: A Journey Towards Psychic Transformation.* Lake Toxaway, NC: Mercury Publishing, 1990.

Talbot, Michael. *The Holographic Universe.* Harper Perennial, 2011.

INDEX

To Write to the Author

If you wish to contact the author or would like more information about this book, please write to the author in care of Llewellyn Worldwide Ltd. and we will forward your request. Both the author and publisher appreciate hearing from you and learning of your enjoyment of this book and how it has helped you. Llewellyn Worldwide Ltd. cannot guarantee that every letter written to the author can be answered, but all will be forwarded. Please write to:

Storm Faerywolf
℅ Llewellyn Worldwide
2143 Wooddale Drive
Woodbury, MN 55125-2989
Please enclose a self-addressed stamped envelope for reply,
or $1.00 to cover costs. If outside the U.S.A., enclose
an international postal reply coupon.

Many of Llewellyn's authors have websites with additional information and resources. For more information, please visit our website at http://www.llewellyn.com